NEPALESE POLITICAL BEHAVIOUR

Ole Borre
Sushil R. Panday
Chitra K. Tiwari

NEPALESE POLITICAL BEHAVIOUR

AARHUS UNIVERSITY PRESS

ISBN 87 7288 483 5

AARHUS UNIVERSITY PRESS
Building 170
University of Aarhus
DK-8000 Aarhus C, Denmark

PREFACE

The idea of this book goes back to the hectic 1990 summer in Kathmandu following upon the uprising in April. The authors became acquainted with one another at garden parties and terrace lunches--often interrupted by monsoon rains--during which the political and intellectual opportunities raised by the fall of the old regime were eagerly discussed. Parties had come into the open, and the new government had set sails for a general election during the Spring of 1991. We decided that such an occasion for probing the mood of the Nepalese public, and for testing voting theories under unusual circumstances, should not be missed.

The authors wish to thank the Danish International Development Assistance (Danida) for funding the election survey, which operated during the Spring of 1991, and to thank the Danish Chargé d'Affaire K.V. Johansen and Mr. Peter Lysholt Hansen personally for their encouragement. Our thanks are extended to the Danish Volunteer Service (DVS) and Mr. Kaj Østergaard personally for their help in many practical matters.

During the fieldwork we were helped by certain key members of the project: the program administrator Dr. Ganga B. Thapa, computer programmer Mr. Ishwar Prasad, analysts Dr. Bharat R. Sharma and Mr. Dev Raj Dahal, along with our eight field supervisors and more than thirty interviewers. We are indebted to all of them for carrying through the project, often under difficult and unforeseen circumstances, and to the more than one thousand Nepalese respondents who spent hours of patiently answering our questions. Of our Nepalese colleagues Dr. Anand Aditya deserves to be particularly mentioned for his active interest in the project.

From the period during which the authors worked together in Aarhus with analysing the data and writing the manuscript, we are indebted to the Danish Council for Research in Developing Countries (Rådet for Ulandsforskning) and to the Institute for Political Science at Aarhus University for providing the facilities for our work. Among our Danish colleagues Dr. Jørgen Elklit gave valuable advice on all phases of the project; Jakob Rogild Jakobsen, who worked with the datafile in connection with his studies, suggested the weighting system which has been used (cf. Chapter 10); and Anne-Grethe Gammelgaard prepared our manuscript for publication.

Of the following chapters Chitra Tiwari wrote Chapters 1, 2, 4 and 5, Sushil Panday wrote Chapters 6, 7 and 8, and Ole Borre wrote the Introduction and Chapters 3, 9 and 10.

CONTENTS

INTRODUCTION

During the training session one of our Nepalese interviewers read aloud a question from our questionnaire which ran, "Some people in this country believe that the king is the reincarnation of Lord Vishnu. Do you think this is true or false?" Then he said, laughing, "Do you realise that one year ago we might all be hanged for asking a question like this?"

Nothing can better illustrate the swift political change, from royal absolutism to free election, which took place in Nepal between April 1990 and April 1991. In one sense the definition of politics suddenly becomes restricted, as an act that used to be considered controversial and part of a conspiracy merely becomes part of an opinion survey. In another sense this definition becomes enlarged, as every citizen can join the field of politics on their own premises.

This book is based on interviews with one thousand Nepalese voters. The interviews were conducted in connection with the Nepalese parliamentary election of May 12, 1991. That was the first election since 1959 in which parties were allowed to participate. The election therefore is the first modern election held in accordance with democratic norms in Nepal, and it came about only after an uprising in April 1990 caused the old political system to collapse. Our interviews provide the first opportunity for studying the political beliefs and behaviour of the Nepalese people. In this regard our survey runs parallel with the wave of surveys that swept over Eastern Europe after the overthrow of the communist regimes in 1990-91. Together, this new wave of election surveys provides a unique opportunity to study democracies in being.

Being the first analysis of Nepalese voters, our study serves more than one purpose. In the first place it conveys some facts about Nepalese voters which were not known before. This task is mainly descriptive. For example, by breaking down the Nepalese electorate into various social categories and measuring the strength of the parties in these groups we shall be able to pinpoint the most important lines of political cleavage in Nepalese society.

Second, because our interview questions are similar to those of other surveys, our study makes possible a comparison of Nepalese voters with those of other societies. In what sense are they similar to voters of other countries, and in what sense do they represent a new and hitherto unknown species of political animal?

Third, the survey becomes a testing ground for empirical theories of voting behaviour and political culture. Such theories have developed over almost fifty years of research. Some of them have their origin in the context of U.S. presidential elections, since the surveys began there in 1940 and have been held regularly since 1948. In the course of the 1960s and 1970s the election survey spread to a number of other Western countries. The addition of new countries caused new dimensions to be incorporated in voting theory. For example, moving from the American two-party system to European multiparty systems, and from an emphasis on the election of a president to an emphasis on the parliamentary election meant that the theory had to be revised. Even more importantly, the repetition of surveys from one election to the next meant that long-term forces and short-term forces influencing the voter's decision could be separated.

Despite these developments, the election surveys up to the end of the 1980s were similar in one respect. All the countries surveyed were comparatively old democracies with well-established political institutions. For example, the parties putting up candidates were several generations old, except that occasionally a new party would be formed to compete with the older ones. Likewise, the voters in these countries had been used to participate in elections from their youth, except for those countries who had gone through a period of fascist rule during the thirties. Except for Spain, no survey had dealt with democratic institutions in being. Theories of how these institutions became established in the first place were mainly based on speculation supplemented by aggregate data such as official election statistics, which is open to different interpretations. The new wave of surveys of democracies in being can replace these speculations and interpretations with more direct evidence.

Our survey continues the tradition of studying the election as the central event in a democracy, and carries that tradition into a new setting. The questionnaire (given in the Appendix) also includes some questions from a five-nation study in 1963 (1) designed to assess the wider political culture of a society. That study operated with certain political attitudes and voter types which occurred in all five countries though in a different mix. Thereby it led to a broad perspective on political development in the direction of a participant democratic culture. In replicating these questions we shall be able to identify Nepalese political culture relative to that of other societies.

As stated above, the base of the analysis in the present book is the voter survey. However, the Nepalese 1991 campaign and election also meant the beginning of party organisation and of a multipartisan parliament. Studies of these important aspects of Nepalese politics have been undertaken in close association with the voter survey. Among other things, some of the questions used in the election survey were also applied to party members and parliamentarians after the new parliament had conducted its first session. We shall therefore at some points be able to compare the responses given by the voters with responses from party members and parliament-arians of the different Nepalese parties. In this way our book contains some elements for a study of political representation and linkages, which attempts to combine mass surveys and elite surveys into one frame of reference.

The book is divided into ten chapters. Chapter 1 contains a historical account of Nepalese politics from the establishment of Nepal as a political entity in 1769 and until the popular uprising in the spring of 1990. This is necessary for an understanding of the present Nepalese party system as well as the leading issues of contemporary Nepalese politics. As will be seen, continuity is at least as characteristic as change. The ostensibly new political institutions including the parties competing in the open for the first time, the election law, the social bases of the parties, and the way in which the parliament operates, all grow out of the past.

Chapter 2 deals with the situation leading up to the election, the results of the election, and the events taking place during the first year of Nepalese politics under the new constitution. One striking fact is how much the election system, taken over from Britain and India, affected both the nomination process and the outcome of the election. Small parties gave up when they saw no chance of winning a constituency; and the absolute majority won by the Congress party, as well as the disaster met by the right wing parties, were both conditioned by the single-member constituency rule.

While Chapter 2 rests entirely on official statistics, Chapter 3 gives the first glimpse of the survey data. The objective is to see how the voters looked at the party system with which they were confronted for the first time. Given the lack of experience, the low level of literacy, and the ethnic diversity of the Nepalese electorate, one might expect very little agreement across the country about what the parties stood for, and very vague perception of the parties except possibly for one's own candidate. On this backdrop the Nepalese voters' perspectives of the party system appear surprisingly consistent.

Having identified the major parties as significant objects in the minds of the Nepalese public, we turn in Chapter 4 to the social factors underlying the voters' choice among them. To what extent do respondent's caste, religion, and residential community determine his or her preference for the parties? Are there significant differences between the poor and the comparatively rich sectors in party choice? Do crosscutting demographic distinction such as age and sex have any impact on the party choice, or is the choice mainly made at the level of the family so as to pertain to young and old, male and female family members alike? Without going into details at this place, it may be mentioned that especially respondents' age and economic status are important in identifying the voter bases of the different parties. This is hardly in line with the simplistic view of Hindu village culture, according to which a few elderly and religious community leaders decide what the rest should do.

3

Chapter 5 analyses the communication process taking place during the election campaign. Again, this analysis rests on accounts from the survey respondents. Since the interviews were made during the week following the election, most respondents still were able to recollect how much they had read or heard about the parties and the election, whether they had attended meetings or received party workers, and who they had discussed politics with. The questions we try to answer are how many and who were mobilised by the election campaign, and whether the different types of communication had any impact on the partisan choice. The general picture is one of bustling activity, almost everybody being drawn into the communication sphere though not of course to the same extent.

Chapter 6 continues with an account of the content side of the messages. It is at least plausible to believe that a great part of the campaign communication dealt with various grievances which the voters either brought up or which were anticipated by the candidates and party workers. The survey contains a particularly rich material at his point since each respondent was invited to state three national political problems and three local political problems, an invitation which was accepted by a large proportion. Furthermore, similar questions were asked of the sample of parliamentarians and party members, so that it can be assessed to what extent the decision-making sectors took over the problems seen by the people.

Chapter 7 focuses on public opinion with regard to some prominent domestic and foreign-policy issues. We find that adherents of the major parties deviate systematically from one another on a number of issues, although on other issues there is near unanimity about which stand to take on the issue. As in the foregoing chapter, there are occasions to study mass/elite linkages since the questions were also applied to parliamentarians and party workers.

Chapter 8 deals with some critical questions in which the respondents have evaluated the government of the interim period as good or bad, comparing it with the previous government from before the uprising. An evaluation of the present government, the outcome of the election, of course cannot be made in the present survey, but in part we need a standard with which to compare possible later surveys, and in part there may be sizeable differences in evaluation among the different sectors of Nepalese society. If particular sectors feel alienated from influence on Nepalese politics, and feel that their interests are not cared for, it is a danger signal for Nepalese democracy. The general impression we get from this chapter is that the interim government was not popular, though most respondents rate it higher than the Panchayat government which it replaced.

Chapter 9 is a broader account of Nepalese political culture, that is, the typical beliefs which Nepalese voters hold about the central institutions of their political system, and their inclination to act on these beliefs. It was mentioned above that with some caution, political cultures can be compared with those of other countries. In doing so, we find the Nepalese culture at the time of the election to be unusually active especially when considering that the major part of the population are living in traditional villages, their lives being very little affected by decisions made by the government in Kathmandu.

Chapter 10, finally, contains some information on the survey itself: how the questions used in the questionnaire were selected, how the sampling of districts and respondents for interviewing was done, what was the experience gained during the interviewing, and how the filled-in questionnaires were coded and made ready for analysis. Since the sample turned out to be distorted, such that educated persons and men were over-represented relative to uneducated persons and women, weighting the sample is necessary for most types of analysis, and the principles of weighting are also laid down in Chapter 10.

It should be realised that fielding an election survey under the extraordinary political and technical conditions of Nepal is very different from conducting a routine survey in a Western country, and the same standards of sampling cannot be expected. Nonetheless we think we can show during the following chapters that a number of conclusions about Nepalese voters can be drawn with some confidence. What is needed is especially a replication of our survey at a later time, most obviously at the next parliamentary election, which should take place no later than 1996. This will determine which of our findings were spurred by the unusual circumstances of the first parliamentary elections, and which are more permanent characteristics of the Nepalese electorate.

CHAPTER 1

THE POLITICAL HERITAGE OF NEPAL

Nepal, known to the world as the country of Mount Everest, has an area of approximately 54,000 square miles and is inhabited by approximately 20 million people. It is a land-locked country surrounded by India in the East, West and the South and it lies South of the Tibetan autonomous region of the People's Republic of China. In view of its geopolitical location, the country was described as a "yam between the two boulders" by King Prithvi Narayan Shah, the founder of modern day Nepal.

The Kingdom of Nepal, as we know today, came into existence in 1769 A.D. when Prithvi Narayan Shah, the king of a small principality of Gorkha successfully annexed several principalities scattered to the West and East of Gorkha. Since Kathmandu valley, which was known as Nepal valley, became the seat of power following the unification, the new country gradually came to be known as Nepal.

Ever since the unification Nepal had been ruled by preemptory and peremptory command (Hukumi Sashan) of Shah Kings. The death of King Prithvi Narayan Shah in 1779 A.D. was followed by political instability in the royal court of Nepal. Several elite families, notably the Thapa, Pande, and Basnyat families, contested for power with the support of the members of the divided royalty. It was a cruel competition for crude power in which one absolute ruler was replaced by another absolute ruler.

The post-unification period was also characterized by expansionist policies carried out by the successors of King Prithvi Narayan Shah. The expansionist policies led to a war with Tibet in 1793 in which Nepal successfully imposed an unequal treaty on Tibet. Nepal entered into yet another war, a humiliating war this time, with the British in the South in 1814. The war ended with a treaty signed at *Sugauli* in 1818 in which Nepal lost almost two-third of its territory which, of course, was acquired through the process of expansion.

The loss in this war heightened the intra-elite conflict marked by palace intrigues, conspiracies and coups. In the process of such political uncertainties a bloody coup occurred in September 1846 in which an army General named Jung Bahadur Rana usurped the power unto himself and instituted the system of hereditary prime ministership in which the eldest male member of the Rana family alone could enjoy the position of the Prime Minister. The competing leaders of elite families such as Thapa, Pande, and Basnyat were totally obliterated. They were either killed or took refuge in India. The Shah Kings were reduced to figure-heads and thrown into oblivion. They became their own prisoners. The Rana family rule remained in Nepal for 104 years until it was toppled by a limited revolution in 1950-51. The Rana family rule was basically a patrimonial system based on primogeniture.

The Fall of the Rana Regime

The wave of political change that swept Nepal around 1950 was not an isolated event. The movement for decolonization and independent home rule that was unleashed throughout the Third World in the aftermath of the World War II led to a drastic political change in Nepal's neighbourhood. India became independent in 1947 after almost two centuries of British colonial rule, and China in 1949 became a communist country after three decades of civil war. With political vacuum around in South Asia and lack of British protection for the ruling Rana government, the upsurge for democracy began to take momentum even in this closed and isolated country of Nepal. The educated Nepalese residing in India, who also had participated actively in the Indian independence movement, organized anti-Rana political organizations and parties, especially in Indo-Nepalese border areas to fight the tyranny of Rana oligarchy. A number of political parties were organized in India in the period 1946-1950 with a view to bringing about democracy by toppling the Rana regime in Nepal. Among these, the Nepali Congress party which had come into existence as a result of the merger of Nepal National Congress and Nepal Democratic Congress, was the largest. It aimed at establishing a constitutional monarchical democracy by ousting the Rana oligarchy. The Nepali Congress, founded and led by Bisheswor Prasad Koirala organized and launched an armed revolution in November 1950 and in February 1951 Nepal began its first experiment in multi-party democracy.

The political change of 1951 came in Nepal as a result of the compromise reached between the King, the Ranas, and the leaders of the Nepali Congress in New Delhi which was arranged by Indian Prime Minister Jawahar Lal Nehru. The compromise which is variously known as "Delhi Settlement", "Delhi Pact" or "Delhi Compromise" in Nepal killed the objective of the revolution. The compromise brought an interim coalition government consisting of the Ranas as well as the leaders of Nepali Congress with the continuation of Mohan Shamshere Jung Bahadur Rana as the Prime Minister of the Coalition government. Therefore, it can be described as a partial revolution in which the political power of the Ranas was reduced to some extent and new forces of change were made partners in the management of political power. The compromise also restored the royal power and prerogatives which the King had lost after the emergence of Rana regime in 1846. In short, the Delhi Settlement widened the scope of political participation while avoiding the massive social upheaval.

Experiment in Democracy

The Rana politics of Nepal was marked by endemic political conflicts and instabilities. There were mushroom like growth of political parties each vying for a seat in the government. King Tribhuvan had promulgated an Interim Constitution and had promised an election to Constituent Assembly to be held no later than April 1953 to draft the constitution for the country. But soon after the formation of a Rana-Congress coalition government, the partners in the government were agreeing to disagree on major issues. The partners in the coalition found it increasingly difficult to function. The interim Rana-Congress government collapsed following a shooting incident by the police in which the Rana Prime Minister publicly accused the Home Minister representing the Nepali Congress for the killing of a student named Chiniya Kazi. The Nepali Congress side tendered its resignation protesting the Rana Prime Minister's statement. The Rana side, too, tendered their resignation the next day.

Following the resignation of the Interim Government, King Tribhuvan invited the leader of the Nepali Congress, Matrika Prasad Koirala, to form the single-party government. Soon the party was divided over such issues like whether the President of the party should be allowed to be the Prime Minister simultaneously. Meanwhile, other parties also claimed the right to form the government. The internecine conflicts between and among parties for political power helped the King to consolidate his power and authority. In this situation, the King appeared the main actor in the Nepalese body politic. In the absence of general elections the actual strength and position of the parties could not be ascertained, and hence the King became the epicentre of politics in Nepal. The formation of several multi-mini political parties, inter and intra-party rivalry, the politics of opportunism followed by the parties in power, and above all the illiteracy and lack of political awareness of the masses were contributing factors in the consolidation of the royal authority. All political parties, instead of going to the people, turned towards the King making the Royal Palace as their safest constituency.

Meanwhile, King Tribhuvan died in 1954 and his son Crown Prince Mahendra assumed the throne of Nepal. The King died without fulfilling his promise to hold the election to Constituent Assembly by April 1953. The new King announced in 1955 that the elections will be held in October 1957. By this time other political forces had become completely impotent, as they could not influence the decision-making process as much as they had aspired to. In five years five different cabinets were formed and none could hold general election for the Constituent Assembly. Such chronic governmental instability contributed to the mushroom like growth of Lilliputian parties all claiming a seat in the government.

King Mahendra was a very different man from his father both temperamentally and with regards to his views about political parties and their leaders. His distrust of politicians and political parties was reflected in a message which he had given as Crown Prince where he had expressed his dissatisfaction with the way politics was managed in Nepal. Upon assuming the throne King Mahendra applied the policy of "divide and rule" and played one party leader against the other. In this situation, heightened by the awareness that the monarch's restored authority might be reduced if an election to Constituent Assembly is conducted as promised in the Royal Proclamation made by his father in New Delhi in February 1951, the King employed delaying tactics to avoid the election to the Constituent Assembly. In December 1957, he further reschedule the election for 1959. He began to float the argument through his cronies that a Constituent Assembly may very well invite further political uncertainties in an illiterate country like Nepal. Therefore, the parties in government, instead of preparing for election, emphasized political awareness of the people. The parties out of power organized a civil disobedience movement in 1958 demanding an election to be held as early as possible. The inexperience of party leaders in establishing and managing modern democratic institutions led to further consolidation of royal power and authority.

In 1959, King Mahendra, acting as custodian of the country and the people, finally promulgated the constitution of the Kingdom of Nepal as his "gift" to the people. The constitution provided for a bicameral legislature with the lower house to be elected directly on the basis of universal adult franchise with voting age limited to 21 years and above. The King retained the emergency powers on to himself, declared himself as sovereign and called for an election to parliament rather than to the constituent assembly as promised by his father in 1951.

General elections were held in March 1959 in which nine parties and 268 independent candidates contested. The general elections were a new and unique experience in Nepal's political history. There were a total of 786 candidates in 109 single-member constituencies. It was a time for all the political parties and individual personalities who claimed a role in the government to assess their relative strength and degree of popular support. In the election, held under the Anglo-American first-past-the-post system, a total of 4,246,468 voters were registered of which only 42.17 percent or 1,791,301 voted. The result of the election went in favour of Nepali Congress party which received absolute majority in the parliament with 74 out of 109 seats. The proportion of the national vote received by Nepali Congress, however, was only slightly over 37 percent.

The parliamentary leader of the Nepali Congress party, B.P. Koirala subsequently formed the government as the first democratically elected Prime Minister. With the formation of this government Nepal embarked on its first experiment in parliamentary democracy. It was also an end of the indecisive and uncertain transitional politics and introduction of a popular legitimate political structure for the first time. This government made attempts to introduce new reforms such as land reform, abolition of the *birta* system (a system in which the land was distributed by the previous rulers for displaying valour in the war, for providing unflinching support and services to the ruler, etc. Such land was tax free.), and certain progressive tax measures based on the party's democratic socialist manifesto. However, re-actionary forces of revival staunchly opposed these measures, and soon chaos and panic prevailed in several parts of the country. Opposition parties, who were routed in the election, went into the streets questioning the fairness of the election, on the one hand, and on the other, they questioned the authority of the Nepali Congress government to make vital decision in view of its minority position in terms of national votes amounting to slightly over 37 percent.

King Mahendra, on the other hand, was dissatisfied with the Nepali Congress government for relegating the Crown to a comparatively minor role in the government. The King also suspected that the socialist oriented Nepali Congress leaders were plotting the gradual abolition of the monarchy.

The Royal Takeover

The elected government of Nepali Congress was dismissed by the King on December 15, 1960, after barely 18 months in power. King Mahendra assumed absolute power which he had reserved for himself in the 1959 constitution. He dissolved the parliament, dismissed the cabinet, imposed a ban on political parties, arrested the Prime Minister and his cabinet colleagues, locked-up thousands of party workers in jails, and suspended fundamental rights of the people. A royal palace dictate charged the government with various misdeeds, including the creation of political instability, the abuse of power, and the encouragement of corrupt practices. The government was further accused of dislocating the administrative machinery, encouraging anti-national elements, being incapable of maintaining law and order in the country and of the adoption of unscientific economic policies. It was also alleged to have violated the sanctity of the constitution and the crown of the country, and to have pursued foreign policy that was detrimental to national sovereignty and independence.

King Mahendra's action against democracy came at a time when military and other forms of civilian dictators were taking over the helms of power one after another in other parts of the Third World. The new leader in post-colonial countries were unsuccessful in managing and institutionalizing the newly introduced western forms of parliamentary democracies. The leadership in these countries had faced the dilemma of modernizing the country while giving unrestrained political freedom

10

to the people. The pluralistic value system which emphasizes tolerance and patience was an unknown commodity in these societies, and hence, the activities of political parties had been obstructionist to modernizing leaders in the government. Moreover, the party activities had given the impression that democracy in other words was mobocracy. As a result, the common people as well as the responsible elite in society was disenchanted with tribal-type partisan strife organized by political parties who claimed to be modern. There were recurring stress on the need of unity, cooperation and strong national leadership. In Nepal, King Mahendra moved to capitalize on these sentiments while fulfilling his own ambitions of using the unrestrained power. But he did not want to put off the hat of "democracy". After two years of emergency rule, King Mahendra appeared with a new constitution with the concept of "partyless Panchayat democracy."

Partyless Panchayat Democracy

The concept of partyless democracy was first advocated by the President of the Philippines Manuel L. Quezon as early as 1940 who discarded the idea that democracy can not exist without political parties. Professor Ricardo R. Pascaul, head of the Department of Philosophy at the University of the Philippines, devoted his time to amplify President Quezon's ideas and came out with a book entitled *Partyless Democracy* in 1952 in which he challenged the Western thesis that political parties are necessary to a liberal political system. President Ayub Khan of Pakistan, in 1958, emerged with the concept of *basic democracy* while Indonesian President Sukarno introduced the concept of *guided democracy*. In Nepal, King Mahendra, while describing the parliamentary system as unsuitable to the political soil and climate of the country, attempted to synchronize the elements described in each of these experiments and introduced the *Partyless Panchayat System.* Panchayats, which have remained as social institutions of five-man councils ever since antiquity in Nepal, were a kind of socio-political forum to discuss local problems and pass decisions of social, religious and political importance. King Mahendra attempted to give it a political shape.

The constitution promulgated in 1962 provided for a four-tiered village, district, zonal and national Panchayat structure. Elections to each of these hierarchical Panchayats were conducted indirectly in which only individual or independent candidates were allowed to contest. The National Panchayat was considered to be the highest legislative body. The King appointed the Prime Minister and other ministers from among the members of this body. The constitution emphasized a decentralization of power from the top to the village panchayats. All fundamental rights, except opposition to the King and the Panchayat system, were guaranteed.

11

In practice, the Panchayat system was basically a puppet of the King. His appointees at various level of government enjoyed more power and privilege than the so-called elected representatives at various levels of Panchayat. The Palace relied on bureaucrats and royal nominees to execute the wishes of the patrimonial monarch. During election time, the candidates to different levels of Panchayats were carefully scrutinized by Zonal Commissioners (royal nominees) and Chief District Officers (home ministry's men in charge of law and order in the districts). The Zonal Commissioners received instructions directly from the palace whereas the Chief District Officers were instructed through the Home Ministry. These officials meticulously worked hard to make sure that Panchayat system's opponents were kept at bay. At the national level, the King, through his rubber stamp national Panchayat, declared that Panchayat system had "no alternative". This was later incorporated in the first amendment of the constitution in 1967. Thus, the door of the political system for the supporters of the multi-party system was permanently slammed.

In order to fill the gap created by the absence of political parties the constitution created five official class organizations of youth, women, peasants, workers and ex-servicemen. With a view to promote participation of intellectuals in the political system a constituency of university graduates was created to elect four members to the National Panchayat. This constituency proved to be the most vocal in opposing and exposing the oppressive character of the regime. Almost all candidates to National Panchayat membership from this constituency vowed to fight for freedom of speech and organization, universal adult franchise, and other liberalization of Panchayat system. Three candidates in the 1967 election demanding reforms in the system were arrested, disqualified to run, and imprisoned.

In order to garner popular support for Panchayat system, King Mahendra set out to introduce certain limited reforms in socio-economic areas. He amended the Civil Code declaring untouchability as illegal after less than a year of his take-over. The Civil Code that was introduced by the first Rana Prime Minister Jung Bahadur more than a century ago had legally institutionalized such social evils as untouchability. By legally eradicating untouchability King Mahendra was able to receive sympathies and support from the so-called untouchable castes such as *Damai, Kami, Sarki, Gaine, Kasain* (tailor, blacksmith, cobbler, minstrel, and butcher) as well as from modern educated individuals some of whom even described the King as progressive monarch.

In economic areas, King Mahendra introduced land reform program in 1964 fixing the ceiling on land holding, and defining the tenancy rights which prohibited the landlords to evict their tenants arbitrarily. The excess land beyond the ceiling was to be confiscated and distributed to landless people. He expected many landlords

12

to siphon off their landed resources towards the establishment of modern industries and accordingly he privately sounded out to many landlords to do the same before the actual implementation of the land reform law. But big land owners, instead of selling their lands to create capital for industrial venture, fragmented the land and registered in the name of each members of the family including the newly born babies and thus avoided confiscation of land by the state. This led to less than three percent confiscation of mostly the unproductive land from the total arable land.

With a centralized political system, King Mahendra moved to establish himself as the modernizing monarch. In 1968, taking a cue from the *White Revolution* of the Shah of Iran, he called the intellectuals and political workers to go to the villages and educate the public in the basics of Panchayat system and its modernization plans. An office of "Back to the Village National Campaign" (BVNC) was established with a view to mobilize the entire gamut of political as well as social aspects of Panchayat system. The Chairman of the BVNC was appointed by the King.

Problems of Panchayat System

But his opponents would not let him do that in the absence of political freedom. Thousands of party activists who had fled into neighbouring India after the royal take-over of 1960 vowed to fight king's dictatorship. Among these the Nepali Congress party organized an armed insurgency employing hit-and-run tactics from across the Indian border. The insurgents in the beginning had the tacit support of the Indian government but later on, as India's relations with China deteriorated to the extent of fighting a war in 1962, the Nepalese rebels were told to lay down arms. Thus, the Sino-Indian border war turned out to be a boon in disguise for King Mahendra who now received more time to consolidate his authority. He, however, continued to face opposition from students from time to time but the regime managed to suppress the student movement rather comfortably.

By 1968 it appeared that Panchayat system was truly a system without alternative. Self-exiled Nepali Congress workers in India were increasingly frustrated over their inability to mount a major offensive against the King's government. Moreover, the Indian government under Prime Minister Mrs. Indira Gandhi had continued to remain indifferent to the cause of democracy in Nepal. New Delhi had taken Beijing as a destabilizing force in South Asia. Such assessment was perhaps based on the nature of China's relations with India and particularly Beijing's support to the extreme communists known as Naxallites in India. The Nepali Congress leadership took this assessment at face value and reminded the King that Chinese activities in the region are detrimental to the national sovereignty of Nepal. Subarna Shamshere Rana, the Acting President of Nepali Congress, in a statement from

Calcutta, offered his unilateral co-operation to the King in the name of endangered sovereignty. B.P. Koirala supported the statement and subsequently King Mahendra released him from jail after eight years. The political prisoners and those in self-exile supporting Mr. Rana's statement were released and allowed to enter Nepal freely.

King Mahendra perhaps thought that the Nepali Congress leaders would join the Panchayat. But once out of jail they sought rapprochement with the King which was promptly denied. Encouraged by the presence of their leaders the previously docile Nepali Congress workers began to organize meetings in different parts of the country. Party leaders like former Prime Minister B.P. Koirala and Ganesh Man Singh were the featured speakers.

In order to counter the growing Nepali Congress influence the King decided to release the senior communist leaders like Man Mohan Adhikary and Shambhu Ram Shrestha from jail. As expected these communist leaders began to emphasize the threat to nationalism coming from India and described the Nepali Congress leaders as stooges of Indian reactionaries. The government deliberately let loose the communists to attack Nepali Congress leaders in many parts of the country. The Nepali Congress leaders, once again, went into self-exile in India.

Meanwhile, a small group of young communists, under the influence of Maoist Naxallite Movement in India began to organize themselves in Far Eastern districts of Jhapa and Ilam. In the name of Maoist line of "annihilation of class enemies" these communists started to kill the local landlords. Political discontent, thus, was gradually heating up.

Panchayat System Under King Birendra

King Mahendra died in late December 1971 and was succeeded by his son Crown Prince Birendra as the King of Nepal. The succession of King Birendra to the throne generated political expectations among the opposition as well as reformists of the Panchayat system. The opposition, mainly the self-exiled Congress and Communist party workers, adopted watch and see attitude while some Panchas like former Prime Minister Surya Bahadur Thapa advocated for the liberalization of the Panchayat system. Many thought that the new king, who had educational exposures from well known elite educational institutions of the world such as Eton College in England, Tokyo University in Japan and Harvard University in the United States, would opt for a new liberal political system. And Surya Bahadur Thapa, who had been out of the King's favour for about four years, perhaps calculated that this was the best time to stage a political comeback. But what these reformists forgot to underline was the fact that King Birendra was also a student of Samuel P. Huntington, a conservative American political scientist who had prescribed centralization and concentration of power as essential element of modernization in developing countries. The King's government quickly arrested the reform seekers, increased spy network along the India-Nepal border to watch the activities of the dissidents living in India, and suppressed student leaders who had gone on strike opposing the government's plan to introduce an education system that aimed at producing students loyal to the Panchayat system.

Huntington also had prescribed three formulas of survival for the traditional monarchies. He had argued that a traditional monarch, in order to survive, must follow either of the three alternatives. First, do not introduce any element of modernity and keep the country under perpetual darkness so that there will be no demand for participation in the system. Second, take the active leadership of the mobilization regime with a view to speed up the plans of modernization. If modernization program yielded fruit there will be less pressure for participatory democracy. Third, give power to the people's elected assemblies and remain as constitutional monarch.

King Birendra followed the second Huntingtonian formula of assuming the active leadership of the regime. His father, in fact, had created *Janch-Bujha Kendra* (an Enquiry and Investigative Centre) at the Royal Palace under the supervision of Crown Prince Birendra. The function of this *Kendra* was to supervise, evaluate, expedite the activities of the different development projects that were introduced in the country. The *Kendra* was a very powerful body similar to the high powered *Imperial Inspectorate* of the Shah of Iran, which could investigate any body and could take action against anybody including the Prime Minister for failing to carry out the royal directives. Birendra, as a King, sought to expedite the development plans introduced by his father and made public his commitment to the continuation of the Panchayat system established by his father.

King Birendra introduced a new education plan emphasizing vocational education. The country was divided into four (later, five) development regions with a view to decentralize the development planning and activities. The King personally took initiative to visit at least one development region every year and observe the performance, and supervise the plan.

Meanwhile, three sensational incidents occurred on the very first year of King Birendra's rule. They were the looting of a police post at *Hariharpur* located at Indo-Nepalese border by Nepali Congress volunteers, the hijacking of a Royal Nepal Airlines plane that was carrying three million Indian rupees belonging to Nepal Rastra Bank by three gun-men belonging to Nepali Congress, and a mysterious burning of the country's biggest palace, the *Singha Durbar*, that houses the Central Secretariat of Nepalese government. While the burning of Singha Durbar has remained an unsolved mystery, the hijacking of the plane and looting of the police post

15

were incidents created to send the message to the King that the opposition was ready to strike if the King did not reconcile with the opposition. In Biratnagar, the country's second biggest town, Nepali Congress undercovers exploded a grenade during the King's official visit but King Birendra survived. Nepali Congress also sent armed volunteers in the Eastern districts of Okhaldhunga and Solukhumbu but they were captured en masse by the Royal Army. Thus, both the opposition as well as the Panchayat government were testing their relative strength.

In view of these developments, King Birendra began to assure the people that there was enough "scope for change" in the system. This generated an expectation among the people that a reform in the regime was on the way. He formed a Constitution Reform Commission in 1975 and the members of the Commission toured the country to find out the kind of reform wanted by the people. But, in the meantime, the political developments in India in which Prime Minister Mrs. Indira Gandhi had imposed an authoritarian Emergency Rule suspending the fundamental rights of the people had an immediate impact in Nepal. The hawks of the Panchayat system who had no desire of any change prevailed and the political system that was expected to be reformed and liberal after the constitutional reform became all the more tight-fisted. "Back to Village National Campaign" was made the constitutional organ whose function it was to mobilize the Panchas and define the scope of Panchayat politics. It introduced the concept of consensual politics. In the name of "politics of consensus" the BVNC members discouraged election to Panchayat bodies. They selected the candidate and declared his/her unanimous victory. In some places, Panchas revolted against the BVNC's selection of official candidates by filing the nomination but they were defeated badly in the election through intimidation, threat, and manipulation of votes.

Mrs. Indira Gandhi's emergency rule made the Nepalese dissidents living in India increasingly difficult to function. As a result, the Nepali Congress leader B.P. Koirala returned to Nepal in late December 1976 with an appeal for "national reconciliation". He was promptly arrested the moment he stepped out of the plane while Panchas and BVNC's rented crowd demanded an execution of the former Prime Minister whom they described as "foreign agent" just outside of the airport terminal. The Panchas were mobilized by BVNC in a way reminiscent of Fascism in Italy. In each officially sponsored Pancha rally slogans like "we will obliterate the opposition to the Panchayat system" were chanted. The opposition parties and leaders were vilified as agents of foreign powers, namely India and China. Before 1975, the opposition leaders were prevented from making speeches at mass rallies by the police but now such responsibility was handed over to the Panchas. In addition to Panchas, the government also activated a student union known as "Nepal Rastrabadi Vidhyarthi Mandal" which was organized in early 1970s by the then

Home Minister and whose function was to harass the opposition minded people by all means. These members of the NRVM, who were paid from the exchequer, acted as official goons and hoodlums inside the campuses threatening professors and students who were not conformists of the Panchayat system. The NRVM members were reminiscent of the Savak agents of the Shah of Iran, Adolf Hitler's Nazi SS troops, and Tun Makud of Haiti's Duvalier.

Panchayat government was becoming increasingly intolerant of dissident views. Protests and strikes in campuses were swiftly and promptly suppressed and the leaders arrested. The dissidents were demoralized by Panchas and Mandalays (a derogative term for the members of NRVM) and as a result they were in a state of hibernation. The year 1978 and early 1979 appeared politically quiet and peaceful. The discontent against the system, however, was simmering and the lid finally blew up in April-May of 1979 when students marching towards the Pakistani Embassy in Kathmandu to deliver protest letter against the execution of former Prime Minister Zulfikar Ali Bhutto by the military junta were brutally treated by the police. This event led to outbursts among students who demanded proper action against the police officers. When the government ignored the demands, students continued to demonstrate in the streets, who were later joined by the workers of different factories. The movement spread like a wild fire in different parts of the country, and on May 23, during an encounter with the riot police, an angry mob of students attacked and burned the buildings belonging to *Gorkhapatra* Corporation that publishes government controlled Nepali language daily *Gorkhapatra* and English language daily the *Rising Nepal*. The mob also burnt the vehicles and part of the building of the Royal Nepal Airlines Corporation. The protesters were heard for the time demanding an end to the Panchayat rule.

The Politics of Referendum

Many thought on the evening of May 23 that the King would impose emergency rule by bringing the army into the streets. The next morning, however, people had something else to hear over the Radio Nepal broadcast. Early in the morning of May 24 at 6:30 King Birendra announced that a referendum would be held to decide the future political system for Nepal in which people will have to choose either the multi-party system or the Panchayat system with timely "reforms". The King guaranteed the freedom of speech during the campaign for referendum. The political parties, while still banned, came out adding the word "banned" in small letters, sometimes invisible, in their party names. Thus, the parties operated, more or less, openly during the campaign. The Nepali Congress and the communist parties immediately began campaigning for the multi-party system while the Panchayat side remained confused for a while because they had no platform or agendas to convince the people. And, the King was not quite clear what he meant by "timely reforms" in the Panchayat system. They felt humiliated and demoralized for a while because their active leader, King Birendra, had put the system under examination without consulting prominent Panchas. But they were energized by King Birendra on December 15, 1979 when he defined the reforms in the system to be instituted in the event of the victory of the Panchayat system in the referendum. He told the nation that in the post-referendum Nepal, irrespective of the victory of either side, there will be a legislature elected through universal adult franchise, the Prime Minister will be elected by the House, and the cabinet will be responsible to the House. If these points, which are indeed a basic element of democracy, are to be found in Panchayat system, the Panchas argued that there was no need to "import" multi-party system from foreign countries.

The referendum was held a year later in May 1980. The results went in favour of Panchayat system with "timely reforms". The Panchayat received 55 percent of the votes as against 45 percent of the multi-party side. B.P. Koirala accepted the verdict of the referendum but other members of his party as well as the communists charged that there were massive irregularities at the polls. In view of the fact that the referendum was conducted by the Panchayat government and not by an independent care taker government, the charges made by the opposition parties could not be ruled out easily. These charges, notwithstanding, the electoral victory in the referendum helped the King to claim legitimacy of the system that was imposed following the royal take-over of the elected government as well as representative institutions.

Politics Under "Reformed" Panchayat System

Following the announcement of the results, King Birendra appealed to the multi-party side to participate in the Panchayat system assuring them of respect for minority views. He also promulgated a "reformed constitution" of the "reformed Panchayat system" in which he inserted, in accordance to the promise made a year earlier, the adult franchise, an elected Prime Minister, and the responsible cabinet. The constitution, however, continued to maintain the position of the King as an absolute ruler and denied freedom of association once again. Under constitutional provision of Special Circumstances the King could rule the country with the help of the appointed Prime Minister and other ministers. The constitution created an all powerful Panchayat Policy and Enquiry Committee (PPEC). The PPEC was similar to the politburo of the ruling communist parties with powers to initiate actions against any member of the legislature if the committee thought that the members had violated the sanctity of the constitution. The constitution also made a provision requiring the candidates for Panchayat bodies to be a member of one of the official class organizations. These constitutional provisions were not acceptable to the Nepali Congress and hence, it did not participate in the May 1981 elections to National Panchayat.

The results of the referendum clearly established the fact that the country was significantly divided over the issue of political system. It also gave the message to the King that multi-party adherents were a force to reckon with. However, a few political cadres belonging to Nepali Congress and also some communists, realizing that the Panchayat had established its legitimacy, decided to join the system. A few of them even got elected to the 140-member National Panchayat in the May 1981 election. The parties, however, officially boycotted the elections.

Notwithstanding the opposition boycott, the May 1981 elections were important in that they were held after 22 years of the first parliamentary general elections of 1959. The total number of eligible voters had risen from 4.2 million in 1959 to 7.9 million in 1981. According to official accounts 63 percent of the voters had voted in 1981 despite the calls for a boycott of elections by the opposition parties. The major difference, however, was the absence of organized political parties, manifestos and campaigns in 1981. It was at best a beauty contest between the candidates.

The National Panchayat which was elected on the basis of universal adult franchise adopted the past policy of "consensual politics" and recommended former Prime Minister Surya Bahadur Thapa to be the next Prime Minister. Mr. Thapa known to represent the liberal within the Panchayat, was also Prime Minister during the national referendum, and much credit goes to him for making the system victorious in the polls. He was alleged to have misused government machinery in order to make Panchayat victorious in the referendum. Hence, the National Panchayat recommended his name for the position of Prime Minister, and the King, despite his personal reservations, accepted him as head of the government.

Prime Minister Thapa, however, soon developed difference with the Royal Palace Officials and the King's brothers whom he described as extra-constitutional organs of power. The palace officials and the royalties on their part mobilized other members of the National Panchayat and by a no-confidence motion voted the Prime Minister out of office in the Summer of 1983. Mr. Thapa's departure from the office was followed by the ascendency of conservative hardliners of the Panchayat system who refused any adjustment with the multi-party side. Lokendra Bhadur Chand, who succeeded Thapa as Prime Minister, even though a soft-mannered gentleman, was considered to be the henchman of the Royal Palace. His government, in the name of the verdict of the people, began suppression of the opposition activities.

The Civil Disobedience

Nepali Congress launched a signature campaign to appeal the King to repeal the Panchayat system and introduce the multi-party system on his own which he was empowered to do so in accordance with the constitution. In May 1985, the party also decided to launch a Gandhian peaceful *Satyagraha* (civil disobedience), which was supported by moderate communist parties, demanding restoration of multi-party democracy. The *Satyagrahis* (civil disobeyers) were arrested en masse but the agitators were spreading their movement to other parts of the country. The King, however, was taking a tough stand. On June 19, 1985, while addressing the National Panchayat the king expressed his determination to discourage any attempt to undermine peace and order in the country and reminded all Panchas that "it was their bounden duty to counter those who sought to create an atmosphere of instability in the country by spreading unnecessary confusion about the system chosen by the people themselves in free exercise of will."

The Bomb Explosion

King Birendra's call to counter the forces of "instability" was challenged by a group which believed that only violence would bring the desired political change. On the very next day, June 20, it exploded bombs at the gate of the Royal Palace, at the entrance of the National Panchayat killing a member a two legislative clerks, and at the lobby of Annapurna Hotel killing three receptionists. Similar explosions had taken place a day earlier in the Southern town of Birgunj killing a woman and in the Western tourist town of Pokhara where the person carrying the device exploded the bomb by mistake. Authorities discovered unactivated explosives in Kathmandu and elsewhere in the country.

Nepali Congress, the largest participant of *Satyagraha*, denied its involvement in the explosions and realizing that someone had stepped in to take advantage of the peaceful movement, the party called off the *Satyagraha*. An anti monarchist organization calling itself *Janabadi Morcha* (People's Democratic Front) led by Ram Raja Prasad Singh claimed the responsibility for the explosions. The spokesman of the group claimed from New Delhi that they had planted 50 bombs as the beginning of their revolution to topple the monarchy and install democratic republic. It was the first time in the history of Nepal that someone had come forward with the proposal for a republic. The explosion was followed by indiscriminate arrest and torture of thousands of suspected party workers (1,750 persons were taken into custody for investigative purpose, according to the Home Minister) belonging to all opposition parties. Security around the Royal Palace and around the houses of Prince Gyanendra and Prince Dhirendra was beefed up so much that the pedestrians were not allowed to walk of the foot path out side of the compound of princely houses. The government finally decided to try 101 persons under an ex-post facto law called Destructive Crimes (Special Control and Punishment) Act, 1985. Four persons, including *Morcha's* leader Ram Raja Prasad Singh, were sentenced to death in absentia by a Special Tribunal.

Opposition Participates in Panchayat Elections

In 1986, Panchayat system conducted yet another beauty contest in the form of general election. The total number of eligible voters had risen from 7.9 million in 1981 to 9.044 million in 1986. The voter turnout declined from 63 percent in 1981 to 60.32 percent in 1986. The Nepali Congress continued to boycott the election while three communist parties, namely, the Communist Party of Nepal (Marxist-Leninist), Communist Party of Nepal (Manandhar faction), and Nepal Labour and Peasants Organization decided to participate in the election with a view to exposing the system from well within its own chamber. In the elections nine communists and eight other non-communists with multi-party leanings were able to defeat the official candidates of PPEC. The communist members to National Panchayat identified themselves as "pro-people Panchas" as opposed to pro-palace Panchas. The King appointed Marich Man Singh Shrestha, a hardliner among the conservative Panchas who had advocated, in 1975, passing a legislation allowing the Zonal Commissioners the authority to inflict capital punishment to the opponents of the Panchayat system, as the Prime Minister, indicating that he will continue to flex his muscle against democracy seekers.

The Nepali Congress, in 1987, decided to participate in local Panchayat elections apparently under the pressure of the rank and file of the party. The participation of communists at both local and national level elections put the Nepali Congress party in a predicament. The ardent supporters of late B.P. Koirala who had believed that the communists had a plan to gradually take-over the entire political system by participating in it, thought that they, too, should enter the Panchayat and watch the activities of the communists. Nepali Congress leaders claimed that their party would capture at least 23 of the 33 municipalities of Nepal. The results, however, turned out to be totally disastrous for the Nepali Congress. Its claim of being the only alternative to the monocratic Panchayat system proved to be wrong whereas the communists captured significant numbers of village as well as town Panchayats.

Corruption and Divided Royalty

The stories of corruption within the establishment is a much talked about topic in Nepal. The involvement of high ranking officers of the army and police as well

21

as bureaucrats and politicians with close links to the Royal Family members in varieties of corrupt activities were mentioned by people here and there occasionally. But it came to the public in 1987 when a newspaper editor, Padma Thakurathi, who was constantly exposing the activities of some members of the establishment engaged in smuggling of gold, narcotic drugs and other contraband, was shot in the head while still in the bed in the early hours of the morning. This incident unfolded a number of scandals in which King Birendra's younger brother's aide-de-camp Colonel Bharat Gurung, a member of National Panchayat Bhim Prasad Gauchan, a member of National Sports Council Jagat Gauchan and the hired assassin Bikas Gurung were all found guilty of attempt to murder by the court. Colonel Bharat Gurung and retired Inspector General of Police D.B. Lama were also found guilty on charges related to drug traffic, smuggling of gold and other contraband, receiving bribes and kick-backs, and influence peddling. Meanwhile, Prince Dhirendra, having difficulties to adjust with his wife, a younger sister of Queen Aishworya, decided to marry another foreign woman he loved. The Queen, however, was not ready to allow him to do so. Ultimately, he resigned his royal title of "His Highness the Prince" and left for London. General people began to interpret these events as an indication of the decline of the royal power and prestige. And King Birendra was described in private whispers as hen-pecked husband.

In fact, King Birendra was surrounded by a few vested interest lobbies represented by Queen Aishworya, Prince Gyanendra and Prince Dhirendra who competed for more power and influence which they need to enhance their shady business deals. Queen Aishworya naturally emerged as more powerful than the two Princes. In this situation, the King was believed to be politically a lame duck but financially and economically he was still at the apex of hierarchy of social parasites fattening themselves off the Nepalese economy. The Royal Family and other lesser royalties comprising about 19 individuals (including the minors) were pocketing more than half a million U.S. dollars annually in the form of privy purse in country whose per capita income was less than U.S. $170 in 1990. In addition to privy purse they made millions of rupees from their investments in hotel and travel agency businesses.

Natural Disaster With Political Implication

In 1988, the government faced two disasters. One was natural and the other was man-made. Entire eastern Nepal was hit by a devastating earthquake (6.7 on the Richter scale) taking the life of 721 persons and injuring 1,551 persons. A total of 66 thousand houses, 1,202 school buildings and 14 college campuses were razed to the ground. The man-made disaster was the stampede at the Dasarath Stadium followed by a sudden rain storm. The stampede occurred when the people trying to escape the rain storm found the gates closed and as a result some 70 persons lost their lives.

Both of these incidents had political implications for the regime. During the earthquake incident, the distribution of relief materials coming from international donor agencies created conflict in certain areas where Panchayat leaders were accused of distributing the humanitarian materials to their own cronies. In this context, Karna Prasad Hyonju, former member of the National Panchayat, was lynched by the people of Bhaktapur, a district with significant communist influence. The government arrested and tortured communist leader Narayan Man Bijukchhe "Rohit" and hundreds of his followers with a motive of vengeance and charged them with the murder of Hyonju. The stadium stampede incident bred hatred and hostile feelings among the people and the government was condemned for failing to provide basic security of the sports spectators and as a result Keshar Bahadur Bista, the Minister of Culture and Education, had to resign.

Rampant Violation of Human Rights

The government's record of human rights violations continued to be dismal. Anyone opposing the government and making indirect remarks against the royalties were indiscriminately arrested and jailed under an infamous Public Security Act without any trial. Some were charged under Treason Act while others were charged under the Organizations Control Act. Amnesty International, in 1987, came out with a special report on human rights violations in Nepal in which it recorded the arrest of two journalists, Harihar Birahi and Keshav Raj Pindali, for publishing an interview with Yogi Narahari Nath in which the Yogi had criticized the King for acting under the influence of the Queen to the detriment of the interest of the state. The Amnesty report also recorded the arrest of the two members of the National Panchayat-Rup Chand Bista and Govinda Nath Uprety. Bista was charged with publishing a poem with a satire of the monarchy while Uprety was arrested and imprisoned for three years for naming the king's brothers among those who he blamed for rigging the elections in his district. Bhup Nidhi Pant, a journalist and lawyer in Pokhara was arrested twice in six months and charged with treason on both occasions. His first crime was to publish king's photo with black ink smeared around the face and second crime was to misspell Queen Aishworya name in vernacular Nepali. Hundreds of students and teachers similarly were arrested and tortured during their respective strikes. There were also reports of disappearance from the police custody.

Two human rights organizations, Human Rights Organization of Nepal (HURON) and Forum for the Protection of Human Rights (FOPHUR) were organized in Nepal to monitor the human rights violations. Both the HURON and FOPHUR comprised of individuals supportive of opposition political cause. HURON was dominated by self-declared democrats while FOPHUR was controlled by persons with leftist proclivities. The activities of the members of both of these organizations were heavily monitored by the government.

The discontent against the cabinet headed by Prime Minister Marich Man Singh Shrestha was on the rise even among members of National Panchayat. Shrestha had reshuffled his cabinet three times in two years in an attempt to pacify the members. Nevertheless, attempts were made in the Summer of 1988 to introduce a no-confidence motion against the government but these attempts were foiled by the palace officials. The government adopted a number of measures to win over the legislators and other important elites of society. Some members were offered lucrative positions in different Commissions formed to study the problems. They were provided with the privilege of importing foreign cars at nominal import duty as well as the privilege of substantial foreign exchange facility. The corrupt political elite was happy to receive this governmental bribe. Many sold these vehicles at market price and made substantial amount of profit-a profit which otherwise would have gone to the national treasury.

Problems in India-Nepal Relations

India and Nepal failed to renegotiate and renew the Treaties of Trade and Transit that were to expire in March 1989. The two countries have remained uneasy partners since the royal take-over of 1960. As mentioned earlier, King Mahendra's take-over would have failed had there been no Sino-Indian border was in 1962. India had switched its support to the King's regime in order to neutralize Nepal from going too close to the Chinese. In the changed strategic context Indian also thought that monocratic political order in Nepal could act as a best buffer between New Delhi and Beijing. Moreover, Indians could easily negotiate (or impose) their interests with one person rather than with democracy with lengthy parliamentary process. Thus, India's support to Panchayat system came as political expediency. King Mahendra, too, understood it quite clearly but moved cautiously to expand Nepal's relations with outside world while keeping the Indians in good humour.

But in King Birendra's time India had emerged as a regional hegemon by dismembering Pakistan and creating Bangladesh, by exploding a nuclear device, and by annexing Sikkim. These developments were taken with alarm in Nepal. King Birendra sought to preserve his independent role in international affairs by distancing himself from India. He rejected the traditional concept of Nepal as an Indian "buffer zone" China arguing that Nepal touches both India and China. He declared Nepal as a "peace zone" and sought international recognition. While majority of the countries of the world including China and the United States supported the King's call, Indians argued that the concept of "peace zone" runs counter to the spirit of the Treaty of Peace and Friendship signed between the two countries in 1950. The 1950 Treaty of Peace and Friendship guarantees Nepal's security against foreign aggression, and in this context Indian argued that Nepal has to define the source of threat in order to be declared as "peace zone". The source of threat as perceived in Nepalese Royal Palace was no other power than India itself. King Birendra, in fact, had wanted to insulate himself with "peace zone" as safety-valve to his monocratic regime.

Nepal's increased political and economic relations with China were not appreciated in New Delhi whose policy makers argued that there has been a violation of the spirit of the 1950 Treaty of Peace and Friendship. New Delhi, in 1988, was infuriated with Kathmandu when the latter bought arms and armaments from China. During the negotiation for the renewal of the Trade and Transit Treaties, Indian reportedly emphasized Nepal's guarantee of the recognition of India's sensitive security interests. While vainly trying to assure the Indians the Nepalese government emphasized that Kathmandu had not violated the terms of the 1950 Treaty of Peace and Friendship and that the purchase of the limited amount of arms and ammunition from China was only an exercise of independence by a sovereign country. Indians did not agree. The attentive public in Nepal, too, became alarmed when trucks carrying Chinese arms including anti-aircraft guns began to roll in the streets of Kathmandu. The public was alarmed because these arms had no use other than terrorizing the opposition public.

Following the expiry of the Trade and Transit Treaties, New Delhi imposed restrictions on trade as well as on movement of goods across the border. Out of the 17 entry points to Nepal, New Delhi allowed only two entry points for Nepal's overseas trade that is conducted via Calcutta port. Indian oil companies refused to sell petroleum, oil, and lubricant (POL products) to Nepal which seriously affected Nepal's economy. It caused shortage of essential consumer items and the people of Nepal faced immense hardship. The streets of Kathmandu were deserted without any vehicular traffic and everywhere people were seen in long lines to buy rationed kerosene, sugar, and other essential consumer items.

Instead of trying to ameliorate the relations, the Panchayt government embarked on a two-track policy. First, it embarked on pursuing a policy of Most Favoured Nation Treatment(MFNT) with India as with other country. Open General Licence (OGL) were issued for third country trade and foreign exchange was made available for the business community. With MFN treatment Nepal was to pay hard earned hard currency even for imports from India which, hitherto, was paid in Indian currency previously. On a second track, the government embarked on whipping

25

up hysteric type of anti-Indian nationalism telling the people that they were suffering because of India's unilateral termination of existing treaties of trade and transit and thereby imposing unjust embargo. It was an attempt to derail popular contempt against the government.

The Panchayt regime missed no opportunity to mobilize world public opinion projecting an image of India as a Gulliver trying to strangulate its Lilliputian neighbour. But neither King Birendra's visit to Czechoslovakia, Finland, and France nor the visits of Pakistani foreign minister, Bangladeshi President and the Chinese Premier in Kathmandu in 1989 could bring any relief to Nepal. King Birendra's meeting with Indian Prime Minister Rajiv Gandhi during the Non-aligned Movement (NAM) Summit in Belgrade in 1989 also failed to bail out Nepal.

Both policy tracks adopted by the Panchayat government gradually began to degenerate. The MFN treatment with India depleted Nepal's reserve of scare hard currency within a couple of months because Indians were not buying anything from Nepal paying hard currency to supplement the depletion. And the government failed to generate anti-Indian nationalism. Because the people by now had begun to hold their own government responsible for their sufferings and questions were raised about the performance of the Panchayat government over the last 30 years.

An Assessment of Panchayat's Performance

King Birendra depended on foreign aid to push ahead his development plans. Development of agriculture, expansion of education, expansion of health centres, development and expansion of transport and communications were the areas in which successive Panchayat governments had given priority. But the achievement of the plans in proportion of the investment were negative. The developmental sector of the economy, which was financed through foreign aid, was plagued by corruption. As a result, despite the investment of billions of rupees in agricultural sector, Nepal, which used to export agricultural products, became itself an importer of food products from the 1980s onward.

In the field of education, hundreds of new schools were opened and as a result the literacy rate of the country jumped from less than ten percent in 1960 to 37 percent in 1990. Higher educational institutions were similarly expanded. By the beginning of 1980 the student population passing the high school examination increased to such an extent that Tribhuvan University, the only university of Nepal with nearly 100 campuses scattered all over the country, was unable to admit all the students who wanted to go for higher education. Neither the government was able to generate employment for these educated persons. As a result the government had to allow private campuses to open with a view to give some cushion to the system. The explosion of student population, however, put the educational system under stress with demands from students for better educational facilities. The standard of education deteriorated as a result of mass admission of students on the one hand, and recruitment of mediocre and under qualified teachers on political grounds in both the schools and university campuses, on the other. The schools and university campuses were politicized in which both the students and teachers were identified as either pro-Panchayat or anti-Panchayat. Allegiance to Panchayat system rather than intellectual achievement became the criteria for the promotion in the university system.

The corruption, particularly in development sector of the economy, created a small class of people in the urban centres of the country with unlimited amount of wealth. It consisted of Royal Family members, their relatives and cronies, politicians, high level bureaucrats in both the royal palace secretariat and the government's secretariat, high ranking officers in the army and in the police. The contractors of international agencies such as the World Bank, the International Monetary Fund and Asian Development Bank conspired and competed against each other to secure the contract by paying substantial amount of bribe in the form of "commission" to politicians and bureaucrats who were close to the royal palace. The share of the money received in this manner was proportionally distributed among officials. The money ultimately found its way into foreign bank accounts in Japan, United States, Switzerland, Hong Kong, Singapore, Dubai, and other countries considered to be the safe heaven to deposit ill gotten money.

This class, in the absence of industrial enterprises, found real estate as another safe heaven to legitimize its ill gotten wealth. Consequently, the land prices started to soar up in geometrical proportion in the urban centres since the 1970s. The ill gotten money also gave rise to irresponsible consumerism in which members of this filthy rich class invested money in such unproductive items as fancy cars, TV screens, and video, all imported from Japan. They also used this money to finance the education of their children in the western countries, particularly in the United States where an estimated 400 students enter every year for self-financed undergraduate study.

While the ruling class was enjoying its ill gotten riches, the middle class and poor people were hard hit by galloping inflation. To meet the pressure of inflation even a saintly person had to compromise his integrity in favour of corruption. Corruption became an established fact of everyday life. Persons who did not want to engage themselves in corrupt practices or were unable to make money while in position of power were considered to be "stupid" by their friends and relatives. In this situation, common people in the street had no appeal of the Panchayat regime's hysteric nationalism directed against India who thought Panchayat system rather than India as responsible for their sufferings. Moreover, the intellectuals of the country were beginning to criticise the Western donor nations for pouring their tax payers' money in Nepal to sustain the dictatorial Panchayat system, and the banned parties were discussing the possibility of launching a mass movement for the restoration of multi-party democracy.

CHAPTER 2

FROM MONOCRACY TO DEMOCRACY

On April 9, 1990, the 30-year-old Panchayat system introduced and led by absolute monarchy collapsed following a massive popular uprising on April 6, 1990. The uprising delivered the *coup de grace* to King Birendra's absolutist regime that had already been battered and broken by 49 days of street clashes, strikes, and demonstrations. The pro-democracy agitators only armed with slogans and leaflets successfully overthrew a monocratic system as well as the absolutism of the monarchy. How did it happen?

Unity of Opposition

The survival of the Panchayat system had been made possible by bitter divisions among the opposition parties. The weakness of the opposition in the form of divisions had been the strength of the Panchayat. There were as many as 19 communist parties and factions, each claiming ideological purity. While each of these groups emphasized the need for leftist unity, the results so far had remained dismal. Communist disunity was the result of the implantation of Marxist-Leninist ideology in a traditional feudal brain. Apart from personality issues, the communist movement in Nepal was divided on other issues such as the Moscow-Beijing line, the identification of the main enemy, and an alliance with the Nepali Congress to fight the tyranny of the Panchayat system. A group led by late Pushpa Lal identified the monarchy as the enemy number one and, hence, consistently argued for an alliance with the Nepali Congress for struggle against the Panchayat system. There were others, who had actually dominated the communist movement of the 1960s and 1970s, and who rejected an alliance with the Nepali Congress arguing that it was the agent of India which was actually the main enemy. To these communists, the King represented the forces of nationalism in Nepal. As a result of such differences in basic strategy, the communists had failed to establish unity among themselves, and in 1980 some groups participated in the referendum, while others called for a boycott emphasizing people's revolution.

The Nepali Congress party, on the other hand, suffered from ego-mania. Its leader B.P. Koirala was an outspoken critic of communism and hence ruled out the possibility of an alliance with them. He always regarded them as forces of subversion and preferred reconciliation with the King to an alliance with the communists. Moreover, he also regarded the communists as royal siblings raised by the King to undermine the Nepali Congress. Many in Nepal believe that the

29

defeat of the multi-party side in the national referendum was mainly due to B.P. Koirala's stubborn rejection of a united campaign with the communists.

The death of B.P. Koirala in 1983 created a political vacuum in Nepal. The Panchayat government thought that the death of the linchpin of the party would lead to a split in the Nepali Congress. However, the unity shown by the party's rank and file during the civil disobedience movement of 1985 said otherwise. Meanwhile, the post-referendum Panchayat government was acting in a politically suicidal manner arresting and torturing the oppositionists belonging to both the Nepali Congress and the communist parties in an indiscriminate manner. In the 1960s and 1970s, the governments used to suppress one group at the cost of another and maintain a balance. The government's policy of wholesale suppression of the opposition quite naturally generated a sense of solidarity. The common experience of suppression, torture and jail sentences led to the reinforcement of a belief among the workers of both parties that only united action could topple the Panchayat government.

On January 15, 1990, seven factions of the divided communist party succeeded in forging the United Left Front. The major partners in this leftist alliance, however, were the Nepal Communist Party (Marxist-Leninist), the Nepal Communist Party (Marxist), and the Nepal Communist Party (Fourth Congress Group). Six other communist factions, known as the extremists, also forged a united front called the United National People's Movement (UNPM). The United Left Front agreed upon a joint movement for the restoration of democracy to be called by the Nepali Congress, while the UNPM chose to participate in the movement with different issues. Finally, on January 18, the Nepali Congress decided to launch the movement on February 18, the day when democracy had first dawned in Nepal in 1951.

The Panchayat government returned to the old tactics of divide and rule. In a bid to create a schism between the Nepali Congress and the United Left Front, on the one hand, and between the United Left Front factions on the other, the government released 11 leaders of the Marxist-Leninist Party who were serving life sentences for their role in the Naxallite movement of 1970-71 in the Jhapa district in which a number of persons alleged to be "exploiters" were annihilated. These leaders had been petitioning the government for a number of years promising to pursue their lives in a peaceful manner. This time, the Panchayat government chose to release them with the expectation that they would drive a wedge to the alliance. Once out of jail, the opposition welcomed them as the Nepalese Nelson Mandelas and, contrary to the expectations of the government, the leader of the group Mohan Chandra Adhikary expressed his readiness to join the peaceful movement.

Movement for the Restoration of Democracy

The scene of the streets of Kathmandu on February 18, 1990 is worth mentioning here. Prominent leaders of the Nepali Congress - Ganesh Man Singh, Krishna Prasad Bhattarai, Girija Prasad Koirala and others - were put under house arrest by the government. Ordinary people were curious as well as scared to go out into the streets expecting violence. All public places, street quarters, and court yards were manned by riot policy. *Sundhara*, a place where people were asked to assemble at noon by the Nepali Congress-United Left Front, was totally cordoned off by the riot police and the pedestrians were diverted to narrow alleys. At noon thousands of agitators had gradually assembled and were moving around the *Sundhara, New Road and Indrachok* area. Although the people numbered thousands, it was quiet and peaceful, and the faces of the people appeared anxious, curious, and scared. Perhaps Kathmandu had never experienced such a tranquil mass. At exactly 12.15 p.m., a sound of clapping was heard in central New Road, apparently to motivate the crowd, and in a second the pro-democracy agitators unfurled a red banner with the slogan "Down with the Panchayat System" and "We Want Democracy". Before the demonstrators had moved barely a tenth of a mile the riot police fired a couple of tear-gas canisters. Enraged by this, the agitators fought the police with rocks and bricks in several parts of the city for the whole day. The agitators also blocked the official procession mobilized by the government to celebrate the Democracy Day throwing rocks and bricks towards the Panchayat ministers and other bigwigs. Outside Kathmandu Valley, Hetauda and Chitawon in the south were the hotbeds of agitation. Agitation spread like a wild fire in other towns in the country. Posters began to appear in the streets of Kathmandu warning the King that he could face the fate of the recently executed Romanian dictator Nicolae Ceaucescu if democracy was not restored in the country.

The government resorted to massive suppression of the agitators. Thousands were arrested and treated brutally by the police. There was no telling of human rights abuses. The arrested persons, especially young boys, were thrown into septic tanks. Many were beaten mercilessly. In the beginning of March, an estimated 7,000 persons were arrested, about a dozen persons killed including some police officers, and hundreds were injured in police firings. Members of the Nepal Red Cross, who wanted to help the injured, were not only denied access to the hospital in Bharatpur but also arrested. The doctors in the hospitals claimed that the police had used dum-dums, a bullet banned by international convention. The Nepal Medical Association demanded a judicial enquiry into the use of these illegal bullets. Members of the Nepal Bar Association marched out of the courts protesting against the illegal arrests. Professors of university campuses went on a pen-down strike and held

31

a mass meeting to protest against human rights abuses, the curtailment of academic freedom and paid homage to those killed by the police. The Nepal Engineers' Association also came out with a statement denouncing the repressive measures taken by the government against a peaceful movement. About 200 writers and artists attempted to demonstrate their protest in a silent procession in front of the Royal Nepal Academy with black bands tied across their mouth, but they were taken into custody. Approximately 1,000 professors, teachers, lawyers, doctors, nurses, engineers and others who were discussing their role in the present context in the auditorium of the Tribhuvan University found themselves surrounded by the police, and everyone in the auditorium was ordered to follow the police officers. These intellectuals were loaded into trucks and taken to the central traffic police station, crammed into one hall where nobody could sit down for lack of space, kept for hours without food or water, interrogated, fingerprinted, and videotaped throughout the night.

The Panchayat government did not make any conciliatory move with the agitators. In order to create division in the pro-democracy alliance, the official media attempted to single out the communists for subversive activities. Every act of violence was billed in the name of communists, even though the Nepali Congress workers had also participated in them. On March 16, King Birendra made a speech in Pokhara in which he reminded everybody that the Panchayat system was the mandate given by the people in the referendum. The government embarked on organizing pro-Panchayat and "anti-subversive elements" rallies and formed "resistance committees" to suppress the agitators. A special command unit comprising the members of the sports council and *Tastravadi Vidhyarthi Mandal* was organized whose job was to terrorize anyone inclined to participate in anti-government demonstrations. Further, on April 1, the King reshuffled the cabinet of Prime Minister Marich Man Singh in which none of the soft-liners were included. However, only five days later the King dissolved the government of Marich Man Singh charging that it had failed to maintain law and order and appointed former Prime Minister Lokendra Bahadur Chand as the new Prime Minister.

The Popular Uprising

Prime Minister Lokendra Bahadur Chand immediately expressed his desire to engage in a dialogue with people with different shades of opinion. But it was too late. The United National People's Movement (UNPM), a communist united front that had refused to be allied with the Nepali Congress-United Left Front alliance, had made a call for the total *Bandh* (general strike) of Nepal on April 6. The streets of Kathmandu were deserted as there were no vehicles running around except official ones and shop-keepers did not open their shops. By midday, people from Kirtipur,

Patan, and Bhaktapur began to pour into central Kathmandu joined by the people of Kathmandu itself. An estimated mass of 200,000 people converged in the streets close to the Royal Palace, shouting the slogans: *"Biray* (derogatory term for Birendra) chor, desh chhod (Birendra thief, leave the country)"; "Birendra is a crook"; "The Queen is cheaper than a whore"; "Bring back all the money deposited in foreign banks". This was the first time in the history of Nepal that the royal family was vilified by the public in such proportions. The general strike, even though called by the UNPM, was actually spontaneous outbursts of the people which turned into a memorial popular uprising.

The demonstrators were fired at by the riot police killing nine persons (by official count) at Durbar Marga, less than two minutes' walk from the Royal Palace, as the crowd swelled and moved towards the Royal Palace. The death toll was estimated to be as high as 500, but the Interim Government that was established in the aftermath of the uprising was able to find names of only 66 persons killed during the people's movement. On the day of the uprising, the Royal Palace was heavily guarded by army units with armoured personnel carriers and mounted heavy machine guns. The King was said to be panicking inside the palace where it is said that a helicopter was ready to fly the Royal Family to an unknown destination. Kathmandu Valley where the houses of prominent Panchayat elites and royal relatives lived was burned and looted. The government called the army into the streets and imposed a 24-hours curfew and issued shoot-at-sight orders at anyone violating the curfew. On April 8, the curfew was relaxed from 8 to 10 in the morning and 5 to 7 in the evening.

Forced by the popular uprising, which was unprecedented in the living memory of Nepal, King Birendra invited Krishna Prasad Bhattarai, the acting President of the Nepali Congress and its General Secretary Girija Prasad Koirala and Mrs. Sahana Pradhan, the chairperson of United Left Front and its member Radha Krishna Mainali into the Royal Palace on the night of April 8, and after a brief consultation, the Royal Palace issued a communique that lifted the 30 year ban imposed on political parties. As the communique of the palace was read out by Nepal television in the middle of the night, thousands of people turned out into the streets, while the curfew was still in effect, to celebrate the victory of democracy over monocracy. The security forces who were unaware of the palace communique fired in a couple of places killing at least one person at Naradevi.

The Formation of an Interim Coalition Government

The Royal Palace communique had only lifted the ban on parties, but the Panchayat government was not dissolved. Prime Minister Lokendra Bahadur Chand's government opened up negotiations with the multi-party side apparently with an expectation that they would join the government. But people were so angry with the Panchas that on April 15 thousands of them rounded the Royal Nepal Academy building where the talks between the Panchas and the multi-party representatives were taking place and demanded an end to them. On April 16, the palace announced the resignation of Pancha Prime Minister Lokendra Bahadur Chand, the King dissolved the National Panchayat, the Panchayat Policy Enquiry Committee, and all six class organizations associated with the Panchayat system, and suspended various clauses of the constitution. The King called the multi-party leaders to the Royal Palace and asked the Supreme Leader of the Nepali Congress Ganesh Man Singh to head the government. Ganesh Man Singh declined the offer on health grounds and proposed Krishna Prasad Bhattarai for the job, a name which was acceptable to the United Left Front leaders too. King Birendra accepted the suggestion and on April 19, 1990 appointed K.P. Bhattarai as the Prime Minister with the responsibility of conducting general elections in the "near future".

Krishna Prasad Bhattarai formed an 11 member Interim Cabinet consisting of four Nepali Congress members, three United Left Front members, two independent human rights activists and two royal nominees. The three United Left Front members in the government represented NCP (ML), NCP (Marxist), and NCP (Manadhar group). This was the first time in the history of Nepal that communists had emerged to become the partners in power. Prime Minister Bhattarai announced that the priorities of the Interim Government was to frame a new constitution and hold general elections for parliament within a year. The Prime Minister also announced that the constitution to be drafted would lower the voting age to 18 years in view of the role played by the youth in dismantling the old order.

Contrary to the popular expectation that the new government would take legal action against the former Panchayat officials who had enriched themselves through corruption and who had committed atrocities during the democracy movement, the Interim Government did nothing except form a commission known as the Mallik Commission to investigate the matter. When the Mallik Commission submitted its more than one thousand pages report and recommended several actions against approximately 150 persons, the Interim Government of K.P. Bhattarai passed the responsibility of taking action against those criminals on to the upcoming elected government.

The government also took over all legislative powers until the new parliament was elected. Prime Minister Krishna Prasad Bhattarai visited India and both governments established status-quo ante in their relations allowing trade to return to the pre-1989 level. The responsibility of signing the actual treaties, being a matter of vital importance as well as a sensitive one, was left for the future government that was to come after the election in Nepal.

The Constitution and the Parliamentary Elections

In November 1990, King Birendra promulgated the Constitution of the Kingdom of Nepal (1990) that was drafted by the Constitution Recommendation Commission after a long debate. The Commission was composed of nine individuals representing different ideological shades with a supreme court judge as its chairman who was believed to be close as well to the King as to the Nepali Congress. The members of the Commission toured different parts of the country collecting the opinion of the people. They also made an educational tour of the Western countries and collected information on several democratic constitutions. But it turned out later that they had made British constitutional conventions and the Indian constitution their point of reference, while drafting the constitution for Nepal.

The constitution making period, i.e. from September to the promulgation date, was a very sensitive time as both political party leaders and the common people were extremely concerned about the emerging power equation in the country. Many expressed concern that the newly acquired freedom could be slipped away in the process of constitution making. The role of the monarchy once again became a matter of hot debate both inside and outside the Commission. Nirmal Lama, a member of the Commission representing the radical wing of the Communist Party, advocated an election to a constituent assembly, but others were not prepared for it. The burden of defending the monarchy was on members representing the Nepali Congress and others with a tilt towards the King. The deliberations of the CRC were constantly leaked to the press by Nirmal Lama apparently to make the public vigilant about the whole process. As the first draft was completed, it sparked off widespread debate. The vested interests around the Royal Palace led by the King's relatives began to lobby for more power to the King, and it was rumoured that the palace circulated a counter-draft of the constitution. By doing this, the palace officials and royal relatives were putting pressure on the Commission as well as on the Interim Government to respect the royal prerogatives and privileges. The lesser royalties were also scared that their titles and privy purses would vanish. The Constitution Recommending Commission and the Interim Government tried to accommodate these concerns and finally submitted the constitution to the King for promulgation.

The constitution defined the multi-party system, constitutional monarchy and popular sovereignty as the fundamental features of the new polity. King Birendra did not appear happy, while promulgating the new constitution which was carried live by Nepal TV. He walked straight to the podium, read the preamble of the constitution, and walked straight back without exchanging a word with the Prime Minister or anybody else present at the ceremony. He was no longer a sovereign.

35

His powers were drastically reduced. Yet, the constitution vested the emergency powers with him. The constitution provided for a parliament consisting of two houses - the Lower House (Pratinidhi Sabha) and the Upper House (Rastriya Sabha). The constitution settled for a first-past-the-post system to elect 205 members to the Lower House, while the single-transferable vote system was introduced to elect 50 members of the Upper House, which consists of 60 members including 10 royal nominees.

The Interim Government issued the main election laws in February 1991, and the Election Commission announced May 12, 1991 as the date for a national election. This was to be the second parliamentary election after the 1959 elections, but it was also the fourth general election in terms of adult franchise. The election law divided the country into 205 single-member constituencies. The constituencies were delimited both in view of population density as well as geographical distance. The framers of the law did not want to make any change in the existing 75 administrative districts. The representation for these districts ranges from 1 to 6 members. The two densely populated districts of Jhapa and Morang in Eastern Terai close to the Indian border have been allotted six members each. The capital district, Kathmandu, is divided into five constituencies. Eleven districts, mainly in the high Himalayas, form a constituency each, one of them (Manang) having as few as 6,249 voters.

The voting age was lowered to 18 years from the earlier 21 years during the 1959, 1981, and 1986 general elections. This led to an addition of about 700,000 new voters in the voters' list registered by the Election Commission for the purpose of National Panchayat elections that were due in 1991. The Election Commission, as in the past, faced a number of problems in the process of voter registration. The lack of a vital statistical record keeping system led to a difficult situation in which the enumerators had no way of assessing the age of voters. Inaccessibility to remote villages in the hills and mountains was yet another painful reality. The secretaries of Village Development Committees, who were employed as enumerators, often had to rely on information provided by the village notables familiar with the village population. In the process some ineligible names were registered and bona fide names were omitted. In many cases, women voters' names were registered by adding 'Mrs.' to their husbands' full names. Moreover, some persons with dual residence were registered more than once, whereas others were forgotten, including the Home Minister Yog Prasad Upadhyaya, as it was revealed when he appeared at the polling station. The voters' lists were published in each district headquarters in late March, and people were given the opportunity of filing claims for inclusion if their names were omitted. This led to an increase of voters from 10,694,535 to 11,191,777 of which 52.7 per cent were men and 47.3 per cent were women.

Thus, the number of voters had increased from 9,044 million in the 1986 Panchayat general election to 11,191 million in the 1991 parliamentary election.

A total of 44 parties that had emerged following the reestablishment of the multi-party system applied for registration, but only 40 were permitted to run in the election. Four parties were refused registration on the grounds that they were organized on communal and sectarian lines. Of the registered 40 parties, only 20 parties contested the election with their 1,126 candidates. In addition, there were 219 independent candidates. Of the total of 1,345 candidates, 80 were women. The parties were constitutionally required to nominate at least 5 per cent women, and actually nominated 7 per cent, though generally not in the most favourable constituencies.

Before the promulgation of the constitution, the leftists as well as the rightist forces were in total disarray. The marathon talks for broader communist unity had produced no results. In late 1990 two major partners of the United Left Front, Nepal Communist Party (Marxist-Leninist) and Nepal Communist Party (Marxist), succeeded in merging themselves into Nepal Communist Party (Unified Marxists and Leninists, UML). The NCP (Marxist-Leninist) was a close-knit party with nation-wide organizational cells, whereas the NCP (Marxist) had more leaders with national and international popularity. That is to say, the Marxist-Leninist party was a party without leaders and the Marxist party, a party without cadres. The merger of the two would provide a sound leadership as well as the organizational network badly needed for the election.

Meanwhile, unity talks were also going on between the communists considered to be the extremists. Of the six partners of the United National People's Movement, three agreed on a merger to become the NCP (Unity Centre). The Unity Centre made further attempts, rather unsuccessfully, to bring other radicals into its fold. They were divided on the vital question of whether to participate in the election at all. The NCP (Masal group) advocated boycott of the election, while the Unity Centre argued for participation "in order to expel the bourgeois democracy from its own chamber". It created an umbrella organization calling itself the United People's Front hoping to accommodate all communists who called themselves Maoists.

The problem of disunity was much more severe and pronounced in the camp of erstwhile Pancha parties. Both parties had emerged in the late spring of 1990 with the same name following the disagreement over the question of leadership. Surya Bahadur Thapa's group refused unity with Lokendra Bahadur Chand's group charging the latter as an agent of the Royal Palace officials, while Chand's group charged the Thapa group as an agent of India. The animosities between these two groups were the results of Panchayat times when the Chand group had masterminded the no-confidence motion against Surya Bhadur Thapa apparently on the instigation of vested interests around the Royal Palace.

Before the election, the major parties were commonly believed to be the Nepali Congress, the Communist UML, and the two National Democratic parties (NDP) led by ex-Pancha Prime Ministers Surya Bhadur Thapa and Lokendra Bhadur Chand. Thus, a four-party system was expected to result from the election, with a dominant Nepali Congress party flanked on the left by the Communist UML and on the right by the NDP (Thapa), while the NDP (Chand) would constitute the right-wing of the party system. Many people expected parliament to be a hung-house with neither party gaining the majority to form the government. The Nepali Congress was definitely considered to be the largest of all, but its capacity to muster the needed majority was doubted by everybody. The question, then, was which party the Nepali Congress would make its ally to form the government.

The election was generally conducted in an orderly way. There were a total of 8,225 polling centres and 6,564 sub-centres, and a total of 62,881 personnel were engaged in conducting the elections. In the election, a total of 7,291,084 voters (65 per cent) voted of which 322,023 were invalid. The international as well as the national teams of observers had only minor irregularities to report. When the results began to pour in from the town areas the day after the election, it immediately became clear that a close contest between the Nepali Congress and the Communist UML was taking place. The two National Democratic parties who were expected to constitute the right wing of the political system were almost wiped out in terms of seats. Neither of their leaders, Surya Bahadur Thapa and Lokendra Bahadur Chand, were able to get elected. An ethnic party, Sadvabana (literally meaning Goodwill) advocating close relations with India, obtained six seats.

The achievement of the communists far surpassed earlier expectations. Of the ten seats allotted to the Kathmandu Valley, the Communist UML and another communist party, the United People's Front won eight seats, including constituency no. 1 where 66-year-old Prime Minister K.P. Bhattarai was defeated by 39-year-old fiery orator and General Secretary of the Communist UML, Madan Bhandari, in a close contest by 751 votes, making international headlines. The Nepali Congress, however, emerged victorious with 110 seats in the final results. Only eight of the 20 parties obtained representation, and only four were moderately successful in getting a fair share of the candidates elected. The two National Democratic parties got only four seats between them. Of the 1,345 candidates, 751 (55.84 per cent) candidates lost their deposits among which 86 candidates were from the NDP (Thapa) and 119 candidates were from the NDP (Chand). Compared with earlier expectations, the political balance was tilted strongly towards the left. The majority obtained by the Nepali Congress was also a surprise to many observers. Its support came

Table 1. Parties, Symbols, Number of Candidates, and Election Results

	No. cand.	No. seats	% seats	% votes
Left wing				
Nepal Communist Party (UML) [Sun]	177	69	33.6	29.3
Nepal Mazdoor Kisan Party (Nepal Labour-Peasant Party) [Drum]	30	2	1.0	1.3
Nepal Communist Party (Dem.) [Sickle]	75	2	1.0	2.5
Samyukta Jana Morcha (United People's Front) [Sickle & Hammer]	69	9	4.4	5.0
Nepal Communist Party (Verma) [Khukuri, or crossed knives]	35	0	0.0	0.2
Nepal Communist Party (Amatya) [Sickle and three corncobs]	15	0	0.0	0.1
Janavadi Morcha (Democratic People's Front) [Oil Lamp]	14	0	0.0	0.0
Centrists				
Nepali Congress [Tree]	204	110	53.6	39.5
Janata Party (Samajbadi) [Moon and star]	15	0	0.0	0.1
Right wing				
National Democratic Party (Thapa) [Cow]	163	1	0.5	5.6
National Democratic Party (Chand) [Plough]	154	3	1.5	6.9
Conservative Party [Spade]	6	0	0.0	0.0
Ethnic and Regional				
Sadvabana Party [Hand]	75	6	2.9	4.3
Rastriya Jana Mukti Morcha [Man]	50	0	0.0	0.5
Others				
National People's Party H [Fish]	28	0	0.0	0.1
National People's Party N [Pair of Oxen]	9	0	0.0	0.1
Nepal National People's Party [Finger pointing to star]	4	0	0.0	0.1
Party of Labourers and Peasants [Pitcher]	1	0	0.0	0.0
All Nepal Political Unity [Bee]	1	0	0.0	0.0
Majority People's Party [Water Container]	1	0	0.0	0.0
Independent Candidates	219	3	1.5	4.4
Total	1,345	205	100	100

mainly from the western part of Nepal, whereas the Communist UML won most of the eastern constituencies. In fact, a totalling up of the votes received by all the communist parties in 25 constituencies suggests that had the communists been united in the election, they would have received extra 25 seats at the cost of the Nepali Congress and would have formed the government! The following table shows the election result in terms of seats and in per cent of the valid votes.

In spite of what Table 1 shows, the three independents have joined the Nepali Congress later on, increasing the party's strength to 113 members. In view of the election of Nepali Congress' General Secretary Girija Prasad Koirala and Communist UML General Secretary Madan Bhandari from two different constituencies, it is more correct to say that only 203 candidates were elected. A by-election was held in February 1992 in two constituencies vacated by Koirala and Bhandari, and in these elections the Nepali Congress and Communist UML were successful in retaining their previous position. Of the 205 Nepalese parliamentarians elected there are seven women - five from the Nepali Congress and two from the Communist UML. The regional strength of the parties is shown in Table 2 below.

Table 2. Regional Strength of Parties in Parliament

Parties	East	Cent.	West	Mid-west	Far-west	Total
Nepali Congress	16	29	32	18	18	113
Communist Party (UML)	31	25	8	5	0	69
United People's Front	1	4	0	4	0	9
Sadvabana Party	1	0	5	0	0	6
Communist Party (Dem.)	0	2	0	0	0	2
Labour-Peasant Party	0	1	0	0	1	2
National Democratic Party (Thapa)	0	0	0	0	1	1
National Democratic Party (Chand)	0	3	0	0	0	3
Total	49	64	45	27	20	205

Out of the eight parties in parliament, six, i.e. the Nepali Congress, the Communist UML, the United People's Front, the Sadvabana party, and both National Democratic parties, succeeded in establishing themselves as national parties by securing more than three per cent of the valid votes polled. The other highlight of the election includes the victory of 16 members of the dissolved National Panchayat. Six winning candidates of the Nepali Congress had also been the winners in the 1959 parliamentary election. Of the eleven ministers in the Interim Government, seven had contested the election but only three got elected.

Second Experiment in Parliamentary Democracy

The Interim Coalition Government resigned after the election paving the way for Nepali Congress' single party government. Girija Prasad Koirala, the younger brother of the first elected Prime Minister B.P. Koirala, was elected as Nepali Congress' parliamentary leader, who subsequently formed the government with 14 other ministers. On the other hand, the UML which had emerged as the strong opposition party in parliament with 69 seats elected the party president Man Mohan Adhikary as its leader in the house and appointed him as the head of the shadow cabinet.

The first session of Pratinidhi Sabha commenced in June 1991. All members in the house except 22 were first timers for a national legislative assembly. That being so, the parliamentary secretariat organized an orientation programme to the members in which they were tutored by bureaucrats and legal experts on how the business of parliament takes place and how the members are expected to follow parliamentary norms, values, and behaviour. A mock election based on the single-transferable vote system was conducted to familiarize the members with the system, the first task in parliament being to elect members to the Rastriya Sabha (Upper House) based on this system.

With the formation of Rastriya Sabha, King Birendra addressed both Houses of Parliament in which he outlined the policies of the Nepali Congress government. But within a couple of weeks the that government faced a major problem when the civil servants went on strike demanding higher salaries to compensate for inflation. Prime Minister G.P. Koirala had asked for a period of one year to sort out the problems of the nation, but the civil servants who were hard hit by the spiralling prices had hardly any patience to wait. Opposition communist parties supported the civil servants' movement, badgered the government ministers inside parliament, and walked out of the house protesting against the government's insensitivity towards the civil servants. The government, however, remained firm and moved to take disciplinary actions against the striking civil servants while condemning the opposition as irresponsible. Inexperienced as they were in parliament-ary practices, the treasury bench as well as the opposition found themselves frequently at loggerheads. The opposition leaders' speeches and their proposals for a coordinated approach to solve the nation's complex problems were not heard by the government ministers. The government, in the first session of parliament, failed to take the opposition into confidence and as a result parliament appeared to be a monkey house.

The crisis of confidence existing between the government and the opposition was once again visible during the winter session of parliament in February-March 1992. The government's signing of Trade and Transit Treaties and other Agreements with India in early December 1991 became a matter of life and death in the Nepali government. The government had made some understandings with the government of India in matters of harnessing the water resources of Nepal for the benefit of both countries. According to the understanding, India was to make feasibility studies in several river valleys of Nepal with a view to generate electricity, provide irrigation facilities, and ultimately control the floods that damage both Nepali and Indian lands. The opposition quite naturally made it a big issue. The leaders of all opposition parties, except the Sadvabana Party which advocates closer relations with India, accused the government's constitutional authority of making agreements and understandings without the approval of two-thirds of the members of parliament. They demanded that all texts of the agreements and understandings be submitted to the house for discussion. The Nepalese have, in the past, felt cheated by India in the Koshi and Gandak river projects. Experts believe that India has reaped more benefits from the Koshi and Gandak river agreements without providing corresponding benefits to Nepal. Given this past experience, the people in Nepal had valid reasons for doubting India's intentions.

The government tried to fizzle out the opposition by presenting a statement of public importance in which the substance of the agreements and understandings were noted. The opposition, however, was not satisfied and insisted on seeing the original draft of the documents and disrupted the proceedings of the house occupying the rostrum and chanting slogans against the government. Finally, the Prime Minister agreed to show the minutes of the meeting held between the authorities of India and Nepal. The opposition members found nothing new in the minutes that was not presented in the government's statement on public importance. Had the Prime Minister consulted the leaders of the opposition immediately after his return from India, this kind of situation could have been avoided. But the crisis of confidence that pervades Nepali society hardly permitted the Prime Minister to do so.

Democracy on Trial?

The performance of the elected government has been much criticized by both the members of the ruling party itself and by the opposition parties. The workers of the Nepali Congress who had put their lives at stake during the thirty years of Panchayat rule have found themselves alienated by the leadership. Their demand for swift action against former Panchayat officials as recommended in the Mallik Commission have not been met by the government. Some informed sources claim that the government cannot and will not take any action against former Panchayat officials because of the "gentlemen agreement" made at the Royal Palace at the time of the transfer of power. Sources close to the old establishment maintain that the very creation of the Mallik Commission was a breach of faith on the part of the Interim Government led by Nepali Congress President K.P. Bhattarai. In light of the government's attempt to appease the traditional elements by either letting them stay in power or by giving new appointments, the theory of a "gentlemen agreement" appears to hold ground. This led to a conflict in the party and the Supreme Leader Ganesh Man Singh himself threatened to resign from the party as well as from politics if the government continued to neglect the sentiments of the people and the party workers.

The general public was dissatisfied with the government for its failure to control market prices and provide basic utility services at lower prices. Prime Minister Koirala's promise to provide economic relief to the people was hampered immediately following India's decision to devalue the rupee by almost 25 per cent against major foreign currencies. Nepal had no choice but to follow the Indian coat-tail because its economy is closely tied with India. As a result, the prices of essential commodities went up. While the government had little control over this development, the government imposed yet another price hike by telling the government-owned corporations and the university to raise the cost of electricity, telephone calls, and college tuition and fees at an alarmingly high rate, apparently after pressure from the World Bank and the International Monetary Fund whose loan is vital for Nepal's development plans.

Despite the poor performance of the government and the opposition's concerted effort to benefit from the inefficiency of the government, there appears to be no alternative to the Nepali Congress party as indicated by elections held for local government bodies in May 1992. In these elections, people voted the ruling party candidates to offices in more than 65 per cent of the country's four thousand or more village development committees. The opposition UML failed to capture more than 26 per cent of the local government positions, while members of the National Democratic parties and other parties received the rest of the positions.

The Nepali Congress party's victory in local elections came as a surprise to many. Political analysts believe that people voted for the party not because it had an excellent record, but because the opposition had acted in a manner that was perceived to be unparliamentary by the attentive public. The ruling party supporters had blamed the opposition parties for not allowing the government sufficient time to make the policies that are important for the nation. Moreover, the opposition's politics of "from the house to the streets" was not much appreciated by members of the responsible intelligentsia. Furthermore, the opposition was not able to reap

43

anything from the government when it supported the strike of civil servants. Similarly, it could not detect any "sinister design" in the minutes of meetings and agreements and understandings between the governments of India and Nepal.

The ruling party's image and popularity was expected to wane in the aftermath of police firing at a protest demonstration organized by the United People's Front on April 6, 1992 killing 14 persons. The demonstrators were demanding the resignation of the government for its failure to check spiralling prices and for "congressizing" the bureaucracy. The UML also entered to fish in the troubled waters following the shooting incident and organized several protest marches all over the country demanding the resignation of the Nepali Congress government. All these demonstrations were taking place on the eve of local elections and therefore many thought that the ruling party was losing its touch with the masses and predicted its defeat in the upcoming local elections by the communists as well as the National Democratic parties. But the effect of these demonstrations turned out to be counter-productive for the organizers themselves as people could not appreciate the unconventional behaviour displayed during the demonstrations. Nepalese people once again gave the mandate to the Nepali Congress party to decide the fate of the nation. But the opposition parties are charging the government for massively rigging the local elections.

In this situation, what can we expect of Nepalese democracy? Many sensible observers are of the opinion that the transition to a democratic way of life is going to be painful in Nepal in view of the contradictions inherent between the traditional cultural norms of Nepal and the dynamics of plural democracy as its is understood in Western democracies. The Western concept of the rule of law that justice should be administered independently of political considerations and that all citizens should be equal before the law is an alien concept for the majority of the Nepali people. While the elites are not tired of paying lip service to this concept, in reality they themselves ignore it. Political party leaders, no matter how democratic and secularist they may describe themselves, use traditional values and norms to consolidate their power and influence. Therefore, it is important to outline some of the basic characteristics of the political processes and dynamics of Nepal that are likely to shape the future of democracy.

Nepali society does not distinguish between political, social, and personal relations. The political behaviour and the range of influence of an individual is determined by his social status and personal ties. As a result, political parties tend to be oriented to some aspects of communal or ethnic framework of politics. They represent the personality of a charismatic leader. Power resides in the person of high officials and not in their offices or institutions. Personal cliques act as intermediaries in decision-making. The personalized nature of power provides the party and government leaders with a high degree of freedom in determining the matters of strategy and tactics. It, in turn, determines the nature of the political loyalty of the followers. Institutions are used to formalize the decisions made by a particular clique in some leaders' living rooms.

The personalized power structure has led to an emphasis on the principle of proximity. In Nepal there is a fierce drive to be near those who are at the top of political decision-making. No one has noticed any change in this tradition even after the emergence of democracy. During the Panchayat time, aspirants for governmental resources used to spend their time in *Chakari* (obsequious attendance) around the homes of Royal Palace secretaries. In post-Panchayat Nepal, they are seen around the homes and offices of Nepali Congress leaders. Once the *Chakariwal* (obsequious attendant) gets a feeling that the person he is doing *Chakari* to is no longer a powerful personality, he quickly withdraws from his regular ritual of *Chakari* to that person and moves on to another person whom he considers to be powerful. This can be illustrated from the fact that these days very few appear in the courtyard of the homes of the Royal Palace secretaries. They have moved to the courtyards of Nepali Congress leaders and ministers. The popular psychology is that those who possess power have to command more influence and accomplish more things than ordinary citizens. People want to be followers of a strong personality who can provide them with security as well as with prestige. If a leader cannot act up to the expectations of his *afno manchhes* (own people), then the leader is considered to be an impotent person and thus worthy of being deserted.

Ideology does not play a major role in Nepalese politics because Nepalis are preoccupied with their own inner world. Dependent relationships (patron-client) determine the extent of a leader's power rather than the ideology. The political loyalty of the followers is governed more by a sense of identification with a concrete group - communal, ethnic or sectarian - rather than with the policy or ideology of the party. The followers expect that the leaders will seek to maximize communal, ethnic, and sectarian interests rather than the ideological interests of the party. Hence, political parties have grown out of a system of patronage politics. Internal conflicts within the party or parties are rarely related to ideology. Caste and kinship ties and factional affiliations related to the need for status and prestige or the desire for material rewards have been the crucial factors in inter-party as well as intra-party conflicts. Reference to ideology is, however, made to legitimize the wishes of the leaders.

The majority of the people in Nepal do not differentiate between a political system and a government. The opposition to the government takes the form of opposition to the political system. This belief, moreover, is augmented by the irresponsible utterances of the leaders of the party in power that the Nepali Congress

45

is democracy and democracy is the Nepali Congress.

Nepali society suffers from a vicious circle of crisis of confidence, sense of insecurity, and behavioural irresponsibility. The personalized nature of power by definition is irrational. Hence, subordinates hesitate to make decisions or implement decisions even though they are empowered to do so without first checking the mood and attitude of the man on top. He does so because he is scared that he could be fired or punished if his actions are not in line with the thinking of his superior. The superior also does not fully trust his subordinates because he has doubt in his mind that subordinates may be playing at the hand of somebody else to discredit or destroy him. Thus, the sense of insecurity coupled with the crisis of confidence naturally leads to irresponsible behaviour resulting in delays in every walks of public life. Democracy has not been able to bring about even a minor change in the state of affairs.

Democracy is essentially a way of life based on the exercise of patience. But patience is a rare commodity in Nepal when it comes to discussions of public importance. The discussions on public policy or any other debates do not take place in a peaceful manner. The authoritarian feudal mentality handed down from generation to generation hardly permits one to listen to another. There is always a tendency to impose one's own opinion on the other. That is why within minutes of the start of a debate, hot exchange of words ensues, and the meeting ends up with personal vilification and at times it even ends up with fist-fights.

There is no consensus as to the legitimate means and ends of political action. There are parties like the United People's Front whose aim it is to expose the "bourgeois character" of the parliamentary system and prepare the way for a people's revolution. There are parties advocating the peaceful transfer of power. Uneven economic development, wide disparities in wealth and income, communal, ethnic and caste related tensions contribute to the lack of societal consensus on fundamental national issues. Unlike the elites of previous Panchayat rule, leaders of the newly established democracy, particularly the Nepali Congress, accept the legitimacy of interest group conflicts. The democratic system as it is understood emphasizes diversity, pluralism, and dispersed power. Different voluntary associations emerge and compete for influence on the political market place. The recognition of interest group conflicts in an essentially traditional society like Nepal which is stronger than the state invites the danger of group polarization, political stagnation, instability, and even civil war. Therefore, the main problem facing the Nepali Congress government today is how to create rules and institutions that can reconcile group conflicts. Particularly important is the development of norms of toleration, compromise, and civility. The indication, so far, is not encouraging.

Nepal lacks the economic and political conditions needed for an effective democratic system. First, both civic values and national integrity structures are weak. Parliament is there, but it is not expected to make crucial decisions. Political party leaders rarely establish close contact with the masses. They are always seen in Kathmandu in the homes and offices of ministers seeking personal advantages. The ties of the leaders to sub-national groups seem stronger than the welfare of the whole society. Under the present condition of economic scarcity and rising expectations of the masses, the Nepali Congress leaders do not seem to be able (or do not seem to want) to develop the procedural consensus needed to accommodate conflicting group claims on limited governmental resources. As a result, democracy once again appears to be on trial.

CHAPTER 3

HOW THE VOTERS SAW THE PARTIES

The study of the 1991 election in Nepal is a study of a party system in being. Many parties and candidates gave up during the campaign, others changed their strategies and appeals in response to these withdrawals. There was no prior parliamentary record neither of the parties nor of most of the candidates with the exception of Nepali Congress and the Communist party, which had participated in the experiment of parliamentary rule in 1959. In the new parties party members and activists had been enroled over a period of little more than half a year. If a party system is defined as the relations of size, coalition and conflict between the parties making up the system, then one can hardly say that a party system existed at the time when the votes were cast.

Still, the Nepalese party system did not emerge all of a sudden out of the blue sky. The image of the Nepali Congress party was shaped by its role in the anti-Rana revolution of 1950, by the events of the brief democracy of 1959-60 when the party was in power, by the activity and messages of the exiled party leaders during their long struggle against the Panchayat regime, and perhaps by its Indian counter-part. The images of the National Democratic parties led by forme prime ministers Lokandra Bahadur Chand and Surya Bahadur Thapa were influenced by their partici-pation in Nepalese government and their defense of the Panchayat system. The image of the Communist party was affected by its activity in the underground move-ment leading up to the 1990 uprising. And even the small parties had historical images, at least to some of the voters, by which the enlightened commentators could fit them into the future party system of Nepal. Thus when parties were at last made legal as one cause of the April 1990 revolution, the unofficial party system came into the open and was communicated to the ordinary voters during the election campaign.

How did the Nepalese voters orient themselves and the parties in such a way as to come up with an ordered and consistent choice, limiting the parliamentary representation to a handful of parties bound to particular competitive relations vis-a-vis one another? What criteria did the voters apply in judging the parties, and were these the same that the political elite employed? These are the main questions to be approached in this chapter.

The Perception of Differences between the Parties

First of all, the efficiency of a party system in bringing public demands upward and giving weight to them depends on the public seeing some important differences between the parties. Whether in the end this leads to actual policies that are responsive to public opinion is another matter, but surely the belief that "parties matter" is where responsive party government begins.

Question 19 in the Nepalese questionnaire read, "Do you think there are important differences in the politics and programs of different parties?" To this, 42 percent in the (weighted) sample answered Yes, 15 percent No, and 43 percent Don't Know. The high frequency of Don't Know responses were expected and natural. Only two parties had had a chance of carrying out their politics, namely the Nepali Congress party and the Communist UML party, and their policies had to be reconciled within the interim government. Therefore it was not the differences between these parties that had dominated the interim period. And with regard to party programmes, few Nepalese voters are able to read them.

It seems therefore more significant that the question resulted in almost three times as many positive as negative replies. Evidently one finds little of the sophisticated and somewhat cynical view, common in Western party systems that no real differences exist between the major parties once they are in government. Such cynicism might perhaps be expected at least among the well-educated strata of the Nepalese people, but as Table 1 makes clear it is the other way round.

Among those having no schooling the relation between positive and negative responses was 2:1, in the middle category it was 4:1, and among the well-educated it was above 9:1. Thus it was the informed opinion that there were indeed important differences between the parties.

Table 1. Perception of Policy Differences between the Parties (Percentages)

	Major Differences between Parties?			
	Yes	No	Don't know	Total
School education:				
No School	33	16	51	100
Primary or low secondary	59	15	27	101
High secondary or more	84	9	7	100
Age of respondent:				
18-29 years	55	19	26	100
30-44 years	38	16	46	100
45 years or more	39	13	48	100
Sex:				
Male	40	16	44	100
Female	43	14	42	99

Looking at the age and sex breakdowns one finds that the perception of differences was most widespread among the young, and that there was no significant difference between men and women in this regard. The new generation, which is also the best educated, are leading in the belief that there is a real choice between policies from the start of Nepalese multiparty democracy.

New Ideas or Tradition?

The party systems of new democracies in developing countries may take one of several forms. To mention three types: (1) the party system may reflect ethnic, religious, or regional identifications; (2) it may be dominated by one party which has been the leading force in the struggle against the old order; or (3) it may become aligned along a left-right dimension, stretching from parties which demand radical change to parties which have been associated with the old order. These types are probably not equally conducive to democracy. In the first type, the centrifugal forces are strong, and violence is often a significant element in the struggle between the parties. The second type is close to a one-party state, tends to suppress opposition, and often leads to corruption and nepotism. The third type is the path followed by most if not all European democracies, and it has generally led to economic success as well as internal political stability, except where radical mass movements of either communist or fascist types have staged a revolution and overthrown the multiparty system.

The emerging Nepalese party system appears to be of the third type, and only has a trace of the two first-mentioned types. The leading Nepali Congress party is checked on its left side by one major and several minor communist parties and on its right by two National Democratic parties. The combined strength of these oppositional forces makes it unlikely that Nepal will develop into a one-party state. On the other hand, the split on both the left and right wings, the comparative weakness of the right wing, and the fact that the strong Marxist-Leninist party, despite its name, is pledged to democracy, makes it unlikely that a revolution or coup against democracy will be undertaken or at least can succeed. Finally, the ethnic or separatist element is present mainly in the form of the rather weak Sadvabana party struggling for closer relations with India.

In this chapter we shall study to what extent this bird's eye view of the Nepalese party system is concordant with the perceptions of the Nepalese voters and political elite. At the first election of a new democracy one might well fear that the ordinary voters either are confused about the relative positions of the parties or else that they have no political perceptions and attitudes of any consequence. In the case of the party system which unfolded during the interim government, our field study sought to investigate this possibility by inviting the respondents to place the major parties along a left-right dimension (Question 21). However, we presumed that this placement had to be done without using the very labels of "left" and "right", which presuppose a European political tradition. Furthermore, the issues of nationalisation of industry, social equality, improvement of work conditions, and building welfare institutions, which are conventionally regarded as the divisive ones in Western party systems, have little reality at the present stage of Nepalese development, nor did they play any significant role during the election campaign. As an agricultural society Nepal does not have any sizeable industrial labour force that can serve as a base for leftwing parties. Consequently we approached the left-right division from another angle.

The more general meaning of left as social change in the direction of greater equality (e.g., Lipset 1960) may serve as a criterion for aligning the parties. As a developing society Nepal is penetrated by thinking in terms of traditional and modern life styles, traditional and modern beliefs, traditional and modern institutions, and so forth. To test whether this developmental framework also puts its stamp on the perception of the parties, Question 21 read, "Some parties want to preserve old tradition while others stand for new ideas, and still others are in between. Where would you put [A] the Nepali Congress party, [B] the United M-L, [C] the NDP (Thapa), and [D] the NDP (Chand)? And [E] where would you put yourself?"

These four parties were chosen because in the beginning of the campaign, when our questionnaire was constructed, it was generally believed that the Nepalese party system would be a four-party system with the Chand party constituting the right wing. As it turned out, the election result was strongly biased toward the left relative to this expectation. Nevertheless these four parties were the four largest and best known parties, and the only ones to put up candidates in the majority of districts.

Table 2 shows that the respondents clearly differentiated between the Communist UML position, the Nepali Congress position, and the National Democratic position in the way we expected. They did not differentiate between the positions of the two National Democratic parties, however. The only difference is that more respondents were able to locate the Chand position than the Thapa position.

More than one-fourth of the Nepalese respondents (in the weighted sample) had not formed perceptions of the Nepali Congress party's position, and in the case of the other three parties it is between one third and one half. This is what might be expected from voters that are quite inexperienced in judging the parties ideologically. Yet the fact that the remaining voters distinguished so well between three positions in locating these four parties means that the Nepalese party system

Table 2. Association of the Major Parties with New Ideas or Tradition (Percentages)

	New Ideas	In Be-tween	Tradi-tion	Don't know	Total
Communist UML	55	5	6	34	100
Nepali Congress	20	23	30	28	101
NDP (Thapa)	2	5	47	46	100
NDP (Chand)	3	8	52	37	100

may be considered an ideological left-right system in its main contour. The overwhelming majority placed the Communist UML as a party of new ideas and the two National Democratic parties as parties of tradition. In the case of the Congress party the votes divided almost evenly among the three positions (with a slight tilt toward traditionalism). It is obvious that this "muddled" position of the Congress party, when compared with the clear positions of the three other parties, is a very realistic assessment, indicating that the Congress party attempts to span the entire range of the spectrum, standing for new ideas in some respects and for tradition in others, and for an in-between position in yet others. We shall return to this subject later in the chapter.

Elite Perceptions of the Party System

How well does this public image of the party system correspond to the image held by the political elite? Since the same question was asked to the elite survey of 100 persons, the two sets of perceptions can be compared directly. Table 3 shows the elite perceptions.

Table 3. Association of the Major Parties with New Ideas and Tradition among Elite Respondents (Percentages=Raw Numbers since N=100)

	New Ideas	In Be-tween	Tradi-tion	Don't know	Total
Communist UML	74	14	2	10	100
Nepali Congress	22	45	33	0	100
NDP (Thapa)	2	21	58	19	100
NDP (Chand)	1	24	63	12	100

It is seen that the agreement is very good, the elite sample being less inclined to give Don't Know responses, and consequently more inclined to give higher figures in the active columns. Granted this natural tendency, the most interesting deviation between the two samples is that the elite tend to place the Nepali Congress in the centre whereas the mass respondents place it more to the right. A slight tendency in the same direction is visible for the two National Democratic parties: the elite sample is not quite so inclined to place these parties on the right as are the general public.

This model of the Nepalese party system can be completed with the positions of the remaining parties by means of the interviews conducted with the parliamentary members during the autumn session of the two houses of the Nepalese parliament. 256 interviews were completed, covering 96 percent of the parliamentarians. These interviews, however, also reveals some interesting deviations from the voters' image of the four parties, as Table 4 shows.

Table 4. *Association of the Parties with New Ideas and Tradition among Members of Parliament (Percentages)*

	New Ideas	In Be- tween	Tradi- tion	Don't know	Total (100%)	No.
Communist UML	50	16	23	11	100	(244)
United People's F	45	8	32	15	100	(239)
NCP (Democratic)	40	15	27	18	100	(238)
NDP (Thapa)	39	20	24	17	100	(235)
Nepali Congress	27	37	35	1	100	(250)
Labour-Peasant	15	10	56	19	100	(227)
Sadvabana	3	3	84	10	100	(242)
NDP (Chand)	2	4	84	10	100	(240)

On the left side, associated with new ideas, we find the Communist UML, the United People's Front, and the Communist (Democratic). However, the NDP (Thapa) unexpectedly turns up on this side too. The Nepali Congress is placed in the centre, just as it is among the voters and the district elites. On the right wing the parliamentarians place the NDP (Chand) along with the Sadvabana party. Somewhat surprisingly the Labour-Peasant party also shows up on the right side, perhaps because it represents the traditional interests of the farm labour population.

Thus, whereas the positions of five parties along the left-right dimension are clear, there are three "dark horses", namely the NDP (Thapa), Sadvabana, and Labour-Peasant parties. Their positions on the left-right axis as we have conceived of them differ from their positions of the modern-traditional axis as the parliamentarians see them. One can speculate that the reason for this divergence is that the left-right axis is not completely coincident with the modern-traditional axis. There may be parties on the right but still associated with new ideas (NDP Thapa) as well as parties on the left though associated with tradition (Labour-Peasants). Finally there are parties not fitting into the left-right scheme at all but definitely associated with tradition (Sadvabana).

Party Choice and Self-Location

The Nepalese voters perceived not only the positions of the major parties as indicated by Table 2. They also perceived their own position when asked to identify with either "new ideas", "tradition", or something in-between. In this self-location there was an unexpected bias in that twice as many placed themselves on the side of new ideas as the number siding with tradition. This simple fact seems to go a long way toward explaining why the traditional forces lost the election, and why the communist forces became an almost equal partner with the Nepali Congress party. The National Democratic parties were far removed from the modal position of the voters, whereas the Communist UML party was at least as close to the modal point as was the Nepali Congress.

As one might expect, siding with new ideas was especially pronounced among the young and well-educated voters (Table 5).

Table 5. Identification with New Ideas or Tradition (Percentages)

	New Ideas	In Be- tween	Tradi- tion	Don't know	Total
Whole sample	42	25	22	11	100
Level of education:					
No School	40	22	24	14	100
Primary	43	33	18	7	101
Second. or higher	58	31	10	1	100
Age of respondent:					
18-29 years	62	21	12	5	100
30-44 years	50	21	14	15	100
45 years or more	28	29	31	12	100
Sex:					
Male	42	28	18	12	100
Female	41	21	26	12	100

The proportion identifying with new ideas rises from 40 percent among those without school to 58 percent among those with secondary school, and from 28 percent among those 45 years and above to 62 percent among the young. The proportion identifying with tradition varies in the reverse way, and in addition it is somewhat higher among women than among men--26 against 18 percent.

We may now relate respondents' self-identification to the partisan choice. Table 6 breaks down the sample by self-location and vote. It indicates sizeable differences between the three groups of voters. The Communist UML and Communist (Democratic) parties together receive 46 percent of the votes among those identifying with new ideas as against only 12 percent among those identifying with tradition. Another party has a profile that is also tilted toward the left, namely the United People's Front, which receives 14 among those identifying with new ideas as against 9-10 percent in the two other categories. Together these three parties form a left wing that takes three-fifth of the voters identifying with new ideas but only one out of four or five in the two other categories.

The Nepali Congress gets less than one-third of the voters who identify with new ideas, but almost half in the two other categories. The two National Democratic parties are more clearly biased toward tradition. Though they take only one-fourth of the vote between them in this category, this is a comparatively strong standing compared with the 8 percent they attract in the categories identifying with new ideas. Finally, the Sadvabana party has a comparatively strong standing in the middle category, where it receives one out of eleven votes. Finally, a few scattered votes in each category, especially in the traditional category, go to independent candidates.

Table 6. Party Choice by Respondents' Self-Perception (Percent)

	New Ideas	In Between	Tradition
Communist UML or Dem.	46	17	12
United People's Front	14	9	10
Total Leftwing	60	26	22
Nepali Congress	31	45	47
National Democratic	8	18	24
Sadvabana	0	9	4
Indep. candidates	1	2	3
Total Non-Left	40	74	78
Total	100	100	100
N (100%)	(383)	(233)	(210)

In statistical terms, the power of respondents' self-placement in predicting his or her partisan choice, is indicated by an eta=0.32. The fact that 60 percent vote leftwing among those respondents identifying with new ideas, in contrast with only 22-26 percent among those identifying with tradition or taking an in-between stand, signifies a strong element of ideology in the Nepalese public, fully comparable with the corresponding vote/ideology relation in more mature democracies. This fact may come as a surprise to those who (with some justification) think of Nepal as a preindustrial and politically isolated oriental kingdom.

Proximity Voting of Congress Voters

As we saw from Table 2, public opinion is divided on where to locate the Congress party: an almost equal number associate it with new ideas, with tradition, and with something in between. But this uncertainty or disagreement about the party's proper position has not deterred people from voting for it in great number. Across the scale of modernism/traditionalism the party attracted between 47 and 31 percent of the voters according to Table 5. There seem to be two possible explanations for such a dispersed distribution of voters. Either the Congress voters do not bother about the ideological position of their party, being perhaps more occupied with other attributes of the party such as its leadership skills or the party's standing as a national symbol. Or, ideological considerations may well count, but voters of different persuasion may interpret their party's stand differently.

We can show conclusively that the latter explanation is superior. In Table 7 we have cross-classified respondents by their own location and by their perception of the Congress party's location, and the table indicates how many voted Nepali Congress in each of these nine cells (the percentage base shown in parentheses).

Table 7. Percent Voting Congress, by Self-Location and Perception of the Congress Party's Position

R's Location	R's Perception of Congress Party					
	New Ideas		In Between		Tradition	
New Ideas	67%	(119)	23%	(120)	14%	(176)
In Between	37	(27)	73	(164)	27	(66)
Tradition	57	(21)	44	(16)	70	(88)

Note: The data are unweighed.

From the first row it is seen that among respondents who sided with new ideas, and who also perceived the Nepali Congress to represent new ideas, 67 percent voted for that party. The figure drops to 23 percent among respondents locating the party in a middle position and to 14 percent among respondents to whom the Nepali Congress stands for tradition. The second row shows that the Nepali Congress received 73 percent among those identifying the party with the middle position, much more than among those putting the party in one of the outer categories. The third row tells a similar story with regard to those with a traditional identification, fully 70 percent of these voting Nepali Congress if they also located that party in the traditional category. In brief, looking along the diagonal we find that 67-73 percent of those voters perceiving the Nepali Congress to share the same position as themselves voted for that party, irrespective of what that position was.

This is an example of what is called proximity voting: the voter tends more to vote for a party the more he (or she) perceives that party to be close to his own (her own) position. This explains why the Nepali Congress can win votes both on the left, in the centre, and on the right (cf. Table 6). There are voters on the left who associate the party with new ideas, and voters of the right who perceive it as a traditional party. What these voters have in common is that they believe themselves to be close to the Nepali Congress party.

The "flat profile" of the Nepali Congress party and of its voters, therefore does not mean that the voters do not judge this party in ideological terms and act on this judgment. Rather, the Nepali Congress party has succeed in conveying different images to voters of different ideological persuasions.

Issues Mentioned by the Parties

The dimension of modernism/traditionalism is a general attitudinal and perceptual dimension which is related to a number of more specific political attitudes, some of which will be discussed in later chapters. At this stage, however, we shall see

Table 8. *Issues Mentioned by the Parties (in Percent)*

	Congress	Communist UML	NDP (Thapa)	NDP (Chand)
Unemployment	11	20	1	1
Drinking water	13	3	3	4
Education	6	8	1	2
Official graft	4	3	0	0
Foreign policy issues	9	7	7	14
Lack of fertilizers	4	2	1	1
Afforestation	3	1	1	0
Irrigation	3	2	1	3
Ethnic problems	1	3	1	1
Other	6	2	2	2
Don't know	40	49	81	72
Total	100	100	100	100

to what extent it is reflected in issues that were brought up by different parties during the campaign. The questionnaire sought to register what, in the memories of the voters, the candidates of the four nationwide parties talked about during the campaign (Question 20). Table 8 summarizes the findings.

According to our respondents, the candidate of Nepali Congress talked especially about drinking water and unemployment, while the Communist UML candidate concentrated on the unemployment problem and the National Democratic candidates-- in particular the candidate of the Chand party--discussed foreign policy issues such as relations with India and China, peace and security, and national sovereignty. It appears therefore that the left wing was preoccupied with unemployment whereas the right wing focused on foreign policy.

The second last row shows that 40 percent were incapable of associating any problem with the Nepali Congress candidate, whereas the corresponding figure was 49 percent for the Communist UML candidate, 81 percent for the NDP (Thapa) candidate, and 72 percent for the NDP (Chand) candidate. One may venture to say that even fewer associated any issue with the candidates of the remaining parties.

Obviously, the agendas of issues are not sufficient for the voters to associate the parties with "new ideas" or "tradition". Other types of information must have prevailed, probably the character of the candidates and the party activists.

First and Second Choice of Party

Of necessity our investigation of public perceptions of the Nepalese parties have been confined to a few major parties. The four parties we have studied as objects of perceptions were the only ones running candidates fairly nationwide, and even so, the two National Democratic parties appeared to have been rather distant objects to most voters, as the previous table has suggested. Given this handicap, is there a way of completing the Nepalese party system as it was seen by the voters?

According to Chapter 2, eight parties obtained representation in the Nepalese lower house at the parliamentary election of May 1991. And even though the Nepalese system of representation is far from proportional, these eight parties were the same that obtained more than one percent of the vote. That is, both in the parliamentary arena and the electoral arena they constitute the Nepalese party system. We are here first concerned with the structure of this party system as seen from the perspective of the voter. Which parties are "neighbours" and which are far removed from each other?

The individual voter rarely is capable of containing an entire map of the party system in his perception. However, many voters have vacillated between two or three parties, and we may use this information to reconstruct a map of party distances.

The Nepalese questionnaire asked, "If somehow you could not vote for your party or candidate, which is the second best party to you?" Failed with this hypothetical situation, almost half of the respndents were unable to come up with an answer. The rest, however, indicated a second choice.

Table 9 lists the parties according to voting support as indicated in the first column. Each of the other columns then indicates the second choice of voters of a particular party. Column (1) denotes the second choices of Congress party voters, column (2) that of Communist UML voters, and so forth. Column (7) denotes the choices made by NCP (Democratic) voters. There is no column (8), since we had only one Labour-Peasant voter in the sample.

Table 9. Second Best Party of Voters of Different Parties

	Vote	(1)	(2)	(3)	(4)	(5)	(6)	(7)
1 Nepali Congress	39.5	-	47	21	3	4	19	5
2 Communist UML	29.5	105	-	11	2	25	9	14
3 NDP (Chand)	6.9	25	10	-	3	7	0	0
4 NDP (Thapa)	5.6	20	6	6	-	3	1	2
5 United People's F	5.0	8	35	0	1	-	0	1
6 Sadvabana	4.3	17	5	1	1	0	-	0
7 NCP (Democratic)	2.5	13	4	1	0	2	0	-
8 Labour-Peasant	1.3	4	9	0	0	2	0	2

Note: The data are unweighed

Now, if the voters of a particular party chose more or less at random among the remaining parties for his or her second best party, the numbers in the column would be distributed approximately evenly downward. Obviously this is not the case, and thus there is some systematic mechanism involved in the choice.

Alternatively one might assume that the voters' second choices went to the remaining parties in rough proportion to the size of these parties, but without regard for the relative locations of these parties. In order to test this assumption we have listed the parties in order of magnitude and indicated their voting strengths in the first column.

When comparing the figures in the other column with the first column, we find that in the case of some of the parties, this assumption is roughly verified. The numbers indeed tend to decrease as one moves down the column. In the case of the Congress party voters, the remaining parties were chosen as second choices according to their strength, except that the United People's Front was chosen by only 8 Nepali Congress voters, less than the numbers choosing the two parties next in line.

The Communist UML voters deviated from the predicted pattern by choosing the United People's Front much more often (35 cases) than the two National Democratic parties, and at the bottom of the list, by choosing the Labour-Peasant party relatively often (in 9 cases).

The NDP (Chand) voters tended to follow the predicted pattern, even choosing the Communist UML much more often than the NDP (Thapa) party (11 cases as against 6). And the NDP (Thapa) voters also followed the predicted pattern, although they are too few to make any conclusion safe.

Voters of the United People's Front, however, deviated strongly from the predicted pattern by refusing to choose the Nepali Congress party except in the case of 4 respondents. It is obvious that the United People's Front and the Nepali Congress voters had a mutual dislike of each other.

The Sadvabana voters chose either the Nepali Congress party or the Communist UML party in the proportion of two to one. This is in accordance with the predicted pattern. Finally, voters of the NCP (Democratic) party (now the Communist United), much like the United People's Front voters, were reluctant to choose the Nepali Congress party.

It seems clear, not only from the correlation between vote and ideology (cf. Table 6) but also from the study of the second choice of the voter, that there existed at the time of the election on the left side a bloc consisting of Communist UML, United People's Front, NCP (Democratic), and Labour-Peasant party. The other four parties are less easy to combine, except that the two National Democratic parties appear close to one another. The Nepali Congress voters do not appear closer to either the two National Democratic parties or the Sadvabana party than to the Communist UML party; and there is nothing to indicate a close relationship between the Sadvabana party and the other non-socialist parties.

However, on the whole the second choices do not seem so structured as to suggest a strict left-right ordering of the parties. If the two National Democratic parties should be considered the right wing of the system, their supporters should be less inclined than they actually are to make the Communist UML their second choice. Vice versa, the Communist bloc should be less inclined to choose the National Democratic parties than they actually are. Furthermore, the Sadvabana party does not fit easily into the centre because of the reluctance of Congress party voters to make it their second choice.

An interesting feature of the table is that the Nepali Congress party is the most preferred alternative for Communist UML voters, and vice versa, that the Communist UML is the most preferred alternative for Congress voters. It is plausible to interpret this fact as suggesting that the psychological distance between these two parties is not so large as to be impossible to cover for quite a number of voters. We began this chapter by pointing out that responsive party systems must offer real alternatives for the voters to choose from; we will end it by suggesting that these alternatives should not be so far apart as to make it impossible for voters to make a marginal decision between them. The Nepalese party system and electorate in their present form seem to pass both tests.

CHAPTER 4

SOCIAL BASES OF PARTISANSHIP

That political attitudes and behaviours are not randomly and evenly distributed in any society has now become a well established fact. Patterns of political thinking and acting tend to be correlated with identifiable social and economic groups. Long before the invention of survey research, political philosophers and practising politicians have acted on the premise that knowing a persons socio-economic characteristics could provide reasonably accurate assessment of his or her political behaviour. Today, the survey research conducted in many countries have confirmed that social and group influences are relevant to an understanding of political life. A persons perception and the evaluation of socio-political environment, partisan loyalty, interest as well as participation in politics is affected by social and group influence. Therefore, this chapter will concentrate on the analysis of socio-economic factors as determinants of voting behaviour in Nepal.

In democracies several groups elect one group of people to political offices. This "one group", once in power, in turn, has to cater the interests of several other social groups. Therefore, a party which aims at running the government after the election must identify major groups of people who contribute to the party's strength at the polls. The party leaders have to ask how many men or women, young, middle aged and older people, farmers, peasants and workers, intellectuals, businessmen and civil servants, urban or rural dwellers as well as members of different ethnic communities will be impressed by the party's policy. They also have to think carefully of whether the mutually conflicting interests of different social groups could be synchronized. In short, the party leaders have to act as a sociologist who classifies people by the roles they occupy in society, by their position in the social structure and by their membership in social groups. The similarity, however, ends here because the sociologist wants to develop the theory but the politician wants to bag as many votes as he possibly can.

In May 1991 the voters in Nepal voted 8 parties in parliament and rejected 12 other parties. Nepali Congress party received most votes and won majority in the parliament and subsequently formed the government. Other parties are in the opposition. Our enquiry now will concentrate on social group support received by each of these parties in parliament. We begin with sex difference.

Party Choice and Sex

The following table (Table 1) shows voters' party preference by sex.

Table 1. Party Choice by Sex (Percentages)

Party Choice	Male	Female	Total
United People's Front	10	13	11
Communist UML	29	28	28
Nepali Congress	36	40	38
National Democratic	19	15	17
Sadvabana	3	4	3
Others	3	1	2
Total	100	100	100

The partisan preference of women voters does not differ markedly from that of men although a slightly higher percentage of women voters have preferred Nepali Congress and the United People's Front. The division of the Communist UML and Sadvabana voters is almost even in terms of sex. A slightly higher percentage of women vote for Nepali Congress and United People's Front. This is largely the result of two factors: Age and region of residence. When age was cross-tabulated by party choice we found that 46 percent of the women in the middle age bracket voted Nepali Congress as against 37 percent men, and 14 percent middle aged women voted United People's Front as against 11 percent men. When region of residence was cross-tabulated by party choice we found that 71 percent urban women voted Nepali Congress as against 40 percent urban men. Similarly, the United People's Front also drew 15 percent women voters from rural areas as against 11 percent rural men. The marginal sex difference in party choice can be explained from the basic fact of everyday life in Nepal that wives almost automatically share many important personal and social values of their husbands and agree on many questions.

Party Choice and Age

Generational differences in party choice are quite visible in Nepal. The younger people are tilted to the left while their elders are tilted to the centre and the right. The middle aged waver between the left, centre and the right but with a slight tilt towards the right and the centre. Table 2 presents the pattern of party choice by age of respondent.

The first column of Table 2 shows that younger voters prefer communist parties (54 percent combined). But older voters in third column prefer centrist Nepali Congress and rightist National Democratic parties (65 percent combined) while the middle aged in the second column are divided almost equally but with a slight tilt towards the centre and the right. A cross tabulation of party choice by age control-

Table 2. *Party Choice by Age (Percentages)*

	18-29	30-44	45 & above
United People's Front	14	13	9
Communist UML	40	30	22
Nepali Congress	30	38	42
National Democratic	9	13	23
Sadvabana	6	3	3
Others	1	3	1
Total	100	100	100

ling for sex shows that 44 percent of young women have preferred communist UMLas against 26 percent for Nepali Congress. This difference is explained by cross tabulation of party choice by education. 42 percent of the women with high school and above education have preferred Communist UML as against 38 percent for Nepali Congress. Among young men 37 percent have preferred Communist UML as against 33 percent for Nepali Congress. We found that it is not the level of education that differentiates men's party choice but it is the region of residence. A cross tabulation of party choice by age controlling for region of residence showed that 37 percent rural men voted Nepali Congress as against 27 percent to Communist UML.

Party Choice and Region of Residence

Region of residence is one of the most familiar factors of distinction among voters. The urban-rural distinction is becoming an increasingly important factor in Nepal especially in view of the process of urbanization. The economy and the politics are increasingly influenced by urban centres that have emerged in various parts of the country in the last two decades. The following table (Table 3) shows the pattern of party choice among urban and rural population.

Table 3. *Party Choice by Region of Residence (Percentage)*

	Urban	Rural
United People's Front	--	13
Communist UML	36	27
Nepali Congress	60	35
National Democratic	2	19
Sadvabana	1	4
Others	2	2
Total	100	100

Thus we see in Table 3 that the ruling Nepali Congress party has overwhelming support in urban areas (towns over 10,000 inhabitants) and substantial support in rural areas. The urban support to the opposition Communist UML is not small either compared to other parties. However, when the United People's Front is counted in, the combined communist strength in the rural areas is higher by 5 percent. The National Democratic parties, being parties in the right spectrum, also draw support from rural areas. The interesting point to note in this table, however, is the absence of support for United People's Front, a party considered to be radical Maoist, in the urban areas. This occurred because the United People's Front did not field candidates in urban areas within our ten sampling districts.

The ruling Nepali Congress party has derived its support mainly from the women (71 percent) in the urban areas as against 40 percent men. In the rural areas, however, there is no significant difference in men-women ratio (36 percent from men and 34 percent from women). More men in urban areas (54 percent) supported Communist UML compared to 26 percent women. In rural areas, however, the sex difference in UML support is negligible (27 percent men and 28 percent women). Thus we see a dichotomy here in that urban women are found to be Nepali Congress supporters while urban men are found to be supporters of Communist UML. What does it mean? How are we to explain it?

The answer again can be found in the age distribution, as 37 percent of the men in both younger and middle aged category supported the Communist UML as against 33 and 31 percent supported the Nepali Congress. Similarly, women in middle age and older age category (46 and 42 percent) have supported the Nepali Congress as against 27 percent supporting the UML. This phenomenon can perhaps be explained in terms of level of education. A cross-tabulation of party choice by education controlling for sex revealed that 39 percent women without schooling and 46 percent women with primary and lower secondary education had voted for the Nepali Congress. The corresponding figure for the UML is 28 and 22 percent respectively.

Party Choice and Education

As in many other democracies, formal education is an important determinant of voting decision in Nepal. People with more education are more often able to understand and appreciate the complexities of politics. They have greater confidence in their ability to be effective citizens and as a result they respond to political events more intelligently. Table 4 below shows the voting pattern among the educated as well as uneducated Nepalese voters.

Table 4. Party Choice by Education (Percentage)

	No Schooling	Primary or Low Secondary	High Secondary and above
United People's F	13	6	9
Communist UML	29	23	36
Nepali Congress	35	48	43
National Democratic	19	15	5
Sadvabana	2	7	5
Others	2	2	2
Total	100	100	100

Thus we see in Table 4 that the ruling Nepali Congress party has received a whopping support from primary and lower secondary education group. But it runs behind the combined communist forces among persons with no schooling and higher education. But on the whole the Nepali Congress party appears to be fairly representative in all three categories of educated as well as uneducated groups. The support of National Democratic parties, however, has declined with the increase in education of the voter.

When party choice by education was cross tabulated controlling for sex we found that more men (49 percent) with at least some schooling had voted for Nepali Congress. The figure for the women in the same education category is slightly lower. Among no schooling group, however, 39 percent of the women were found to have voted the Nepali Congress as against 32 percent of the men. The higher percentage of uneducated women voting for the Nepali Congress may be related to the influence of other family members. Among highly educated 42 percent of the voters women are found to have voted the UML as against 30 percent of the men. The gender difference among the UML supporters in the no schooling category, however, is small (28 percent women and 30 percent men).

Party Choice and Occupation

Now we turn to Table 5 to see the occupational support received by each of the parties in Nepalese parliament. While our survey had identified more than 13 occupational categories, we have, nevertheless, merged many of the categories to fit within the five categories for the purpose of analytical convenience as shown in the table.

Table 5. Party Choice by Occupation (Percentages)

	Farmer	Worker	Business	Professional	Inactives
United People's F	12	17	18	10	3
Communist UML	24	23	32	41	25
Nepali Congress	39	48	38	40	46
National Dem.	19	11	11	4	10
Sadvabana	3	1	1	2	13
Others	3	1	--	3	4
Total	100	100	100	100	100

Table 5 provides an interesting account of the occupational support to different parties. Communist parties, who claim to be the vanguard of workers and peasants, have ironically trailed behind the Nepali Congress in receiving the support of workers and farmers. Nepali Congress has received 39 and 48 percent support from the farmers and workers as against 35 and 40 percent of the combined communist parties. A cross-tabulation of party choice by occupation controlling for sex revealed that 43 percent men and 34 percent women from the farming community had voted Nepali Congress as against 32 percent men and 41 percent women for the combined communist parties. The cross tabulated data reveal that men from farming community prefer Nepali Congress while the women prefer the communists. The same is the case in the working class where more men (52 percent) are found to have voted Nepali Congress as against 29 percent for the combined communists and more women (52 percent) are found to have voted the combined communist parties as against 43 percent for the Nepali Congress. But the aggregate support of the farming community as well as the working class to the Nepali Congress has disproved the claims of the communists that they are the party of workers and peasants. The Communist party as the party of workers and peasants, according to this data, has become a myth rather than a reality.

Interestingly, the combined communist forces have pushed the Nepali Congress party behind in receiving support from business community which hitherto is believed to be against communist ideology. The combined communist parties have received 50 percent support from the business community as against 38 percent of Nepali Congress. A cross-tabulation of party choice by occupation controlling for sex revealed that there is no difference in the voting pattern of both sexes. Fifty-four percent of the men and 46 percent of the women from the business community are found to have voted the combined communist parties as against 34 percent men and 41 percent women for the Nepali Congress. This is perhaps because of the predominance of small business holdings in Nepal whose owners feel threatened by Indian business houses. The owners of small business holdings might have found communists as their friends who advocate limiting the activities of Indian commercial interests in Nepal. Nepali Congress, on the other hand, rightly or wrongly have been perceived as a party with pro-Indian attitudes.

The combined communist forces have also received more support from the modern professional groups such as teachers, doctors, engineers, nurses, etc. compared to Nepali Congress. It may be due to the antipathy of intellectual class against the performance of Interim Government. Even though the Interim Government was a coalition of Nepali Congress, the communists, royal nominees and independent human rights activists, the blame for the inefficiency of the government basically went to the Nepali Congress whose leader was the Prime Minister of the coalition government. Members of the professional class who had played a major role in the pro-democracy movement had demanded legal actions against the members of the erstwhile Panchayat regime. The record of Interim Government in this area remained utterly dissatisfactory among the intelligentsia of the country. As a result, this group appears to have voted communist parties in larger proportion (51 percent combined) compared to 40 percent for the Nepali Congress. Moreover, there is an uniform pattern of voting among men and women. Fifty percent men and 52 percent women from the professional group have voted the combined communist parties as against 40 percent each from both sexes for the Nepali Congress.

What was the pattern of voting by different age groups within different occupations? To find out the answer we, unlike in the previous table, divided the occupation groups into farm and non-farm groups. We then cross-tabulated party choice by age controlling for family occupation. We discovered that 49 percent of the people in the age category 18 to 29 years from the farming occupation voted for the combined communist parties. The corresponding figure for the Nepali Congress is only 34 percent. Forty-one percent of the middle aged and 43 percent of the old aged people supported Nepali Congress as against 39 and 28 percent supporting the combined communist parties. We also noticed that 26 percent of the older people belonging to farming occupation supported the National Democratic parties. Thus, we see that the percentage of votes to communist parties declines with the rising age of voters whereas the Nepali Congress's percentage of votes increases along with rising age among the farming population.

Among the non-farm population the pattern of support is clearly in favour of communist parties. Sixty-eight percent of the voters being 18 to 29 years old supported the combined communist parties as against 17 percent voting for the Nepali Congress. The increase in age, which was an advantage for the Nepali Congress in the case of farming population, did not at all affected the voting pattern as we found that 58 percent of the middle aged and 44 percent of the older non-farming people voted for the communist parties as against 26 and 38 percent of the Nepali Congress. We also found that older people from non-farming occupations have provided the bulk of the support (14 percent) to the National Democratic parties.

Party Choice and Religion

The majority of the people in Nepal are Hindus, and hence the Constitution of the Kingdom of Nepal has described the country as a Hindu Kingdom. It is, in fact, the one and the only Hindu country in the world with 89 percent of the population as Hindus. There are roughly 9 percent Buddhists and less than 2 percent Muslims. Christianity is a microscopic minority whose population barely exceeds a couple of thousands.

We must admit at the outset that our survey data is not proportional to the national strength of each of the religions mentioned above. This has happened because two out of ten of our sample districts were found to be predominantly Buddhist. The district of Rasuwa, for example, have many Buddhists and very little Hindus, and the same is true of the district of Sindhupalchok. Similarly, Muslims are found over-represented in the sample. It is again due to the heavy concentration of Muslim population in another of our survey districts, Banke. Notwithstanding this disproportion in the sample, it may be safe to say that religious issues have not traditionally been in the forefront of Nepalese politics. There is religious harmony between the majority of Hindus and the minority of Buddhists. Nevertheless some parties have received more support from a particular religious community than from others. The following table shows the pattern of party choice among different religious communities.

Table 6. Party Choice by Religion (Percentages)

	Hindus	Buddhists	Muslim
United People's Front	16	--	8
Communist UML	20	54	15
Nepali Congress	43	21	51
National Democratic	15	25	8
Sadvabana	4	--	10
Others	2	--	9
Total	100	100	100

Table 6 shows that the majority of Hindus and Muslims have voted Nepali Congress while the majority of Buddhists have voted Communist UML. Table 6, however,

69

does not show any Buddhist influence on the United People's Front. This again is perhaps due to our choice of sampling districts. The major support base of the National Democratic parties is found among the Buddhist population. The victory of two candidates of the National Democratic parties to parliament from Rasuwa and Sindhupalchok district can perhaps be attributed to this support of the Buddhist religious community.

Why are these different parties popular among different religious communities? The answer perhaps can be found in religious/secular orientations of different parties although we do not have any statistical evidence to support this judgement. Communist parties are secular in their orientations and hence had advocated for the deletion of the term "Hindu Kingdom" from the constitution at the time of constitution making in 1990. The Nepali Congress, while still professing secularism, was not prepared to delete the "Hindu Kingdom" but it had emphasized religious freedom to all the other religious communities. The two National Democratic parties and the Sadvabana party were in favour of inserting the term "Hindu Kingdom" in the constitution. These debates that had taken place during the constitution making appear to have been the decisive factors for partisan choice of different religious communities.

The Buddhist community appears closer to communist parties perhaps because of the inherent similarities in egalitarian outlook of Buddhism and Marxism. Moreover, the communists had fought a hard political battle to free the constitution from Hinduism, which if successful would have been in favour of other religious communities including the Buddhists. The Muslim minority, however, distances itself from the communists perhaps because of the mutually incompatible values of Marxism and Islam, and hence is found closer to Nepali Congress.

Party Choice and Social Status

Nepalese society, as any other society, is divided into several social levels or strata. There are both "haves" and "have nots". As analysts of the political system we believe that the knowledge of political preference of both of these classes of people is important and crucial for an understanding of the dynamics of Nepalese politics. The problem, however, is to identify and locate the appropriate class or classes of people. Respondents would not ordinarily identify themselves as belonging to a particular class or they have the tendency to hide the fact or provide false statement on their economic status. Therefore, we constructed an index by which the social status of an individual or group of people could be measured. In the Nepalese voters survey we asked the respondents to provide information on their possessions of modern items such as radio, television, telephone, car, motorcycle, refrigerator,

70

washing machine, and bicycle. We then classified people with 4 or more items (2 percent of the weighted sample) as A or rich, people with 3 items (4 percent) as B or upper middle class, people with 2 items (11 percent) as C or middle class, people with only one item (43 percent) as D or lower middle class, and people with none of the items mentioned (40 percent) above as E or poor. The following table provides the index of social status and the party choice.

Table 7. Party Choice by Social Status (Percentages)

	A	B	C	D	E
United People's F	--	--	1	13	14
Communist UML	15	21	29	28	30
Nepali Congress	73	59	52	39	30
National Democratic	7	8	5	15	23
Sadvabana	4	9	13	3	1
Others	--	3	--	3	2
Total	100	100	100	100	100

Thus, we see in Table 7 that support for Nepali Congress declined from Class A to Class E, that is, from the rich to the poor. In Class A it is almost five times the support for the Communist UML whereas in Class E it is the same as that of the Communist UML, and considerably less than the support for the combined left wing. On the basis of this data, it is fair to say that the Nepali Congress is the party of rich people but also enjoys support from the majority of the middle classes. Forty-four percent of the poor people have supported combined communist forces as against 30 percent of the Nepali Congress. Similarly, 41 percent of people from the lower middle class have supported combined communist parties as against 39 percent of the Nepali Congress. But the middle, upper and rich class voters have chosen Nepali Congress by 52, 59 and 73 percent as against 30, 21 and 15 percent of the combined communist parties. It is interesting to note here that the United People's Front has not received any support from rich and upper classes of voters, indicating that the rank and file of the party is basically composed of poor and lower middle class people.

The status consciousness is reflected clearly in the selection of party among different age groups. A cross tabulation of party choice by age controlling for status revealed that younger and middle aged voters in poor and lower middle class category have supported the combined communist parties by 58 percent as against 29 percent supporting the Nepali Congress while the old age voters have supported the Nepali Congress by 38 percent as against 32 percent supporting the combined communist parties. The younger voters who have 2 to 8 status denoting items are slightly tilted towards combined communist parties (36 percent) as against 33 percent of Nepali Congress. The middle aged and older voters with 2 to 8 status items, on the other hand, have overwhelmingly supported Nepali Congress by 60 and 64 percent as against 31 and 18 percent of the Communist UML. The United People's Front, the radical wing of the Nepalese communist movement, has no support whatsoever from either the middle aged or the old aged people who have 2 to 8 status items.

The pattern of lower status people voting the communist parties and higher status people voting the Nepali Congress was found in particular among Buddhist religious group. The percentage of lower class people voting the combined communist parties is substantially higher (55 percent) as against 18 percent of the Nepali Congress. The second choice of lower class Buddhists arc the National Democratic parties with 27 percent support. Among the higher class Buddhist voters, however, the support margin is very narrow with 51 percent for the Nepali Congress and 49 percent for the combined communist parties and none for the National Democratic parties. The support pattern, however, is not the same as regards Hindu voters. Hindu voters in lower status group support Nepali Congress by only one percent more (40 to 39) but a whopping 57 percent voters of higher status group support Nepali Congress as against 24 percent of combined communist parties.

Ethnicity, Caste and Party Choice

A person's caste, ethnic origin and tribal relations have traditionally been crucial considerations in the Nepalese political system. Traditionally, the state in a Hindu society is ruled by a Chhetri King with his Brahmin advisors. There is no exception to this tradition even in modern day politics of Nepal. Besides Brahmins and Chhetris, Newars of Kathmandu valley have been influential in the politics of Nepal. Newar influence in politics is mainly due to their involvement in business since antiquity. Moreover, they were an ethnic nation by themselves in the valley of Kathmandu before they were defeated by the Chhetri King during the unification of the country. Because of their rich culture and heritage, Newars were gradually assimilated in the ruling establishment of the post-unification Nepal. The ruling elite of Nepal have traditionally come from these three castes and that is why Nepal is often described as a country ruled by a closed aristocracy of Brahmin-Chhetri and Newar stratum.

King Prithvi Narayan Shah, the founder of the modern day Nepal, however, had made it clear that the country was a "common garden of four castes and thirty-six races". The thirty-six races that the King referred are actually many tribal ethnic communities living in the hills and plains of Nepal. While saying so he was either acutely aware of the possibility of dominance of a particular caste or ethnic community over the others and wanted to avoid it or he was simply trying to show himself as the friend of other ethnic tribes in order to neutralize their hostile feelings against Brahmins and Chhetris. Despite the founder's dream, other castes and ethnic communities were left behind in the realm of politics and administration of the country. The hill tribal groups, such as Gurungs, Magars, Rais, Limbu, who are famous for their fighting bravery, have been serving in the army and the police in the lower level positions. The Terai tribal communities have remained traditional agricultural communities. With the dawn of democracy in 1951, several of these tribes were exposed to modern day political verbiage leading to higher demand for political participation and representation in the national politics. As a result, leaders and chieftains of different castes and ethnic communities in Nepal began to articulate communal demands and sentiments and thus became politicized.

Some efforts were made by different political parties in the 1951-60 period to recruit into their ranks members from different ethnic communities. As a result, 20 percent of the members of the 1959 parliament was composed of the leaders of the minority tribal communities from both the hills and Terai. Most of them were members of the Nepali Congress. The Panchayat elections, too, increased the level of participation of ethnic communities but there is no way to measure the basis of the choice of voters because of the nature of partyless elections.

Tribal societies, as is well known, are organized in a kinship basis. It is very much like the extended family which is the basic unit for major decisions. The likelihood of bloc voting based on ethnic considerations is very high in Nepal. When voting is done in accordance to family decisions it violates the spirit of individuality which governs the electoral system of Western democracies. But it is extremely difficult to determine whether voting in Nepal is an individual act

Table 8. *Party Choice by Caste and Ethnicity (Percentage)*

	BR	CH	NE	MT	TT	AR	OT
United People's Front	18	21	9	4	3	20	2
Communist UML	27	11	44	22	15	25	54
Nepali Congress	43	48	42	56	32	36	17
National Democratic	8	19	5	14	22	17	24
Sadvabana	2	1	--	--	21	--	4
Others	3	--	--	3	8	3	--
Total	100	100	100	100	100	100	100

Note: BR = Brahmin; CH = Chhetri; NE = Newar; MT = Mountain Tribes; TT = Terai Tribes; AR = Artisans; OT = Others

or it is a group act. It is a complex process. While we can produce statistics on the voting pattern of different ethnic communities, we cannot, however, quantify the reasons why particular community voted particular party. The table above shows the party choice of different castes and ethnic communities in 1991 elections.

We see in Table 8 that Nepali Congress has received substantial support from across the board of all the castes and ethnic communities. But when we compare the support of Nepali Congress vis-a-vis the combined communist parties we see that the party has lagged behind the combined communist parties by 2 percent among the Brahmins, by 11 percent among Newars, 9 percent among artisans (artisans are those people who are known as Damai, Kami, Sarki, etc. and who mostly do manual work. They were previously described as untouchables but "untouchability" has been rendered illegal since 1962, and the continuous use of the term will have demeaning as well as undemocratic flavour. Hence, we have selected the word "artisan" to describe this category of people), and 39 percent among "others". It is, however, ahead of the combined communist parties among Chhetris, Mountain Tribes (such as Gurung, Magar, Thakali, Tamang, Rai, Limbu and Sherpa) and Terai Tribes (such as Tharu and others) by 16, 30 and 14 percent respectively.

A cross tabulation of party choice by ethnic group controlling for sex revealed that more men from Brahmin (50 percent), Newar (57 percent), Artisan (50 percent) and "others"(53 percent) voted combined communist parties as against 36, 22, 31 and 16 percent respectively for the Nepali Congress. The Nepali Congress, however, has received substantial support from men of Chhetri caste (57 percent), Mountain Tribes (58 percent) and Terai Tribes (37 percent). But more women from Brahmin (50 percent),Chhetri (43 percent), Newar (55 percent), Mountain Tribes (54 percent) and Artisan (46 percent) are found to have voted Nepali Congress as against 40, 38, 43, 26, and 34 percent respectively for the combined communist parties. The communists are found strong only among the women of Terai Tribes (27 percent) and "others" (57 percent) category as against 16 and 18 percent respectively of the Nepali Congress.

When party choice was cross tabulated by ethnic group controlling for age we found that younger people in 18-29 years of age group in all ethnic categories except Chhetris and Terai Tribes had voted predominantly for combined communist parties. Thus, younger Brahmins (59 percent), Newars (80 percent), Mountain Tribes (53 percent), Artisan (51 percent) and "others" (68 percent) are found to have supported combined communist parties as against 28, 19, 47, 49 and 17 percent respectively for the Nepali Congress. Even among Chhetris and Terai Tribes, the margin of difference is negligible. In each categories, the Nepali Congress is ahead by only one percent i.e. 40 and 31 percent as against 39 and 30 percent of the combined communists. Thus we find that younger people, irrespective of their ethnic origin, have a tendency to vote leftist parties.

Among the middle aged people (30-44 years of age group), combined communist parties have received substantial support from Brahmin (50 percent), Newar (49 percent), Artisan (52 percent) and "others" (60 percent) as against 36, 31, 32 and 11 percent of the Nepali Congress. The Nepali Congress, however, has received substantial support from the middle aged Chhetris (58 percent), Mountain Tribes (66 percent), and Terai Tribes (33 percent) as against 29, 27 and 21 percent of the combined communist parties. Thus we see that middle aged voting among Mountain Tribes is in reverse order compared to their young voters. The support to Nepali Congress from Chhetris and Terai Tribes is substantially consolidated as we move to middle age from the young age.

As we move to older age group we find a completely different picture. All ethnic categories except Artisans and Others have supported Nepali Congress. Thus, 49 percent Brahmins, 44 percent Chhetris, 53 percent Newars, 33 percent Mountain Tribes, and 37 percent Terai Tribes have voted Nepali Congress as against 40, 29, 33, 14, and 13 percent respectively for the combined communist parties. The interesting point to note here is that the radical wing of the communist party, the United People's Front, has not received any support from among the older people of Mountain and Terai Tribes. Among Artisans and Others, however, the combined communist parties have receive 35 and 41 percent support as against 24 and none for the Nepali Congress. Another interesting point to note here is that older people from the Artisan group are found to have voted the National Democratic parties by 28 percent. If we are to separate the communist parties and compare the voting percentage, the National Democratic parties are on top among the older people from the Artisan group.

To simplify the analysis of ethnic support to parties by age we present the following table.

Table 9. *Ethnicity, Age and Preferred Party*

	18-29 yrs	30-44 yrs	45 & above
Brahmin	CP	CP	NC
Chhetri	NC	NC	NC
Newars	CP	CP	NC
Mountain Tribes	CP	NC	NC
Terai Tribes	NC	NC	
Artisan	CP	CP	CP
Others	CP	CP	CP

Note: CP = Communist Parties; NC = Nepali Congress

Thus, we see in Table 9 that Chhetris and Terai Tribes have voted Nepali Congress across the board while the Artisan and Others have voted the communist parties across the board. In these cases we see the entire ethnic community tilted towards either of the parties and hence we do not find age as a determining factor of voting. But in the case of other castes and ethnic groups age has played a role in the voting. As we have seen, young and middle aged Brahmins and Newars are supportive of the communist parties while older Brahmins and Newars are supportive of the Nepali Congress. Similarly, younger people from the Mountain Tribes appear supportive of communist parties but their middle age and older people are clearly supportive of the Nepali Congress.

A cross tabulation of party choice by ethnic communities controlling for region of residence revealed that all ethnic communities living in urban areas with the exception of Artisans have overwhelmingly supported Nepali Congress while the Brahmins, Newars, Artisans and Others living in rural areas have supported communist parties in a similar fashion. The Chhetris, Mountain Tribes, and Terai Tribes have supported the Nepali Congress in both the urban and rural areas while the Artisans alone are supportive of communist parties in both urban and rural areas.

A cross tabulation of party choice by ethnic communities controlling for economic status revealed that higher percentage of poor people (i.e. those who do not have any of the items that are considered status symbols) among Brahmins, Newars, Artisans and Others have supported communist parties while more Chhetris, Mountain Tribes and Terai Tribes from the same class have voted Nepali Congress. Among the lower middle class, too, this tendency is clearly visible with the exception of Terai Tribes favouring the communist parties. The greater percentage of middle class in all ethnic communities, with the exception of "Others" have voted Nepali Congress, and when we move up to rich people we interestingly find Terai Tribes equally divided. The higher percentage of Artisans in the middle class had voted for the Nepali Congress but more richer Artisans are found to have voted the communist parties. All other castes and ethnic groups from richer people have voted Nepali Congress in higher proportions. However, there is no relation between ethnicity and economic status when it comes to Chhetris and Mountain Tribes because they are found to have voted the Nepali Congress in greater proportions across the board. There is no such pattern, however, in the case of communist parties.

Conclusions

The social cleavages that are most important in generating political conflict in Nepal seem to be of the following four types.

First, a generational cleavage pitting the young against the old. The combined left vote runs to 54 percent among those below thirty years of age, but only 31 percent among those of forty-five years upward (Table 2).

Second, a property cleavage that sets the relatively propertied families apart from the poor families and individuals. As indexed by the possession of private consumption goods, the propertied show a left wing vote of 15-20 percent, none of which goes to the extreme left. In the other end, the dispossessed have a left wing vote of 44 percent, one-third of which goes to the extreme left (Table 7).

Third, a religious cleavage according to which the Buddhist minority is positioned to the left (with 54 percent leftwing), and the Moslim minority to the right (23 percent leftwing) of the Hindu majority (Table 6).

And fourth, an ethnic cleavage in which Brahmins and Newars show a leftist vote of 53-55 percent whereas ethnic groups of the southern Terai plain as well as groups of the high Himalayas have a leftist vote of only around 20 percent (Table 8).

Putting it crudely, it thus appears that the left wing opposition is mainly composed as a coalition between the young and well-educated Brahmins and the proletariat. Conversely, the ruling majority including the moderate right wing should be thought of as consisting of a coalition between the older propertied class and the uneducated farm population. This is certainly not an uncommon cleavage system in a developing country.

CHAPTER 5

CAMPAIGN AND MOBILIZATION

Election campaign is an interesting event in which a large number of people actively participate in the discussion about the political life of a nation. It attracts the attention of the whole nation and frequently, the attention of the international community as well. The campaigns for election reveal many unknown facts about the political process and provides an understanding of the dynamics of the political process. It arouses voters' curiosity, identifies national as well as local issues of importance and disseminates information on those issues. It provides alternative choices for the voter by discussing and debating the advantages and disadvantages of a particular policy advocated by rival political groups. It politicizes and mobilizes the people in order to integrate them into the mainstream of the political system.

Viewed from the lens of political parties and candidates, the election campaign provides them the opportunity to bring the scattered supporters of the party into one fold, to win the hearts and minds of neutral voters, and to make new supporters by either stealing, converting or demoralizing the supporters of the rival parties. If one is to view election campaign from the point of view of the political system, it is a necessary part of the political process that allows its citizens a participatory role in the system which, in turn, identifies the individual with the political system.

In Nepal, an election campaign is as fascinating as national festivals or fun fairs. Just like in India, it is a *Tamasa* that extends from the remotest villages to the national centres of power in Kathmandu. It brings larger number of people out in the streets than any other national festivals and it is featured by all sorts of traditional methods employed to modern political purposes. Almost every Nepali is aware during the campaign that something unexpected might happen. The data from our survey shows that 53 percent of the voters worked in campaign in one way or the other.

Political parties and independent candidates officially start their campaign for election with the publication of their manifestos identifying different national and local issues and describing party or candidate's position on these issues. These documents are very important in that they put the position of parties and candidates on record which the voter can compare before making the decision. In post-election period, the manifesto issued by the party at the time of election serves as a tool to evaluate the performance of the government vis-a-vis its campaign promises. But since the vast majority of the Nepalese voters are illiterate, the influence of manifestos on them is very little.

In May 1991 elections all political parties and independent candidates were able to campaign openly all over the country with posters, handbills and wall painted slogans. The electoral law has set the limit of campaign expenses to Rupees 75,000 (US$1,500) per candidate. But the system has not devised a mechanism to control and monitor the actual spending. Conservative estimates of spending incurred by one candidate ranges from couple thousand Rupees to several million Rupees. The money is spent to organize mass rallies and meetings in both urban and rural area in order to arouse voters' curiosity, identify issues of debate and disseminate information. Sound trucks are frequently used to call the people to attend the rallies. The campaign is launched in such a way that attracts attention of the people more than any other national event. It takes the form of fun fair unmatched by any other national festivals. People participate in one form or the other in campaign activities.

Parties devise their own strategies of campaign. The individual strategies may be different but the pattern of campaign is just about the same. All parties avoid sophistication of language in view of the overwhelming illiteracy in the country. Messages to voters through slogans and graffiti on the walls are made as simple as possible. Different campaign techniques to suit the socio-psychological temperament of the Nepalese society are employed by parties and candidates. The campaign strategists adopt techniques and strategies that are visibly observable, clearly audible and emotionally and sentimentally touchable. All available spaces in cities, town and bazaars are painted with election symbols and names of the candidates; posters carrying the pictures of party leaders are posted; party flags are displayed in almost every house and shop; arches and gates are built across the thoroughfare of the towns and cities; small banners and leaflets are distributed. Clearly audible campaign techniques include the use of sound trucks and cassette players to relay the speeches of leaders as well as to relay the revolutionary songs. In remote villages, where the party's bigwigs have little time to go, documentary films and video cassettes from the big mass rallies of Kathmandu and other urban centres are shown. In order to give personal touch to the campaign, party workers, candidates and other campaigners visit door to door seeking votes. The POLSAN data-bank shows that 77 percent of the voters surveyed said that they were visited by different party workers in their homes. These door visitors inform the voters of their serial numbers in the electoral roll which later on makes it easy for the election officials to locate the voters' name quickly and handover the ballot paper. As the election day nears festival-like rallies and processions with folk dances with political propaganda are organized. The survey data shows that 24 percent voters participated in meetings "many times" while 50 percent said they participated "a few times".

Election time violence is not unusual in Nepal. In fact, many observers believed that the May 1991 election would be marked by rampant violence. In order to ensure that the parties and candidates conduct campaign in an orderly way without impinging upon the right of another party or candidate, the Election Commission, after consulting political party representatives and with their approval, published a 21-point code of conduct. While the code of conduct helped to minimise the incidents of violence, it could not stop the violence altogether. As the campaign got into full swing, reports of violence came in from almost half of Nepal's 75 districts. An estimated 40 persons lost their lives between September 1990 and the election day, and thousands were injured. The clashes mainly occurred among the supporters of the Nepali Congress, Communist parties, and ex-Panchayat parties, each blaming the other side for perpetrating violence and thus maintaining a "holier than thou" attitude.

Effect of Campaign on Voting

In this chapter we will explore and analyze the following questions: What were the techniques of campaign and the medium employed? Did the election campaign reach everybody, or only a minority of politically interested? Did the personal discussion about politics engaged everybody? And what were the effects of campaign in generating political interest, in making the party symbols known, and in guiding people toward a particular party? To answer these question we will analyze such variables as media exposure, political discussions among various groups and participation in mass meetings by cross tabulating independent variables such as age, sex, education and urban/rural residence.

Medium of Campaign

The role of television and newspapers in the campaign in disseminating political information in Nepal is doubtful. The viewership of television and the circulation of newspapers both are very limited. Nevertheless, in order to find out the influence of each of the media of campaign among the voters, the survey asked a question on voters exposure to radio broadcasts, newspaper readership, someone reading the campaign materials for the voters, mass meeting attendance, and finally door-to-door visit by candidates or party workers. The following Table (Table 1) shows the campaign media exposure by sex.

The table below shows no significant difference between the two sexes in radio listening. The interesting thing to note as well as difficult to explain, however, is that more women have read newspaper than men. Similarly, there is marginal difference between the two sexes in terms of someone reading the campaign materials. But when it comes to attending the mass meetings more men are found to attend "many times" than women although more women are found to attend mass meetings

Table 1. Campaign Media Exposure by Sex (Percentages)

	Male	Female
Followed radio		
Many times	11	10
A few times	52	53
Read newspapers		
Many times	4	5
A few times	27	29
Somebody read to me		
Many times	3	2
A few times	32	35
Went to meetings		
Many times	13	10
A few times	43	51

"a few times" than men. The high level of participation among women demands an explanation. Ordinarily the task of child rearing and house keeping is the woman's repsonsibility and may be thought to severely restrict their political activity. It is possible, therefore, that it is only because of the constant encouragement by men that so many women have attended to the campaign and turned out to vote. Nepalese women reflect in their own behaviours and attitudes the expectations of the broader society that they better be confined to the business of a housewife. But Nepalese women never had to organize the women's liberation movement to get voting rights. Moreover, the constitution and other laws of the country have given special attention to women with a view to promote their participation. Nevertheless, the suffragette's desired role for emancipated womanhood is still not only realized but also not wanted by many women themselves.

The Radio Nepal, which can be heard all over the country is controlled by the government, and equal access to it is not available. In May 1991 elections, the Radio Nepal was believed to have covered the campaigns of the Nepali Congress more than any other party simply because the communication minister in the interim government happened to be from the Nepali Congress party. Despite the reach out capacity of Radio Nepal and the government's manipulation of it for the ministers' party in power, the overall impact of radio in campaign appears negligible in terms of its number of listeners. The survey shows that 37 percent of the voters "never listened" to radio, 52 percent "listened a few times" and only 11 percent responded that they had "listened many times". A combination of "many timers" and "a few timers" gives us a figure of 63 percent voters that was exposed to radio and television broadcasts.

The weighted sample of the survey shows that 68 percent of the Nepalese voters have "never read" newspapers, 28 percent have "read a few times" and only 4 percent have "read many times". Even the combination of many timers and a few timers does not make the figure (32 percent) impressive in terms of newspaper reading. But the figure comes closer to Nepal's literacy rate.

Given the illiteracy of the majority of the people of Nepal, the survey tried to find out the whether and to what extent the voters were made aware by the campaigners by reading the campaign materials from the newspapers. The question asked was: did anybody read from the newspapers to you? We found out that the majority of the voters (64 percent) were not read any materials by any campaigner. Table 1 above shows no substantial difference between the two sexes in terms of the information received through someone reading.

Mammoth political rallies and meetings are among the most visible technique of election campaign. They raise public enthusiasm about the election and a curious voter always tries to attend meetings organized by rival parties, listen to their case and compare one party's issue with that of another party. We wanted to assess the impact of mass meetings on the voters by asking a question: "Did you go to meetings where the candidates or the party spokesmen made speeches?" The response to this question suggests that this method of political campaign is most effective in Nepal. Table 1 above shows the participation of voters in political meetings and rallies. And, it is clear from the table that more men attended political meetings "many times" than women but more women attended "a few times" than men. It also shows that majority of the people (58 percent with many timers and a few times combined) were following the politics by attending the mass meetings.

A cross tabulation of the same variables by age is given in Table 2 below.

Table 2. Campaign Media Exposure by Age Group (Percentages)

	18-29 years	30-44 years	45+ years
Followed radio			
Many times	12	9	11
A few times	55	52	52
Read newspapers			
Many times	6	5	3
A few times	29	26	29
Somebody read to me			
Many times	2	3	3
A few times	33	30	36
Went to meetings			
Many times	17	12	8
A few times	48	45	49

Table 2 shows that younger as well as older persons listened to radio broadcasts more often than the middle aged, although the difference is marginal. When newspaper readership was cross tabulated by age we found out that 68 percent of the total respondents "never read" while 28 percent read "a few times" and only 4 percent read "many times." As in radio listening the above table shows that the younger generation of population reads newspapers more than the middle aged and the older. A cross tabulation of variable "Somebody read" with age shows that middle aged and older people were read "many times" a little more than the younger ones but younger and older people were read "a few times" more than the middle aged. The table clearly shows that the campaigners were not able to reach out to 64 percent of the voters of each age group even by way of reading campaign materials published in the newspapers. With regard to the proportion of the age group attending meetings Table 2 above shows that more younger people attended many meetings (17 percent) than middle aged (12 percent) and older people (8 percent). But it goes in the reverse order in the case of "a few times" attenders. The data suggests that the campaign attracted more voters in the young and middle aged category than among the old.

The following table (Table 3) shows the results of cross tabulation of same variables by education.

Table 3. Campaign Media Exposure by Education (Percentages)

	No School	Primary School	Lower Second.	High School	Higher Educ'n
Followed radio					
Many times	9	13	13	17	33
A few times	47	63	75	69	62
Read newspapers					
Many times	2	6	5	16	33
A few times	17	46	64	68	61
Somebody read to me					
Many times	3	1	2	3	6
A few times	31	35	41	47	46
Went to meetings					
Many times	9	11	18	29	42
A few times	43	58	59	54	46

The data in Table 3 suggests that radio communication is an effective channel for educated persons. The data shows that 33 percent of the highly educated persons followed politics in the radio "many times", as against only 9 percent of those with no schooling. That 47 percent of those with no schooling followed radio broadcasts "a few times" is yet another interesting aspect of Nepali communication system.

The table shows a significant relationship between newspaper readership and the level of education. Newspaper readership, is substantially and rather understandably higher among educated persons. The table shows that 33 percent of the highly educated persons follow newspapers while only 2 percent among the non schooling category follow the newspaper.

Table 3 above also shows the extent of campaign workers reading the newspapers to different categories of educated and uneducated voters. Evidently, newspaper material was read not only to illiterates but even more to well-educated. And why should this not be the case? Quoting a news item or an argument to an educated friend or family member is a normal occurrence also in Western election campaigns, though rarely measured in surveys.

Finally, Table 3 shows the rate of meeting attendance by the level of education. Thus, we see in the table that more highly educated voters went to meetings than those with no schooling. The 44 percent with no schooling who attended meetings is also quite significant in terms of political participation by uneducated people.

Table 4 below will show the scale of campaign media exposure when cross tabulated by urban or rural settings.

Table 4. Campaign Media Exposure by Urban/Rural Setting (Percentages)

	Urban	Rural
Followed radio		
Many times	16	10
A few times	55	52
Read newspapers		
Many times	10	3
A few times	44	26
Somebody read to me		
Many times	4	2
A few times	47	31
Went to meetings		
Many times	15	11
A few times	45	47

Table 4 shows that more urban than rural residents followed radio broadcasts many times as well as a few times. The table shows a contrasting newspaper readership in urban and rural settings. The table clearly shows that three times more urban dwellers follow politics many times through newspapers as against their rural counterparts.

Thus, the radio and newspapers which are considered to be the most effective media of campaign in the Western countries play very little role in Nepal's elections. Television, which went into air only a decade earlier, has an estimated 600,000 viewers and hence its role can not be assessed for the purpose of national campaigns. Similarly, newspapers, even though they carry campaign news overshadowing all other news, have very limited role in influencing the large masses of the electorate during the campaign in view of the illiteracy of the country.

Table 4 also clearly shows that more urban than rural voters were mobilized by the campaign workers by reading materials many times as well as a few times. This suggests that the campaigners focused more on urban centres than in the villages. The table also shows the scale of mass turnout in urban and rural settings. We see that more voters in the urban areas went to meetings "many times" compared with their rural counterparts. But more rural than urban voters went "a few times" to meetings.

Did the mass meeting as a tool of campaign have any effect on voters' decision to vote? When did the voter decide to vote? This question has fascinated researchers of voting behaviour for many years. Researchers concentrate on timing of voting decision with an expectation that it may give some indication of other aspects of electoral process and voter motivations such as the degree of traditional primordial or loyalties, including loyalty to a particular party, the influence of campaign on voters and the long range nature of voting behaviour. We cross tabulated the mass meeting attendance by time of decision and found that 46 percent of the voters had already decided how to vote before attending the meetings; 28 percent had decided during the campaign period; and the remaining 26 percent had decided during the last days of the campaign.

Now, what about the effect of mass meeting attendance on party choice? we again cross tabulated the mass meeting attendance by party choice and found the figures shown in Table 5.

The data show that voters belonging to communist camps other than the UML attended mass meetings much more than voters belonging to other parties. If we are to lump all varieties of communists into one group we see that they received 63 percent of those voters who attended mass meetings many times but only 38 percent of those attending a few times or not at all attending. In the latter group especially the National Democratic and Sadvabana parties received disproportionally many votes. Thus mass meetings probably had an effect in mobilizing the left wing rather than the right wing.

85

Table 5. Effect of Mass Meeting Attendance on Party Choice (Percentages)

| | Mass Meeting Attendance | | |
	Many times	A few times	Never
Communist UML	22	25	26
Other Communists			
(UPF,CPN(U),NLPP)	41	13	12
Nepali Congress	31	47	31
National Democratic	2	12	24
Sadvabana	1	1	6
Others	3	2	2
Total	100	100	100

Door-to Door Campaign

Door-to-door campaign was yet another medium employed by parties. This type of campaign was normally followed a few days before the actual voting day. The party workers and volunteers visit the doors of as many voters as possible and inform them of the voting day and schedule, and remind them of their duty to vote as a democratic citizen. The party workers help the voters find out their names in the electoral roll and tell them the serial number of their name so that voter as well as the election official will find it easy on the polling booth. The survey found that no less than 70 percent of the voters were visited by campaign workers. The following Table 8 shows the frequencies of visits from party workers and the percentage of votes received by the parties.

Table 6. Door-to-Door Campaigning by Actual Voting (Percentages)

| | Visited by Campaign Workers from | | | | |
	None	Cong.	UML	Other	Two or more
Communist UML	37	14	65	3	19
Other Left					
(UPF;CPN(U);NLPP)	19	7	6	35	13
Nepali Congress	29	72	15	19	37
National Dem.	15	6	14	29	22
Sadvabana	0	0	0	7	6
Others	1	0	0	6	3
Total	101	99	100	99	100

In those categories where we can isolate the respondents exposed to Nepali Congress party workers (second column) and those exposed to Communist UML party workers (third column), there is a remarkable association between having visits from a party and actually voting for that party. Seventy-two percent of those visited by Nepali Congress workers voted Congress, and 65 percent of those being visited by Communist UML workers voted UML. If we interpret this as an effect of campaigning, the effect is astounding. However, it is very likely that party workers have campaigned in neighbourhoods where they expected to be friendly received, and one may as well interpret these figures as resulting from the activists' success in locating their own voters. A more detailed investigation of the campaign would be needed to separate these two tendencies.

Group Political Discussions

Now we turn towards our second question. Did the personal discussions about politics engage everybody? To answer this question we have seized on a number of conversational groups such as family, friends, neighbours, colleagues at work, housewives, students, social workers or volunteers, school teachers, religious leaders, local notables and others. Political discussions with family, friends and neighbours will be given separate treatment and will be cross tabulated by independent variables such as sex, age, school education, and urban/rural origin. Other variables like discussions with colleagues at work, housewives, students, social workers, school teachers, religious leaders, local notables and others will be lumped together under the heading "discussion groups" and will be cross tabulated by the same independent variables. We begin from discussions that occurred between family, friends and neighbours. The following Table 7 illustrates the extent of discussion that took place.

Table 7. Talked with Family, Friends and Neighbours, by Sex (Percentages)

	Male	Female	All
Family	67	77	71
Friends	52	42	47
Neighbours	53	62	58

Table 7 shows that more than 71 percent voters talked politics within their families, 58 percent talked with neighbours and 47 percent talked with friends. The breakdown by respondent's sex shows that more women than men talked about politics with family and neighbours, but more men than women discussed it with their friends.

That people should engage in political talk with family and neighbours in Nepal is quite understandable in view of the role that family and kinship ties play in social relations. That more men talk politics with their friends than women is a clear illustration of the role men play outside of the house where they have opportunity to meet many friends.

Table 8 shows that especially younger people engaged in discussion with friends and neighbours while the middle aged and older people discussed with family more

Table 8. Talked with Family, Friends and Neighbours, by Age (Percentages)

	18-29 Years	30-44 Years	45 Years or More
Family	63	75	74
Friends	57	47	44
Neighbours	56	57	59

frequently than with friends. The data substantiates the fact of traditional social life in Nepal that the younger persons play relatively docile role in the family discussions. It is the seniors in the family i.e. the middle aged and the older people who are supposed to take part in discussion, and the younger members have to listen. In this context the participation by 63 percent of the young persons in family talk is in itself a surprise. The next table will show the influence of education on political talks within family, friends, and neighbours.

Table 9. Education and Political Talks (Percentages)

Education	Political Talk Groups		
	Family	Friends	Neighbours
No schooling	69	40	55
Primary	79	63	63
Lower secondary	80	70	67
High school	74	80	71
Higher education	73	80	68

Table 9 shows that higher educated people engage in political discussion with their friends more often than with their family and neighbours. Those with primary and lower secondary education with family followed by friends and neighbours. People without schooling discuss with family, followed by neighbours and friends. The following table shows the extent of political talk in urban and rural settings.

Table 10. Political Talk in Urban or Rural Settings (Percentages)

	Urban	Rural
Family	75	71
Friends	52	47
Neighbours	64	57

Table 10 shows that political talk in the family was more frequent in urban areas than in rural areas although the difference is marginal. Similarly, higher frequency of talk between friends and neighbours in urban area can be explained by the fact the urban people have more time to mix up than the rural ones. The latter are too busy in the agrarian fields and they live in sparsely populated areas.

We also tried to find out the frequency of political discussions among different groups and hence made an index of eleven different groups mentioned earlier. We lumped them into five groups and cross tabulated with sex. Table 11 indicates the result.

Table 11. Group Discussion by Sex (Percentages)

	Male	Female	All
None	5	4	4
1 group	37	29	33
2 groups	22	18	20
3 groups	27	33	30
4 or more groups	10	16	13
Total	100	100	100

Thus we see in Table 11 that no less than 96 percent of the voters in Nepal had engaged themselves in group discussions one way or the other. 33 percent people participated in discussion with one group, followed by three groups, two groups and four or more groups. More men discussed politics in one or two groups while more women discussed it in three groups or in four or more groups. The data speak for themselves: there is no substantial difference in the rate of participation by men and women in political discussions. Moreover, it also suggests that informal political discussions among different groups is much more effective means of political mobilization than other formal means. In the next table we will see the extent of different age groups participating in discussions with family friends and neighbours.

Table 12. Group Discussion by Age (Percentages)

	18-29 Years	30-44 Years	45 Years or More
None	5	3	4
1 group	26	34	35
2 groups	23	17	21
3 groups	31	33	28
4-11 groups	15	13	12

When age was cross tabulated with eleven other discussion groups we found the picture shown in Table 12.

Table 12 shows that there is only marginal difference in term of participation by different age groups in political group discussions. Higher numbers of middle aged and older people appear to discuss politics in one group, while more younger and middle aged discuss it in three groups. The following table gives a picture of group discussion among different levels of educated voters.

Table 13. Group Discussion by School Education (Percentages)

Education	Discussion Groups				;	
	None	1	2	3	4+	Total
No school	5	37	21	27	10	100
Primary	2	27	16	39	16	100
Low secon.	3	18	23	31	26	100
High school	1	20	14	37	29	100
Higher educ.	0	14	19	27	40	100

Among all respondents 96 percent of the voters engaged themselves in group discussions one way or the other. Voters with no school most frequently discussed in one group, while voters with primary, lower secondary, and high school education most frequently discussed in three groups. The highly educated persons most frequently discussed politics in four or more groups. We now go on to see the extent of group discussion among the voters of urban and rural residence.

Table 14 shows that higher numbers of voters in both urban and rural areas engage in group discussion with one and three groups. The frequency of urban voters discussing in three groups is higher while rural voters' frequency of discussion is with one group. This is explicable in terms of density of population.

Table 14. Group Discussion in Urban or Rural Settings (Percentages)

| | Discussion Groups | | | | | |
	None	1	2	3	4	Total
Urban	3	29	18	32	19	100
Rural	5	34	20	30	12	100

However, an inexplicable pattern of group discussion was found in the individual districts. We call it inexplicable because the voters in the two highly educated and politically conscious districts of Chitwon and Tanahu are found to have discussed politics less frequently in groups than their counterparts in other less developed districts. In our sample districts we found that voters frequently engaged themselves in more than one group discussion . The average number of groups in which respondents discussed politics in the districts sampled was as follows: Doti (3.22), Banke (2.26), Rukum (1.74), Rupendehi (2.03), Tanahu (1.89), Chitwon (1.73), Rasuwa (1.80), Sindhupalchok (2.09), Saptari (2.36), and Ilam (2.92).

Campaign and Political Interest

Now we turn to our third question: what were the effects of the election campaign in generating political interest, in making the party symbols known, and in guiding the people toward a particular party? Let us start from the level of voters' political interest.

In the weighted sample 15 percent voters are "very interested", 25 percent are "somewhat interested", 23 percent are "only a little interested" 28 percent are "not interested at all" in politics and 9 percent belong to "don't know" category. Thus we see that the majority of the Nepalese electorate have little or no real interest in politics. We see on the basis of this finding that 37 percent of the Nepalese electorate have no interest in politics and national affairs and that 85 percent of them are not "very interested". When we combine the percentage of somewhat interested and only a little interested we find that 48 percent of the Nepalese voters show some form of interest in politics. What makes these voters show some form of interest in politics? The purpose of our enquiry here will be to analyze the factors that may have influenced the voters in generating political interest.

A voters' political interest depends among other things on his level of awareness which is determined by campaign exposure, and the level of his or her education. Therefore, the variable "interest in politics" was cross tabulated with the number of media such as radio, newspaper, mass meeting, and someone reading for the voters, controlling for education. We divided the educational group into three i.e.

Table 15. Interest in Politics of No Schooling Group by Media (Percentages)

| | No. of Media R Was Exposed to | | | | | |
	None	1	2	3	4	All
Very interested	5	14	11	18	34	12
Somewhat	9	15	34	38	37	22
Only a little	17	30	12	31	22	22
Not at all	51	31	34	8	--	32
Don't know	20	9	8	4	7	12
Total	100	100	100	100	100	100

no schooling, primary and secondary education, and high school and more. We found the following result.

Thus, according to Table 15, among the uneducated voters the number of media exposure has increased the level of political interest. For example media exposure has led to the reduction of disinterested voters from 51 percent to zero. Therefore we can safely generalize that the voter exposed to multiple media shows more interest in politics than the voter who is not exposed to media. The following table will show the scale of political interest among those who have primary and lower secondary education.

Table 16. Interest in Politics of Primary and Lower Secondary Education Group by Media Exposure (Percentages)

| | Number of Media R Was Exposed to | | | | | |
	None	1	2	3	4	All
Very interested	3	11	29	14	30	19
Somewhat	19	16	26	39	40	30
Only a little	24	33	21	41	17	28
Not at all	54	29	24	6	13	22
Don't know	--	11	--	--	--	2
Total	100	100	100	100	100	100

Table 16 shows that the increase in educational level has increased the proportion from 12 percent to 19 percent in the "very interested" category. And while only 56 percent had shown some form of political interest among the uneducated, the figure for this category has risen significantly to 77 percent. The pattern of media effect in generating voters' political interest is just about the same as in Table 16 above i.e. the higher the number of media exposure the higher the level of political interest. Our third group, educated people who have high school and beyond education, basically shows the same tendency.

Voters who are exposed to multiple media show higher interest than voters who are exposed to none or only one or two media. We find that the number of "very interested" rose from 18 percent to 39 percent when they were exposed to multiple media. Similarly, the percentage of those showing some interest increased from 20 to 51 percent when exposed to multiple media. The table will not be shown because the group size is rather small.

Now we would like to see the extent of influence of multiple media use on voters in their party choice.

Table 17. Party Choice by No. of Media (Percentages)

	No. of Media R Was Exposed to				
	None	1	2	3	4
Communist UML	24	21	30	26	18
Other Left	14	15	15	20	12
Nepali Congress	25	39	39	41	62
National Democratic	32	13	13	11	5
Sadvabana	4	6	3	--	2
Indep. candidates	--	6	--	2	--
Total	100	100	100	100	100

Table 17 above clearly shows that the voters who voted for the Nepali Congress, followed by Communist UML voters, were exposed to more media than the voters of other parties. The interesting point to note in this table, however, is that the voters belonging to National Democratic parties did not use media as often as other voters. This perhaps can be explained in terms of the environment of campaign where National Democratic parties were discouraged by other parties. These parties had become the symbol of repression during the Panchayat time, and hence they were disliked by many politically conscious people. Their mass meetings were disturbed, campaign materials were confiscated, and party workers were discouraged and even threatened by other party campaigners. As a result, there were less mass meetings and other forms of campaigns on behalf of these parties.

Now we turn towards the role of group discussions in generating political interest. Here also we use education as control variable. We begin with the no schooling group.

Table 18. Interest in Politics by Group Discussion among No Schooling Group (Percentages)

| | Number of Discussion Groups | | |
	0-1	2-3	4-11
Very interested	6	18	15
Somewhat	12	27	39
Only a little	12	31	23
Not at all	50	19	15
Don't know	20	6	8
Total	100	100	100

Table 18 shows that voters in the no schooling group who are involved in 2-3 group discussions express higher political interest than those involved in only

Table 19. Political Interest by Group Discussion Among Primary and Lower Secondary Education Group (Percentages)

| | Number of Discussion Groups | | |
	0-1	2-3	4-11
Very interested	10	21	29
Somewhat	20	29	44
Only a little	27	32	15
Not at all	36	18	12
Don't know	7	--	--
Total	100	100	100

one group discussion. Similarly, we find more voters in the "somewhat interested" category among those engaged in more group discussions. The following table will show the impact of group discussion on voters with primary and lower secondary education.

We see in Table 19 that participation of voters with primary and lower secondary education in multiple group discussions have raised the percentage of "very interested" and "somewhat" interested in politics from 30 to 73 percent. Finally, among the well-educated the same tendency can be noted (table not shown). The number of very interested rises from 25 percent among those engaged in 0-1 group discussion to 43 percent among those engaged in 4-11 discussions.

Table 20. Party Choice by Group Discussion (Percentages)

Party Choice	No. of Discussion Groups					
	None	1	2	3	4	Total
Communist UML	24	27	24	27	13	24
Other Left	--	19	19	14	8	15
Nepali Congress	46	32	29	41	56	38
National Dem.	23	17	19	13	20	17
Sadvabana	6	1	6	4	2	3
Indep. cands.	--	3	3	1	--	2
Total	100	100	100	100	100	100

Hence we find that participation in group discussion, like exposure to mass media, has an impact on political interest independently of the impact of school education. Now we turn to see the impact of group discussion on voters' party choice. In Table 20 we find that Nepali Congress and Communist UML voters have participated in group discussions more frequently, followed by other left voters and voters of National Democratic parties. We also see that there are less participation among Communist UML voters in 4 or more groups compared to Nepali Congress and National Democratic parties. Another important aspect of this table is that none of the voters of Other Left parties were left without group discussion indicating the cadre oriented nature of these parties.

Conclusions

The election campaign mobilised very large sections of the Nepalese population. Roughly half of our respondents were reached by radio broadcasts and rallies organised by the parties, and more than one third were reached by newspaper items which they were able to read or which others read to them. The mass media campaign engaged men and women, young and old in almost the same proportion--but definitely it engaged the well-educated far more than the poorly educated (Table 3). In addition, door-to-door campaigns by party workers appear to have been both intense and successful in generating support (Table 6).

All of this campaigning aroused discussion in families and groups of friends, neighbours, and colleagues. And the effect of media exposure and small-group discussion in arousing political interest and leading to voting turnout cannot be doubted. Even among the uneducated, one third described themselves as very or somewhat interested in politics (Table 15), a proportion that rises to two thirds

95

or more among those exposed to several media (Table 15) and to more than one half among those engaged in several group discussions (Table 19).

The Nepali Congress party was particularly successful among those exposed to multiple media, whereas the leftwing parties were successful among those using a few media, and the National Democratic parties drew support disproportionally from those not exposed to any medium (Table 18). Roughly the same picture emerges if instead of media exposure one looks at exposure to political discussion at the personal level (Table 22), except that the Nepali Congress also did well among those not taking part in discussions.

CHAPTER 6

AGENDAS OF VOTERS AND PARTIES

The one year interim period of all-party government was marked by constitutional reform, restructuring of old feudal bureaucracy, and hectic preparation of general elections for parliamentary seats. In such a transitional situation, it is important to analyze which issues are considered the most important by voters, as such "issue priorities" can be meaningful platforms for public policy formulation. Also, the study of differences in perception between party members and voters regarding issue priorities can be meaningful, as it provides valuable information on the degree of responsiveness parties have toward the electorate.

However, given the short time-frame in which the parties have functioned in Nepal, the Nepalese public at best can assess the performance of the government in a limited way. The issue priorities of voters may therefore be far removed from government policy. Furthermore, in an environment of newly evolving multiparty democracy as in Nepal, where political norms and values are in the formative stage, the place of issues among the determinants of voting behaviour may not be clearly identifiable. We should not be surprised to find that issue stands do not explain why voters vote in one way and not the other way.

In the present study, the analysis of issue priorities will be carried out on the basis of the question, "In your opinion, what is the most important problem facing Nepal today?" This was the opening question in the interviews both with voters, party members, and members of parliament. For the voters and party members the next question was, "Thinking now of your village or town, which is the most important problem which you are facing here?" Hence at the national level we may employ three sets of data on voters, party members, and parliamentarians; at the local level only the voters and party members are included. We shall study the cross-sectional views of these different sets of respondents in order to explore the possible linkage between the input and output side of policy formulation. In attempting to do this, we distinguish between the problems as perceived by those who are directly affected by governmental actions (the general public), by those who are in the opposition parties, and by those in the ruling party who are likely to influence the formulation of governmental policies. In many newly established democracies, the ruling party is often under strong pressure to meet rising public demands (and expectations) lest the opposition parties capitalize on the failing of the government by winning over the voters in the next round of national elections. Nepal is no exception.

We shall here analyze these problems by exploring those variables such as age, level of education, place of origin and party affiliation, in order to explain who these voters are and also briefly mention how the parties and parliamentarians differ in their perceptions of these problems. Broadly, we shall try to answer the following questions:

* To what extent do the parliamentarians and parties represent the mass public (the voters)?

* What issues are favoured by which parties?

* Are there differences in perception between the rural and urban population and between regions with regard to the priorities of issues?

Of our survey data, the first set is based on the representative national sample of voters (N=1000) taken a few days after the national election in Nepal. The second and third set are based on the representative national samples of party members (N=805) and parliamentarians (N=256/265) taken eight months later. Only those few available variables on socio-economic status and party choice are used from the first sample.

Cross Sectional Views on National and Local Problems

In an emerging developing society such as Nepal, the problems facing the nation are innumerable, ranging from the dire need for safe drinking water to mass illiteracy. These problems are largely rooted to psycho-cultural factors, traditional values, mismanagement of resources, low level of economic development, difficult terrain, landlockedness, work ethics, governmental inaction, feudal politics, and a vicious cycle of poverty. Indeed, if one were to list the entire range of problems as identified by the Nepalese respondents, the list can be very exhaustive. There are more than sixty problems identified by all three sets of respondents. These problems are found to be highly variegated and they can have different degrees of impact on the Nepalese polity. Compositely, the problems affect nearly all sectors of national life -- the social, political, economic, and developmental. The following is a list of problems that were mentioned by the Nepalese respondents:

Education	Agriculture
Tenancy	Ethnicity
Unemployment	Industrialization
Exploitation	Price Rise
Black market	Food and shelter
Alcoholism	Landlessness
Dowry	Self reliance
Market economy	Planning

Confidence crisis	Official graft
Favouritism	Dual landownership
National sovereignty	Afforestation
Drinking water	Migration, Citizenship
Health and sanitation	Intra-party discord
Electricity	Communication
Peace and security	Roads and transportation
Relations with India	Community development
Political instability	Technology
Political consciousness	Modernization
Migration	Politicization
Political integration	Violence
People-oriented govt	Political culture
Work permits	Democracy
Poverty	Ecology
Citizenship	

In the references to these problems we find striking variations between our sampled respondents from the three sets (Table 1 and Table 2).

National Agendas of Voters, Party Members, and Parliamentarians

It is seen that the general voters identify "unemployment" as the number one national problem which is considered by party members to be the second most important problem and by parliamentarians to be the third. To the latter groups, the problem of "price rise" seems to be more important. This implies that the newly elected government has, over a period of one year, encountered a new set of economic problems and the economic situation of the country has deteriorated further. The third problem facing Nepal is "poverty" which is a well-known problem as the country ranks among the ten poorest countries in the world with a gross national product per capita of less than $170. By and large, the three major national problems fall in the economic sector and it is this sector which has been identified by a large percentage of respondents in all three sets of data. In the case of parliamentarians, a larger majority (65%) confirm this to be true, much more than the fractions of party members (45%) and voters (27%). See Table 1.

Next to the economic problems, there is a wide array of social, political, and developmental problems which the general public perceive. There are five problems identified in the political sector which may be seen as domestic and foreign policy issues. The voters and party members perceive "official graft" to be the major domestic political problem which has been overlooked by parliamentarians. The parliamentarians see "political consciousness" and "political culture" to be important political problems instead. Also, there are two other political problems which may be treated as foreign policy issues, namely threat to national sovereignty and peace

99

Table 1. National Problems As Identified by Three Sets of Actors (Percentages)

Problems	Voters (N=1000)	Parliamentarians (N=256)	Party Members (N=805)
Price rise	--	24	19
Unemployment	27	16	14
Poverty	--	19	12
Economic development	--	6	--
Food and shelter	--	--	4
Official graft	6	--	6
National sovereignty	4	3	4
Peace & security	3	--	3
Political consciousness	--	4	--
Political culture	--	3	--
Education	14	--	3
Exploitation	--	--	5
Lack of drinking water	13	--	--
Lack of fertilizers	9	--	--
Lack of irrigation	7	--	--
Other	17	25	30
Total	100	100	100

Note: Problems that are identified by less than 3% of the respondents are put under 'other'.

and security. All three actors perceive national sovereignty under some kind of threat, though by small percentages of respondents, and similarly the situation of peace and security has been questioned only by the voters and party members.

It is important to see that the voters have identified education to be the second largest social problem which has also been identified by a small percentage of party members. One other problem seen in the social sector is "exploitation" which has been seen by a small percentage of party members only. The parliamentarians, on the other hand, do not mention any social problem at all.

Lastly, about the developmental sector which concerns the public very much, it is only the voters who have identified three major problems, namely lack of drinking water, fertilizers, and irrigation. Though these problems are of local nature, it is understandable that the Nepalese voters identify them as national problems. In a largely agricultural country such as Nepal they are of utmost importance, concerning agricultural production and livelihood of the people.

Local Agendas of Voters and Party Members

The voters have perceived many problems which are treated as local and national problems such as unemployment, official graft, peace and security, education, lack of fertilizers, drinking water, and irrigation. The problem of protecting national sovereignty is seen as a national problem. By implication, the party members seem more in touch with the people (the general voters) than we can say of the parliament-arians who do not see any problems in the social and developmental sector. It is also clearly evident that the general voters are more concerned with problems they face at the local level. Many of the local problems fall in the developmental sector and in a developing country like Nepal these problems can have special significance to political parties during the time of election as more than three-quarters of voters originate from the rural population (see Table 2).

Table 2. Local Problems Identified by Voters and Party Members

	Voters (N=1000)	Party Members (N=805)
Unemployment	16	9
Price rise	--	19
Poverty	--	5
Official graft	7	9
Peace and security	3	3
Education	7	4
Lack of fertilizers	10	4
Drinking water	21	7
Irrigation	11	7
Roads and Transport	4	7
Health and Sanitation	6	--
Other	15	26
Total	100	100

Note: Problems identified by less than 3% of the respondents are put under "other".

Party Differences

Let us look into both national and local problems by analysing the differences in perception between parties and between parties and voters. We shall here analyze the problems under four sectors - economic, political, social, and developmental.

[A] Economic Sector
The backbone of Nepalese economy is agriculture. With little less than 85% of the population involved in farming, the mode of agricultural production is basically traditional. Since the middle sixties, the use of modern implements, pesticides, fertilizers, and advanced seeds was started and it is today applied on a limited

scale and there is a large chunk of farming land yet to receive benefits of modern methods and technical know-how. Over the past two decades, the volume of international assistance through multilateral agencies has steadily flowed in the construction of agricultural infrastructures such as agricultural banks, cooperatives, irrigation, and other support agencies yet the economy of the country staggers, producing inadequate food for the country's growing population of twenty million.

Furthermore, it has limited natural resources which consist of large potential of untapped high current mountain streams and rivers, copper, lead, mica, and few precious stones. The bulk of its export earnings come from garments, carpets, herbs, hides, handicrafts, metal works, finished jewellery, and precious stones. It imports mainly manufactured goods, edible oils and grains, petrol, diesel, kerosine and other items of daily use.

It has a very low per capita income of $ 170 with a limited purchasing power to sustain a decent livelihood for many. By Western standards there is no comparison to what an average person earns as a regular average annual salary in Nepal and what is given out per month as minimum social benefit allowance for the unemployed in a welfare state. Both are nearly equal in terms of market prices.

It suffers basically from unplanned management of the economic sector. Eight national plans have been implemented over a period of 30 years and priorities were targeted on the building of infrastructures.Some of the important areas of resource allocation were agricultural sector, road buildings, electrification, and education. Despite various assistance and generous support from the international agencies, multi-lateral donor groups, and friendly countries, there is still the lingering problem of inadequate infrastructures for all round development of the country.

In our surveys it is seen that the problem of unemployment is strongly mentioned by both party members and parliamentarians (Table 1). Among party members, the Nepali Congress accords the highest priority to unemployment at the national level and following half way behind are the left-wing parties (Tables 3-5). The National Democratic members fall behind in mentioning this problem at both the levels. Comparing the voters against party members on the issue of unemployment, there is a wide perception gap between them at both national and local level, except in the case of Nepali Congress and its supporters. Also, the gap between party members and voters can be seen in perceiving the problem at two different levels. For the voters, the problem of unemployment exists at both national and local level but the party members see it to be national.

In the first sample on the study of voters the problem of unemployment is identified as the top national problem facing the nation. All other problems in the economic sector as pointed out by the party members such as price rise, poverty and food and shelter are not in the voters' agenda. Unemployment, when analyzed by voters' party affiliation to all three major political parties (leftwing, Nepali Congress, and National Democratic), is rated to be the biggest national problem (Tables 3-5).

Table 3. *Identification of National and Local Problems by Leftwing Party Members (N=345) and Leftwing Voters (N=365)*

| | National Problems | | Local Problems | |
	Members	Voters	Members	Voters
Price Rise	15	--	17	--
Unemployment	12	30	8	18
Poverty	11	--	6	--
Economic Development	--	--	--	--
Food & Shelter	4	--	3	--
Official Graft	8	4	9	4
National Sovereignty	3	1	--	--
Peace & Security	--	3	3	2
Education	3	12	5	12
Exploitation	11	--	6	--
Drinking Water	--	13	5	17
Fertilizers	--	12	3	11
Irrigation	--	5	5	10
Health & Sanitation	--	3	--	6
Roads & Transport	--	--	3	2
Others	32	11	27	18
Don't Know	--	6	--	--
Total	100	100	100	100

Table 4. Identification of National and Local Problems by Congress Party Members (N=234) and Congress Voters (N=350)

	National Problems		Local Problems	
	Members	Voters	Members	Voters
Price Rise	18	--	18	--
Unemployment	22	18	9	14
Poverty	16	--	5	--
Economic Development	4	--	--	--
Food & Shelter	3	--	--	--
Official Graft	6	8	8	7
National Sovereignty	3	6	--	--
Peace & Security	--	3	--	2
Education	4	15	4	4
Exploitation	--	--	--	--
Drinking Water	--	15	11	30
Fertilizers	--	3	--	9
Irrigation	3	7	9	11
Health & Sanitation	--	4	4	8
Roads & Transport	4	--	12	2
Others	17	19	20	13
Don't Know	--	2	--	--
Total	100	100	100	100

Table 5. Identification of National and Local Problems by National Democratic Members (N=181) and National Democratic Voters (N=156)

	National Problems		Local Problems	
	Members	Voters	Members	Voters
Price Rise	29	--	25	--
Unemployment	9	18	7	10
Poverty	7	--	3	--
Economic Development	--	--	--	--
Food & Shelter	3	--	--	--
Official Graft	3	8	9	3
National Sovereignty	8	4	--	--
Peace & Security	10	3	4	2
Education	--	10	--	5
Exploitation	--	--	--	--
Drinking Water	--	15	9	30
Fertilizers	--	10	9	8
Irrigation	--	12	4	25
Health & Sanitation	--	--	--	6
Roads & Transport	3	--	9	--
Others	28	3	21	11
Don't Know	--	17	--	--
Total	100	100	100	100

By percentage count, the leftwing voters have scored the highest percentage in identifying this problem (30%). The Nepali Congress and National Democratic voters are found to trail behind. In descending order the leftwing voters consider unemployment to be the main problem at the local level, followed by the Congress and National Democratic voters.

By age, the younger age group of voters (1 in every 3), scoring the highest percentage in all the age categories, identify unemployment to be number one national problem. In ascending order the emphasis to this problem falls slightly as the age of the respondents goes up. In all age categories unemployment is rated to be the biggest national problem. At the local level this problem falls to third position in all age groups (Table 6).

A similar pattern is noticeable in the perception of party members who identify the problem at the national level. At the local level the young and the old aged party members are slightly more concerned about this problem than the middle age party members.

Table 6. *Identification of National and Local Problems by Voters' Age*

	18-29 Years		30-44 Years		45+ Years	
	Nat'l	Local	Nat'l	Local	Nat'l	Local
Unemployment	32	14	27	16	23	14
Education	21	13	14	7	8	4
Official Graft	7	4	7	7	6	6
Drinking Water	8	21	12	21	17	27
Fertilizers	6	8	6	15	13	11
Nat Sovereignty	2	0	5	--	3	0
Irrigation	5	9	5	9	8	16
Peace & Sec	1	1	2	2	4	2
Roads & Trans	0	3	--	1	2	1
Health & Sanity.	2	7	4	5	2	6
Others	11	20	10	17	9	13
Don't Know	5	--	8	--	5	--
Total	100	100	100	100	100	100

By level of education, there is very little variation in perception of the problem among voters, except that the voters with higher education slightly give more importance to this problem at the local level than the less educated voters (Table 7).

Table 7. *Identification of National and Local Problems by Voters' Level of Education*

	No Schooling		Primary or Low second.		Higher Education	
	Nat'l	Local	Nat'l	Local	Nat'l	Local
Unemployment	26	15	28	13	28	18
Education	13	7	12	7	17	9
Official Graft	5	7	10	4	11	9
Drinking Water	15	25	9	23	3	13
Fertilizers	10	10	8	16	1	6
Nat Sovereignty	2	--	7	--	8	2
Irrigation		7	13	5	10	19
Peace & Security	3	2	2	2	5	4
Roads & Transport	--	--	1	4	5	5
Health & Sanitation	3	6	4	4	2	10
Others	9	15	11	11	19	15
Don't Know		7	--	3	6	-- --
Total	100	100	100	100	100	100

The party members, on the other hand, with lower level education give more importance to this problem at both national and local level than those with higher education. Between the voters and party members, there is a slight perception gap especially among the educated groups (Tables 7 & 8).

Table 8. *Percentages of Party Members (N=805) Identifying Unemployment As National and Local Problems by Level of Education*

	National Problem	Local Problem
None or Primary	18	5
Up to Higher Secondary	14	9
Higher Education	12	9

By place of origin, voters from the Terai point out unemployment to be the biggest problem at both local and national levels. This is also true for respondents originating from the mountains. When respondent's place of origin is controlled by urban-rural dichotomy, those from the rural sector see this problem slightly more than those from urban areas (Table 9).

Table 9. *Issue Priorities by Voters' Place of Origin*

	Local Problems		National Problems	
	Mountain	Terai	Mountain	Terai
Unemployment	16	20	29	30
Education	5	9	11	7
Official Graft	5	8	7	5
Drinking Water	27	8	14	7
Fertilizers	10	15	7	10
National Sovereignty	--	--	4	7
Irrigation	12	18	8	6
Peace & Security	--	--	--	3
Roads and Transport	--	3	--	--
Health & Sanitation	4	--	--	3
Other	21	19	11	22
Don't Know	--	--	9	--
Total	100	100	100	100

Unlike the voters, the sample on party members shows four additional problems identified in the economic sector. These problems are price rise, poverty, food

107

and shelter, and economic development (Table 2). In cross tabulating national and local problems by parties there is an unanimity of views of the parties in identifying price rise as the most acute problem at both local and national levels (Tables 3-5). By percentage count, the National Democratic members give the highest priority to this problem, followed by members of Nepali Congress and leftwing parties (Tables 3-5). In the case of Nepali Congress, the problem of unemployment tops the list of national problems, superseding price rise by a marginal difference of 4% only. Also, at both the national and local levels the intensity of this problem (price rise) is strongly felt by all the parties. With the other economic problems the percentage points between the two levels is slightly higher (Tables 3-5).

The problem of poverty which is considered the second largest national problem by parliamentarians occupies third position on the priority of parties and the voters do not mention this problem at all (Table 1). The party members on the other hand mention this problem at the local level with a lesser degree of intensity compared to other problems.

In the following discussion we shall analyze other problems at the national and local level which do not fall in the economic sector but other sectors -- political, social, and developmental -- which the voters have given higher priorities.

[B] Political Sector
Politically, the Nepalese society can be described as a marginal case between two types -- traditional and modern. It is a transitional society moving away from traditional and feudal structures to more advanced, differentiated and pluralistic society. Both traditional and modern values mix and modern public institutions are found to be quite inefficient. Often rules and regulations are twisted for personal benefits and personalities play influential role in the administration of public policy. Politics in this kind of environment is more authoritarian than democratic.

In all three samples the problem of national sovereignty is perceived to be a national problem by 3-4% of the respondents. Voters originating from the Terai accord much more importance to this problem than those from the mountains. Within the educational category, voters from the higher education bracket apparently are more concerned than those from other levels of education. This problem is seen mainly among the Nepali Congress and Sadvabana voters and understandably it has not been treated as a local problem. Among the eight parties, the National Democratic party shows a much higher concern for this problem than any other parties. Among parliamentarians, the United People's Front leads all other parliament-arians; this is because of the stand it takes against Indian hegemony in the region and seeks greater independence in the formulation of foreign policy.

Closely related to this problem is the problem of peace and security at both national and local level which has been identified by 3% of both the voters and party members and not by parliamentarians. Among party members, the National Democrats show greater concern for peace and security as a national problem -- a result of the difficulties which this party and its supporters faced during election campaigns from opposition parties. A small section of party members from this group and leftwing parties (3-4%) has pointed out this problem at the local level as well.

The next set of national problems in the political sector deal with political culture and political consciousness which are mentioned by a small group parliament-arians (7%) who represent the Nepali Congress and Unified Marxist Leninist parties in both the Houses of Parliament (Table 1). A negligible percentage of party members, less than 3%, mention these problems but the voters do not see them to be of any importance.

Finally, The next problem in the political sector which is seen by the voters and party members is the problem of official graft. During the Panchayat era the government officials in high positions of bureaucracy were known to have amassed huge fortunes and the general public went around with meagre resources and without employment. Those with low salaries were unable to depend on one income. Strangely enough, the parliamentarians do not see this problem to be important at all.

In Tables 3-5 there is a commonality of perception between the Sadvabana voters and party members in identifying official graft to be of lesser importance at the national level but which is treated as a very important problem at the local level. The perception of National Democratic voters and party members on the other hand is found to be in reverse; what is treated by the voters as national problem is treated to be a local problem by the party members and vice versa. At both the national and local levels there is a perception gap between the two groups: The percentage figure of party members pointing it to be a local problem than national problem is higher than the percentage figure of voters who see it as a national problem. The left-wing voters see this problem to be of lesser importance than voters from other parties but the leftwing parties, unlike other parties, see it as an important national problem. The perception gap between the two groups exists significantly. The Congress voters and Congress party have similar perception on the issue at both the local and national levels. There apparently seems a smaller gap between the two groups of actors. Also the problem is comparatively better understood by the two groups. It may be mentioned here that the Terai voters, especially those originating from the rural Terai than urban Terai, see the problem of official graft slightly more than the respondents from the mountain at the local level.

Regarding the problem at the national level, voters from the mountain mention the problem but none from the Terai. Also, at the local level, the older party members perceive this problem to be important (1 in 10 cases) than the younger party members (1 in 14 cases) and the voters give a lower importance to this problem (1 in 16 cases) and age as an independent variable does not explain voters' perception of the problem. The opposite is true at the national level. Younger party members give slightly more importance to this problem (1 in 12 cases) than we can say of the older members (1 in 20 cases). On the other hand, the perception of voters does not significantly differ between the different age groups.

[C] Social Sector
There are several factors which affect voting and the social environment to a large measure play an important role in determining voter's behaviour in an emerging democratic society. The social environment, as commonly understood, deals with a whole range of variables that are both hidden and open. Education is one such explicit variable which not only produces informed voters but also it is the very foundation on which democracy has any meaning in terms of participation.

In Nepal the total percentage of literate population is approximately 35-40% of 20 million population who can read and write. The low percentage of literacy is accredited to, of the many factors, lack of primary schools in physical terms and the social environment of castes, ethnic culture, tradition, and even religion which influences the decision to learn, read and write or send children to school.

There are two major problems identified in the social sector -- education and exploitation (Table 11). The problem of education is seen by voters and party members (especially those originating from Kathmandu) and not by parliamentarians.

Comparatively, the voters give much higher importance to the problem of education than party members do. There is a perception gap between the two actors on this major issue. At both national and local levels the problem is seen nearly in equal footing by all the parties except for the National Democratic parties which is separated on the issue much more from the voters. By voter's origin of place, problem of education is felt slightly more by the mountain voters than the Terai voters though the problem exists in both the regions.

Following closely is the problem of exploitation which is seen as a national problem by a small number of party members only; who, by and large, originate from leftwing parties. The members of the United People's Front (1 in 5) accord much importance to this problem; its percentage figure is higher than that of the Communist UML members (1 in 10). The voters do not report this problem.

110

[D] Developmental Sector

The last set of national and local problems falls in the developmental sector which is seen largely by voters. It is this sector which clearly shows the perception gap between party members and voters. Party members see developmental problems at the local level which are considered important after the economic problems. The parliamentarians on the other hand do not mention any of the problems in this sector.

Let us look into each of the development problems as perceived by the voters and compare them with the perception of party members.

First, the problem of drinking water is considered to be important to the voters not only at the local level (1 in every 5 cases) but also at the national level. The importance of this problem is felt more by the voters supporting the Nepali Congress and National Democratic parties than the left-wing voters. The Sadvabana supporters do not see this problem to be important even at the local level. The party members on the other hand treat this problem to be local and the parties in general have similar perception, except for the Nepali Congress party which perceives this problem to be of lesser importance (Tables 3-5). Party members from Kathmandu Valley seriously take this problem (1 in 6 cases). In the case of the voters from the mountain, the problem of drinking water is considered to be more acute in the mountain than in the Terai though Terai urban areas seem to face the problem too.

Second, on the voters' list of priorities at the national level, the problem of fertilizers is identified. The party members see this problem at the local level which is fairly treated by two groups -- Left-wing and National Democratic. The Nepali Congress party fails to see this to be of any importance; not even at the local level (Tables 3-5). By voters place of origin, the problem is seen to be acute in the rural sector of the mountain and the Terai than in the urban parts of the mountain.

Third, the problem of irrigation is identified by the voters. To them it is an important local problem. In the order of importance given to this problem, the National Democratic members top the list closely followed by Sadvabana.

The leftwing and Nepali Congress voters see this problem to be important in lesser degree (Tables 3-5). The rural parts of the Terai clearly show an acute need of irrigation at both the national and local level.

Finally, the last two problems in the development sector -- roads and transport and health and sanitation are mentioned as local problems by the voters. The party members mention the problem of roads and transport and not health and sanitation and give slightly more importance than the voters.

Especially party members originating from mountain consider this problem to be more acute than the Terai members. Unlike the party members the Terai voters give higher priority to roads and transport than the mountain voters. The

111

dissimilarity in perception between the two groups is clearly seen when districts are compressed into mountain and Terai (Tables 3 and 9). At the local level the problem of health and sanitation is seen in the Terai but at the national level, both the mountain and the Terai voters see the problem though by a small percentage of voters.

Mass and Elite Voters

Now we come to the next discussion on the perception between the mass and elite voters. Once again we notice the perception gap between the two groups (Table 10).

Table 10. Issue Priorities by Mass (N=1000) and Elite Voters (N=100)

| | National Problems | | Local Problems | |
	Elite	Mass	Elite	Mass
Price Rise	4	--	--	--
Unemployment	22	16	27	16
Poverty	4	--	--	--
Economic Development	--	--	--	--
Food & Shelter	--	--	--	--
Official Graft	8	4	5	7
National Sovereignty	11	3	3	--
Peace and Security	--	--	3	3
Political Consciousness	6	--	--	--
Political Culture	--	--	--	--
Education	--	14	7	7
Exploitation	--	--	--	--
Lack of Drinking Water	3	13	8	21
Health & Sanitation	--	--	4	6
Lack of Fertilizers	--	9	10	10
Lack of Irrigation	9	7	8	11
Ethnic Problems	4	--	5	--
Roads and Transport	--	--	4	4
Political Stability	5	--	--	--
Other	18	17	16	15
Total	100	100	100	100

There is little commonality between them in the identification of problems at national and local level. As for instance, at the national level problems such as price rise, political consciousness, ethnic problems and political stability which have been identified by the elite (by one out of five) are not at all mentioned by the mass. Neither problems such as education and lack of fertilizers mentioned by the mass (one out of five) are referred by the elite. In two other major problems seen by either of the group -- national sovereignty pointed out by the elite (17%) and drinking water by the mass (13%) -- there is a wide perception gap between them. It is apparent from Table 10 that the elite and the mass do not come to agree in fifty percent of the case in identifying national problems. In the remaining fifty percent cases only two problems -- lack of irrigation and official graft -- are somewhat closely identified by both the groups.

How do the elite see the problems at the local level? Do they perceive the problems similar to the mass? The answers are more in the affirmative. By and large many of the problems perceived by the mass are similarly perceived by the elite. In one important area the elite have failed to see a major problem identified by the mass -- the problem of drinking water.

Proximity of Agendas

In discussing the extent of proximity between parties and the electorate, between party members and parliamentarians, between parliamentarians and voters, and between elite and mass, we can draw a few inferences from Tables 1, 2, 3, 4, 5, and 10 (Table 11).

Table 11. *Proximity Between Respondents in Identifying National and Local Issues from Four Sets of Data*

	Percentage Points in a Scale of 100
[A] Perception of National Problems	
Mass and Elite	42
Party Members and Voters	53
Parliamentarians and Voters	64
Party Members and Parliamentarians	25
Congress Party Members and Congress Voters	49
Leftwing Party Members and Leftwing Voters	69
National Democratic Party Members and National Democratic Voters	78
[B] Perception of Local Problems	
Mass and Elite	20
Party Members and Voters	40
Leftwing Party Members and Leftwing Voters	48
Congress Party Members and Congress Voters	41
National Democratic Party Members and National Democratic Voters	56

113

First, the party members and parliamentarians are found to be the closest in comparison to other groups of respondents. Second, between party members and parliamentarians, the former groups is closer to the voters than the parliamentarians. Third, Between the parties, the Nepali Congress party members are more closer to the electorate in perceiving problems at both national and local level than the leftwing party members and National Democratic party members. Fourth, there is a visible gap between the elite and the mass in perceiving national problems than local problems. Finally, in all sets of respondents the perception of local problems by the party members is closer to the level of voters' perception but not so when national problems are to be perceived.

It may be observed here that the probable reason for the narrower perception gap between the mass and the elite could have been due to the passage of time between the two surveys. As seen from the preceding discussion on party differences, many problems have been identified by party members and parliamentarians which are not in the agendas of voters.

Conclusions

From the preceding discussion on the problems facing the economic sector what can we infer? Basically, there is a perception gap between the parliamentarians/party members and voters in identifying the economic problems. The lack of representative-ness of party members to their constituencies can be inferred. As many of the problems are identified to be economic which are closely related to the problems in the developmental sector -- there is apparently a need for careful planning of the economy. Also, given the changed political environment, the party members have greater responsibilities to their constituencies and they cannot have a different perception from that of the voters; i.e., if they represent voters as a responsible party.

It may be said here that the voters have identified several national problems unlike the parliamentarians party members and elite. They perceive a wide range of problems which fall in all the sectors of national life. Between the parliamentarians and party members, the latter group seem more closer to the voters' way of looking at problems at the local level. Also, the elite are found to be more closer to the voters than the party members in identifying local problems though there is almost no commonality between the elite and the mass in perceiving national problems. The voters have perceived many problems which are treated as local and national problems such as unemployment, official graft, peace and security, education, lack of fertilizers, drinking water, and irrigation. In one problem -- the problem of protecting national sovereignty -- is seen as a national problem by all four sets of respondents. By implication, the party members seem more in touch with the people (the general voters) than we can say of the parliamentarians who do not see any problems in the social and developmental sector. Comparatively, the Nepali Congress members are quite close to the voters in perceiving the local problems. The leftwing parties seem to address problems that are at the national level than at the local level which the voters are more concerned with. Many of the local problems perceived by the voters fall in the developmental sector and in a developing country like Nepal (see economic sector above) these problems can have special significance to political parties during the time of election as more than three-quarters of voters originate from the rural population.

CHAPTER 7

PUBLIC ACCEPTANCE OF FOREIGN POLICY ISSUES

In this chapter we will focus on issues of foreign policy concern that are of vital importance to landlocked Nepal in safeguarding its national interests, territorial integrity, and independence as a sovereign nation and the well-being of its predominantly illiterate and poor people. We shall here concentrate on five major issues which have enjoyed the attention of national leadership; which have been commonly discussed at the popular level, and which vitally concerns Nepal's national interests. These issues cover Nepal's relations with India and China, introducing work permits for non-Nepalese, keeping Nepal-India border open, and maintaining Gorkha recruitment abroad. Some of the independent variables which will be employed to study the perception of the Nepalese voters on these issues are geographic origin, age, level of education, and party affiliation. The attitude of members of different parliamentary parties on these issues will also be studied in order to analyze cross-sectional views between the party members and the voters. Briefly, a few references to parliamentarians will be casually discussed in order to grasp a more comprehensive picture of how these issues are perceived by the Nepalese people in general, by those who can influence the legislation of bills in the Parliament either in support of or against them, or by those who can agitate in the streets along with the voters.

Nepal's Relations with China and India

In the aftermath of British withdrawal from India in 1947 and the parallel rise of communist power in China under Mao's leadership in 1949, the Rana rulers of Nepal who had ruled the country for more than a century were suddenly deserted without strong allies in the neighbourhood. The threat of forceful overthrow of its oligarchic rule by the suppressed people and the fear of subsequent loss of property and privileges enjoyed by the closely knit Rana families were important factors for the quick establishment of friendly relations with India, its southern neighbour. As a result, the Treaty of Peace and Friendship was signed in 1950 between Mohan Shumsher, the outgoing Rana Prime Minister of Nepal, and C.P.N. Sinha, the representative of the Government of India. This treaty has been the guiding force in shaping the relations between the two countries. In matters of trade, transit and defense the treaty has closely linked Nepal to India. Despite increasing diplomatic relations with a large number of countries (numbering more than one hundred), including China, and despite the opening up of the country to the outside world since 1950, (Nepal became a member of the United Nations in 1955), it has not officially made any attempt to alter the Treaty. Several reasons may be cited for the lack of initiative on the part of Nepal, or the intransigence shown by India, towards modification of the Treaty. Probably the dictates of geography, security, and market forces may have restrained bold foreign policy initiatives from either of the parties. Just exactly how the Nepalese mass and the elite perceive the subject of relations with India and China, can be seen in the voters' sample (Table 1).

Table 1. *Proposal on Improvement of Relations with China and India by Mass and Elite in Percentages*

	With India		With China	
	Mass	Elite	Mass	Elite
Good and important	74	90	46	69
Good and unimportant	11	8	30	28
Bad proposal	2	1	3	1
Don't know	13	1	21	2
Total	100	100	100	100

It is seen that the Nepalese people in general consider the relations with India to be more important than with China. In the case of comparison between the elite and the mass on the question of improvement of relations with both the countries there is less than half the total respondents at the mass level who consider relations with China to be "good and important" whereas with India nearly three quarters of them see so. Also, the elite in both the cases differ significantly, affirming relations with India to be not only more important than with China by a margin of 21% but also 30% of the elite respondents see improvement of relations with China to be "good but unimportant" - this is three times the number who see improvement of relations with India in such vein. What can we infer from these figures? Apparently there is a slight cleavage between the elite and the mass in perceiving Nepal's relations with its two neighbours. The elite are for improvement of relations with both the countries: 9 out of 10 cases with India and 7 out of 10 cases with China; whereas the mass perceive improvement of relations with India to be more important (7 out of 10 cases) than with China (4 out of 10 cases). The perception shown by the elite here reflects a desire for a more balanced foreign policy approach which has been interpreted by many Nepalese intellectuals as a policy based on political pragmatism. Whatever the defense for or argument against it, this position reflects a long tradition adopted by the rulers of landlocked Nepal since the very beginning

117

of the country in 1769. Regarding the position taken by the mass, several factors are responsible if not for strategic reason - social, political, economic, and place of origin. See Table 2 to study district origin of the mass.

Table 2.   *Proposal on Improvement of Relations with China (C) and India (I) by Districts*

	Good and Important		Good but Unimportant		Bad		Don't Know		Total	
	C:	I:	C:	I:	C:	I:	C:	I:	C:	I:
Bordering China										
Sindhupalchok	80	79	9	3	2	2	9	16	100	100
Rasuwa	41	55	36	26	--	--	23	19	100	100
Bordering India										
Banke	39	79	60	21	--	--	1	--	100	100
Rupandehi	85	98	14	2	1	--	--	--	100	100
Chitwan	57	64	16	10	8	5	19	21	100	100
Saptari	17	100	69	--	9	--	5	--	100	100
Ilam	65	86	24	14	--	--	11	--	100	100
Interior Mountain Districts										
Tanahu	59	85	31	9	10	6	--	--	100	100
Doti	22	96	37	4	3	--	38	--	100	100
Rukum	22	34	3	2	4	5	71	59	100	100

Looking into the respondents' district origin, there seems to be some degree of influence of this variable on the issue. Though the variable itself may not be an explanatory factor in determining the voters' perception, the activities of political parties in the district can, to some extent, reflect partisan type voting on the issue. As for instance, where the left political parties have influential party bases, there seems a tendency among the respondents to propose relations with China to be no less important. In Terai district of Chitwan and mountain district of Ilam, which have demonstrated strong left electoral strength during the parliamentary election of May, 1991, there are higher percentages of respondents who prefer to have closer relations with both China and India though with the latter the percentages are higher by over 60 and 80 percentages. Similarly in Rupandehi district of western Terai where the left parties have demonstrated some strength in four out of five constituencies in the national election, there are high percentages of respondents, proposing relations with both China and India to be good and important. However, where the left parties have been less influential in the national election as in Saptari district of eastern Terai, there is an exceptional picture. All the respondents clearly propose relations with India to be vital whereas with China there is about one-sixth of the respondents. Within district category, Rasuwa (a mountainous and backward region of Nepal) reveals a small size of respondents preferring good relations with China (2 out of 5 cases) though the number of respondents preferring good relations with India are still higher. As regards to Rukum there is some room to speculate because many responses fall under "don't know" category.

What about party affiliation of respondents? Does this variable have any influence on the respondents' perception? There seems to be a tendency of certain types of voters affiliated to political parties. Clearly there are some interesting characteristics in the sample. See Table 3.

Table 3.   *Proposal on Improvement of Relations with China and India by Party Affiliation*

	Good and Important	Good but Unimportant Proposal	Bad	Don't Know
With China:				
Leftwing	53	26	1	20
Nepali Congress	38	38	5	19
National Democratic	55	15	--	30
Sadvabana	33	46	17	4
All voters	47	30	3	20
With India:				
Leftwing	60	18	5	17
Nepali Congress	88	3	--	9
National Democratic	70	13	--	17
Sadvabana	100	--	--	--
All voters	75	11	3	11

The left voters prefer to have a balanced foreign policy relations with both China and India. Those voting for the National Democrats, parties generally considered rightist but professing a liberal political and economic philosophy, and which have party members largely from the previous partyless Panchayat system, have a tilt towards India for improved relations compared with China (70 as against 55%). The Nepali Congress voters overwhelmingly prefer to be closer to India than China.

119

The Sadvabana voters originating mainly from the Terai prefer India to China: With regard to India it is all of them and with China, it is 3 out of 10. It may be inferred that a good number of Sadvabana and Nepali Congress voters are not at all interested in improving relations with China.

From the preceding interpretation a question naturally crops up which has been in the minds of many Nepalese: Do the Terai people differ from the mountain people on this important foreign policy issue? A clear picture does emerge from the sample when the issue is cross tabulated with respondents' place of origin (Table 4).

Table 4.   *Proposal on Improvement of Relations with China and India, by Region*

	With China		With India	
	Terai	Mountain	Terai	Mountain
Good and important	46	46	83	71
Good but unimportant	41	25	9	12
Bad proposal	5	3	1	2
Don't know	8	26	7	15
Total	100	100	100	100

Comparatively, the Nepalese people originating from the Terai do not significantly differ from those originating from the mountain region on the question of improving relations with neighbouring countries. In both the set of questions, there is a greater preference of relations with the adjoining southern Indian state than with China. There are several explanations that look apparent in the shaping of foreign policy perception of the Nepalese people. The most plausible explanation is the proximity with India in terms of access, interaction, language, trade, culture, religion, and even ethnicity. To look for differences between the two groups of people would be of marginal importance. Both the Terai and mountain people consider relations with China to be good and important. However, there are one-fourth of the respondents originating from the mountain region who have not been able to comprehend the question and an equal proportion are of the opinion that improvement of relations with China is good and important which is a much higher figure in comparison to the respondents originating from the Terai. Thus the myth regarding mountain people preferring China to India can be dispelled. The Chi square values for both proposals prove that the respondents' place of origin have significant correlation with their preferences. In the case of preference for greater improvement of relations with India, the association between the two variables is even higher, nearly double in strength, than in the case of China.

The next question is to ask if education is an important variable in influencing the respondents' position on the above issue. Apparently there is some degree of influence on perception. Respondents with higher education prefer improvement of relations with both India and China whereas those with lower education prefer India much more. Also, there is an inverse relationship between the level of education and preferences: those with lower education generally tend to prefer China less than India and those with higher education want improvement of relations with India. See Table 5.

Table 5. *Proposal on Improvement of Relations with China and India, by Level of Education*

| | Good and Important | | Good but Unimportant | |
	China	India	China	India
No schooling	44	72	31	11
Primary	49	80	27	9
Low secondary	55	78	35	14
High secondary	59	82	29	12
Higher education	62	82	32	15
All respondents	46	75	30	10

Finally, on the question of relationship between age and preferences we can say that there is a significant relationship in one case and not in the other (Table 6).

Table 6. *Proposal on Improvement of Relations with China and India, by Age*

	Good and Important	Good but Unimportant	Bad Proposal	Don't Know
18-29 years				
China	57	30	5	8
India	78	14	4	4
30-44 years				
China	57	30	5	8
India	78	14	2	6
45 years or more				
China	48	31	4	17
India	81	8	2	9

Note The Kendall-Tau b value for the proposal on improvement of relations with China is 0.07. In the case of India the relationship is not significant.

Keeping Nepal-India Frontier Open

The issue of maintaining an open frontier between Nepal and India has its root in the 1950 Treaty of Peace and Friendship.

For over four decades the border has remained open to the nationals of both countries to travel without visas or passports for trade, employment, pilgrimage, education, etc. The frontier stretches about 720 km from the west to the south and to the eastern border of Nepal with India. There are more than 17 entry points at the border through which goods are transported. During times of strained relations between the two countries, the flow of Nepalese goods for import and export have been blocked by the Indian customs in violation of the Treaty and international law. It is not uncommon for India to flex its muscles over the small country by resorting to economic blockade and political intimidation. What is often found to worry the Nepalese government is the management of the border where smuggling of goods and cheating of customs are quite common and which has created an underground economy of smugglers mainly originating from India. In several pockets of the country, this underground economy runs nearly parallel to the country's main economy, influencing prices of goods in the Nepalese market to rise and fall. Also, every year there are innocent village women and children smuggled into India for sale which has damaged the social psyche of the Nepalese people. At any rate, the challenge of maintaining the open border exists as there is a lurking fear in the minds of Nepalese elite that Nepal will be overwhelmed in the near future by increasing population migration from India. Though the economic liability of continuing the open border cannot be overlooked, the political cost of maintaining the existing status quo of the border may prove troublesome in the existing multiparty environment as the data clearly reveal differing perception between the mass and elite and between leftwing parties and parties at the centre or right of the political spectrum.

On the Nepalese side of the border there is a large population of mixed linguistic groups who have close ties with the people living across the border in India. Social, economic and cultural relations in the form of marriage, religion, and market have bound both people together. To them any closure of the border can cause much hardship.

Let us now look into how the Nepalese voters see the issue. Do voters with different political affiliation perceive the subject differently? To what extent does the respondents' origin of place explain the issue? Do the younger voters have more favourable attitude to the existing status quo of the border than the older voters? Does respondents' level of education explain anything on the issue? To what extent do the elite differ from the mass?

Broadly, half of the sampled mass population want to continue the existing situation of keeping the frontier open. The elite on the other hand are not so enthusiastic to do the same. Only one third of them are interested in continuing the existing status quo on the border. Another one third of the mass respondents are split in two, indicating the proposal to be bad or non-issue (meaning "good but unimportant"). Whereas, the elite in significant percentages see the proposal to be quite unimportant and even bad. See percentage breakdown of responses in Table 7.

Table 7. *Proposal on Keeping the Nepal-India Border Open Seen by Mass and Elite Voters*

	Mass	Elite
Good and important	53	30
Good but unimportant	17	40
Bad proposal	16	27
Don't know	13	2
Total	100	100

Age as an explanatory variable on the proposal is not significant in knowing the perception of the voters. It may be mentioned that half the younger population and a little over half of the older population above 45 years of age want to maintain the existing status quo on the border. The figures are nearly close to the overall sample breakdown in Table 7. Those in the younger and middle age brackets are slightly more in favour of changes to the present situation than the older people.

Next, when level of education is cross tabulated with the proposal once again the relationship between the two variables is not significant. It may be mentioned that those with higher education are less favourable to maintaining an open border than those with lower levels of education. The figures are close to the sample breakdown in Table 7 except for those falling in the higher education bracket. Less than half of them (45%) consider the proposal to be important but about one-third of them categorically state the proposal to be "bad" -- this percentage figure is the highest in comparison to respondents falling in different categories such as no schooling, primary school, low secondary, and secondary.

Which variables then are significant in determining the respondents' perception on the issue? Table 8 and Table 9 show that the respondents' place of origin and party affiliation are significant variables.

123

Table 8.   Proposal on Keeping Nepal-India Border Open, by Origin Geographical Region

	Mountain	Terai
Good and important	47	68
Good but unimportant	22	9
Bad proposal	16	21
Don't know	15	1
Total	100	100

Table 9.   Proposal on Keeping Nepal-India Border Open by Affiliation to Parties

	Leftwing	Congress	NDP	Sadvabana
Good and important	48	61	42	81
Good but unimportant	17	17	22	19
Bad proposal	24	10	16	--
Don't know	11	12	20	--
Total	100	100	100	100

In Table 8 two thirds of the Terai people favour the border to remain open and about half of the mountain people say the same. Interestingly, one fifth of the Terai population call the proposal "bad", a figure slightly higher than among those from the mountains. The table confirms that respondents' place of origin is an important explanatory variable on the proposal. In Table 9 affiliation to parties does determine what position the respondents are likely to take on the proposal. Respondents affiliated to Sadvabana party, the party far right of the political spectrum and which is well known for its support on the issue, strongly want the border to remain open (8 out of 10 cases). This is followed by voters affiliated to Nepali Congress, the party at the centre of the political spectrum (6 out of 10 cases). About voters affiliated to the leftwing National Democratic parties the support to the proposal declines to about 1 in 2, and 2 in 5, cases respectively. These two parties comparatively have higher percentages of voters who do not support the proposal at all: 1 out of 4 cases among left voters and 1 out of 6 National Democratic voters. It may be noted that the correlation of respondents' preferences, when controlled by party affiliation and place of origin, is higher among left voters than among voters from other parties.

Introducing Work Permits for Non-Nepalese

The third national issue, introducing work permits for non-Nepalese is closely related to the issue of open border discussed in preceding paragraphs. The percentage breakdown for this variable is as follows (Table 10).

Table 10. Proposal on Introducing Work Permits for Non-Nepalese as Seen by Mass and Elite

	Mass	Elite
Good and important	61	54
Good and unimportant	15	28
Bad proposal	9	17
Don't know	15	1
Total	100	100

The majority of voters (6 out of 10 cases) prefer the introduction of work permits in Nepal. In about 1 in 4 cases the voters say the proposal is unimportant or bad. Regarding the elite, 1 in every 2 cases say the proposal to be good, which is slightly more than what the mass respondents hold. However, a more conservative position of the elite is seen when they state the proposal to be unimportant and bad. Just who are these voters in favour of and against the proposal? By age, the majority of young, middle aged, and old voters want the work permits to be introduced. However, the young voters are more strongly in support of the proposal (7 out of 10 cases). The correlation of age and preference demonstrates a moderate strength. What about the respondents' level of education? Superficially, there seems to be a linear rise in support for the proposal; i.e., the higher the level of education the greater is the support to it. But this kind of proposition should be cautiously interpreted, as there exists a very weak Tau-b between level of education and the proposal. Similarly, the respondents' place of origin categorized as mountain or Terai does not explain much, except that nearly an equal percentage of both mountain and Terai people support the proposal by nearly 6 out of 10 cases. The very fact that even the Terai people show significant support for the proposal clearly indicates important policy relevance of the issue. Finally we come to party affiliation (Table 11).

The general support to the proposal by a majority of the voters clearly indicates the popularity of the issue. Voters identifying with the Nepali Congress party show the highest percentage of supporters to the proposal and also within this group of party affiliation 1 in 5 cases consider the proposal to be good but unimportant,

Table 11. Proposal on Introducing Work Permits to Non-Nepalese by Party Affiliation

	Leftwing	Congress	NDP	Sadvabana
Good and important	61	64	54	48
Good but unimportant	10	21	10	20
Bad proposal	14	7	7	22
Don't know	15	8	29	10
Total	100	100	100	100

the highest percentage of such category of respondents compare to other types of voters. By implication we may infer that the public expect some kind of policy implementation from the ruling government headed by the Nepali Congress party-- to move in the direction of reforming the existing 'open policy' towards non-Nepalese immigrants. The Pearson correlation is fairly strong between place of origin (mountain and Terai) and party affiliation (Table 12).

Table 12. Proposal on Introducing Work Permits for Non-Nepalese by Place of Origin, Controlled for Party Choice

	Leftwing		Congress	
	Mountain	Terai	Mountain	Terai
Good and important	52	76	63	54
Good but unimportant	16	1	24	22
Bad proposal	12	18	6	14
Don't know	20	5	7	10
Total	100	100	100	100
N	179	81	227	51

	National Democrats		Sadvabana	
	Mountain	Terai	Mountain	Terai
Good and important	54	34	100	44
Good but unimportant	12	--	--	22
Bad proposal	6	22	--	24
Don't know	28	44	--	10
Total	100	100	100	100
N	128	14	2	29

126

Comparatively the voters associated with leftwing parties differ from voters of Nepali Congress when place of origin (mountain and Terai) is controlled by party affiliation. In the former case even the Terai left voters (3 out of 4 cases) prefer the proposal much more than the left voters originating from the mountains (2 out of 4 cases). In contrast, the Nepali Congress voters originating from the mountains (6 out of 10 cases) prefer the proposal slightly more than the Nepali Congress voters originating from the Terai (5 out of 10 cases). This difference in perception raises a fundamental proposition: the association between the party and the voters is higher among leftwing parties than is the case with Nepali Congress voters.

Maintaining Gorkha Recruitment Abroad

Since the signing of Sugauli Treaty between Nepal and British India in 1818, the process of joining the British army in India voluntarily began. Officially the tradition of Gorkha recruitment in India goes back to more than hundred years in 1885 when the Rana Prime minister Bir Shamsher permitted the British to enter few points in eastern Nepal to recruit the mountain people for the British-India army. This policy of the Rana prime minister, the purpose of which was to seek favour from the British in order to stay in power, has continued to the present despite the overthrow of the Rana system in 1950 and subsequent change of governments over the past four decades and the withdrawal of the British from India. Just like other issues discussed above the issue of continuing this policy has featured much debate among the intellectuals and politicians as it is thought to damage the self esteem of the Nepalese people and threaten national interests. In the villages from where the Gorkhas have been supplied abroad, the general public reaction is different, not so much against the policy as the young recruits bring home lucrative earnings which are considered important for improving the conditions of the rural families. The other side of the story is pathetic. There are difficulties faced by families who live separated from their sons and who sometimes lose them when they are killed in some unknown wars. Some records in the past have shown of villages with hardly any young men but only widows.

The Gorkha soldiers have fought in big and small wars in different parts of the world. They are well known for valour. During first and second World Wars they fought in the European theatres along with the British. In recent times they fought in the Falkland wars on the side of the British too. Their number in the British army today has been reduced to less than 10,000 and in India there are an estimated 125,000 Gorkhas serving the Indian army. The recruitment of Gorkhas in both the Indian and British armies are based on treaty relations and the continuation of this tradition is sometimes treated as "historical legacy".

In the sample a question was asked to examine the attitude of general voters towards maintaining Gorkha recruitment abroad. The percentage breakdown of responses is shown in Table 13.

Table 13. *Proposal on Maintaining Gorkha Recruitment Abroad As Seen by Mass and Elite*

	Mass	Elite
Good and important	25	12
Good but unimportant	26	26
Bad proposal	31	61
Don't know	18	1
Total	100	100

The table shows a divided opinion between positions, stating the proposal to be important and unimportant among the mass respondents. Another thirty percent totally reject the proposal. The remaining percentage of respondents have no opinion on the question. Regarding the elite, a large majority of them see the proposal to be bad (6 out of 10). Also the support for the proposal is far less than what is shown by the mass respondents (nearly 1 out of 8).

Let us now look into the age variable (Table 14). How do the young, middle aged, and old voters see the issue? Do the respondents from lower educational level differ in perception from those with higher education? The data reveal an interesting pattern of responses from the young to the old. Every one out of five cases among young to middle aged voters support for the proposal slightly less than the overall percentage figure of 26. The older voters above 45 years give slightly more support to the proposal though the difference from the younger voters is only a few percentages. However, half the younger voters in 18-29 years age bracket consider the proposal "bad", the percentage figure expressing the similar opinion declining in the older age brackets. It may be said here that the correlation between age and preference is fairly weak which is also true for the variable of education. But on the educational variable (Table 15) there is an interesting feature when seen in comparison with the preceding analysis; i.e., those with lower level education do not consider the proposal attractive enough, and the four responses of this group are fairly evenly divided. But the majority of respondents with higher education consider the proposal bad, a figure which declines as level of education decreases. Once again we notice the elitist opinion here which differs from the other categories of voters.

Table 14. Proposal on Maintaining Gorkha Recruitment Abroad by Age (Percentages)

	18-29 Years	30-49 Years	45 Years or More
Good and important	24	22	27
Good but unimportant	19	28	25
Bad proposal	50	42	34
Don't know	7	8	14
Total	100	100	100

Table 15. Proposal on Maintaining Gorkha Recruitment Abroad by Level of Education

	No School	Primary Second.	Low Second.	High Educ.	Higher
Good and important	25	30	21	23	8
Good but unimportant	26	23	28	24	21
Bad proposal	29	28	45	47	59
Don't know	20	19	6	6	2
Total	100	100	100	100	100

Probing into two other independent variables similar features as seen earlier can be clearly noted. The association between attitude and party affiliation is fairly strong (Table 16).

Table 16. Proposal on Maintaining Gorkha Recruitment Abroad by Parties

	Leftwing	Congress	NDP	Sadvabana
Good and important	17	36	18	23
Good but unimportant	32	20	29	48
Bad proposal	37	27	31	3
Don't know	14	17	22	26
Total	100	100	100	100

Clearly the left voters are against maintaining Gorkha recruitment abroad compared to Nepali Congress voters. In 1 in 3 cases the left voters, closely followed by National

Democratic voters, consider the proposal "bad" whereas in similar ratio the Nepali Congress voters consider the proposal "good and important". Interestingly enough the Sadvabana voters tend to choose the middle position of considering the proposal good but unimportant. Reinforcing the traditional notion of left party beliefs, respondents' place of origin controlled by parties also explains the earlier hypothesis (Table 17). The place of origin as a single first variable does not establish a close association with attitude. A weak Pearson r is found. But when place of origin is controlled by party affiliation, there is a fairly strong association especially for the voters affiliated to left parties. In these parties the Mountain voters take a more positive stand than Terai voters, while the opposite is true of Nepali Congress voters. Among the National Democratic voters it is again those coming from the Mountain region who favour the proposal. Finally, the ten Sadvabana voters from Mountain aras have no opinion.

Table 17. Proposal on Maintaining Gorkha Recruitment Abroad by Place of Origin Controlled by Parties

| | Leftwing | | Nepali Congress | |
	Mountain	Terai	Mountain	Terai
Good and important	15	19	31	41
Good but unimportant	49	3	16	43
Bad proposal	21	67	31	14
Don't know	15	11	22	2
Total	100	100	100	100

| | National Dem. | | Sadvabana | |
	Mountain	Terai	Mountain	Terai
Good and important	21	--	--	24
Good but unimportant	28	35	--	52
Bad proposal	28	47	10	3
Don't know	23	18	90	21
Total	100	100	100	100

Now we come to the last part of the analysis. The national issues discussed above are likewise seen by party members and parliamentarians. In the sample of 805 cases representing all eight parliamentary parties the perception of party members originating from the central committees to the local committees seemingly reflect the opinion expressed by the elites more than the mass, except on the first issue related to improvement of relations with China and India. On this issue, there is an overwhelming support of party members, no matter what parties they represent, for a balanced approach in relations with the two neighbours (Table 18). The two last columns show that the parliamentarians would like to see the 1950 treaty and 1965 agreement with India abrogated, implying alteration in Nepal's existing foreign policy so that the relations with both China and India are set on a more balanced footing.

Table 18. *Proposal on Improvement of Relations with China and India for Party Members, and Proposals on Abrogation of 1950 Treaty and 1965 Agreement for Parliamentarians*

| | Party Members | | Parliamentarians | |
	China	India	1950	1965
Good and important	91	92	66	73
Good but unimportant	7	6	13	11
Bad proposal	1	1	13	6
Don't know	1	1	8	10
Total	100	100	100	100
N	804	804	240	243

On keeping the border with India open, the parties and parliamentarians have similar perceptions, and their perceptions differ from those of the voters by having a large proportion opposing the proposal (Table 19). Nearly half of all the party members and parliamentarians consider keeping the border open as a bad proposal whereas only 1 in 6 cases at the mass level consider it so.

Table 19. *Proposal on Keeping Nepal-India Border Open by Parties and Parliamentarians and Voters*

	Party Members	Parliamentarians	Voters
Good and important	37	41	53
Good but unimportant	14	11	17
Bad proposal	47	46	17
Don't know	2	1	13
Total	100	100	100
N	805	243	897

Interestingly, the perceptions of the party members on the issue vary extensively when further divided between the leftwing parties and the Nepali Congress. The left parties overwhelmingly want nearly total change in the existing status quo of the border by regulating it unlike the Nepali Congress who do not significantly oppose the present situation. About the parliamentarians, more radical changes are sought by left parliamentarians than their counterparts who are stationed at different levels of party hierarchy.

A similar picture is found regarding the issue on introducing work permits for non-Nepalese.

Table 20. *Proposal on Introducing Work Permit for Non-Nepalese as Seen by Parties and Parliamentarians*

	Party Members	Parliamentarians	Voters
Good and important	61	63	61
Good and unimportant	18	12	15
Bad proposal	20	21	9
Don't know	1	4	15
Total	100	100	100
N	805	246	911

On introducing work permits for non-Nepalese, there is the same overall division of perception between the parties and parliamentarians. However, the left parliamentarians once again are found to be more radical than the party members in comparison to the parliamentarians from the Nepali Congress. As evident in Table 20 every 1 out of 5 party members and parliamentarians consider introducing work permits as a bad proposal, a ratio slightly higher than what is found at the mass level.

Table 21. *Proposal on Maintaining Gorkha Recruitment Abroad As seen Party Members, Parliamentarians, and Voters*

	Party Members	Parliamentarians	Voters
Good and important	29	30	25
Good but unimportant	18	18	26
Bad proposal	50	48	31
Don't know	2	4	18
Total	100	100	100
N	805	899	247

Last but not least, the proposal on maintaining Gorkha recruitment abroad is supported as a good and important proposal only by 1 out of 3 respondents in both the sample on party members and parliamentarians. In these two samples, however, every 1 out of 2 respondents want the recruitment abroad to discontinue. The leftwing party members and parliamentarians are overwhelmingly against the proposal. Here again we see the cleavage between these two categories of respondents and the general mass. See Table 21.

Conclusions

Synopsis of Mass/Elite Differences

The preceding tables have revealed some important similarities and differences between ordinary voters, local elites, party members, and parliamentarians with regard to foreign policy orientations. An overview of these similarities and differences can be gained from Diagram 1. The X axis of the diagram indicates the issue orientations of the mass respondents as percent who consider a proposal good and important minus percent considering the same proposal bad (disregarding those considering it good but unimportant or having no opinion). Thus the X axis indicates what may be termed the net balance of opinion among the voters, ranging in theory from −100 if everybody considers the proposal bad, to +100 if everybody considers it good and important.

On the Y axis are plotted corresponding net balances for local elites, party members, and parliamentarians, each with different legends. Thus if one of these elite groups is plotted above the diagonal, this indicates that this group is more positive than the mass respondents on that particular issue; if plotted below the diagonal, the group is less positive than the mass respondents. In this sense we can speak of the diagram as suggesting a representation function, the diagonal representing complete agreement between mass and elite.

The overall impression one gets from looking at the diagram is that of a positive relationship, that is, the same issue positions that are favoured by the mass are also favoured by the elite. Good relations with India is a highly valued position, Gorkha recruitment a rather unpopular one. It is true that in this pattern good relations with China deviates by being more popular among the elite groups than in the general population. As one may say, this is an elite-driven issue, whereas by contrast the desire for an open border toward India tends to be mass-driven. The general picture, however, is one of a fairly well implemented representation function.

Next, one may wonder how the relative correspondence between elite and mass comes about. On the face of it one might have expected that the party members served as an intermediate political stratum between the candidates and the voters.

Unfortunately, we do not have information about the parliamentarians' positions on Nepal's relations with India and China, which in the interview were replaced by their positions on two treaties (cf. Table 18). On the other three issues, however, the party members seem to be much closer to the parliamentarians than to the voters, at least when we look at their average position across parties. A more detailed analysis of the representation process goes beyond the limits of the present study.

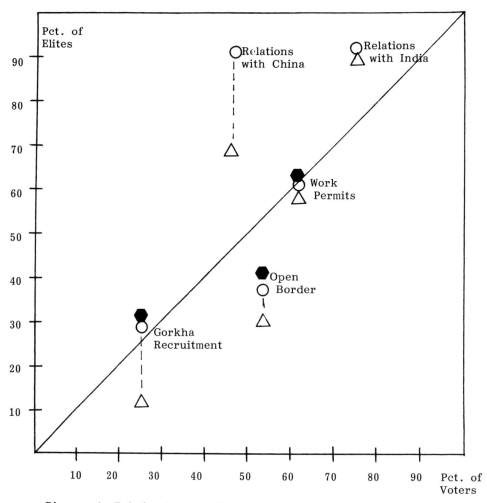

Diagram 1. Relation between Issue Positions of Mass Respondents (X) and Three Types of Elite Respondents (Y) on Foreign Policy Issues. Percent Who Consider Different Proposals "Good and Important".

O = Party members, ⬡ = Parliamentarians, △ = Local elites

134

CHAPTER 8

PERFORMANCE OF GOVERNMENT

The transformation of partyless politics to a multiparty system was the most striking phenomenon of 1990 which fundamentally changed the Nepalese political system in three important ways. First, the power of the king was reduced to symbolism. By limiting the monarchy to a figurehead and transferring the real power of the king to the people or at least the political parties, the elected parliament was empowered to decide the actual affairs of the state. Second, political parties were legally recognized to assume a political role in mobilizing the electorate towards party programs and policies and the elections would be competitively contested on the basis of adult franchise. Third, the democratic rights of the people were guaranteed by the constitution. These were important features which characterize the recent political transformation.

The new democratic order which has emerged as a result of these major shifts calls for a change in the political behaviour of the citizenry. In the new set up, the electorate, the political parties and the government have important roles to play. The electorate by remaining vigilant over their rights decides which party or parties will best serve their interests. By voting in the election, they choose the party they desire to form the government. The parties, on the other hand, perform the role of articulating agents in arousing public sentiments either in support of or against one party or the other, or the ruling government. Within a given set of rules defined by the constitution, the party in power acts in meeting public demands in a democratic society. In failing to do so, the ruling party loses the confidence of the people and sometimes the mandate to rule altogether. The result is that an early election may be called.

We shall here discuss the attitudes of the electorate toward the performance of the government during the interim period. Several independent variables will be analyzed to study the attitude of the electorate. Following are the questions raised in this chapter: How do the voters measure government performance? Is there any impact of the decisions taken by the national government in Kathmandu at the local level, in towns and villages? Is there any difference in attitudes of the electorate toward the previous partyless Panchayat government and the present government? How do the social positions of voters influence their evaluation of the government? Finally, do mass media spread dissatisfaction?

Measuring Government Performance

In a study of this kind it is important to remember that the measurement of government performance in totality is not possible; i.e., the integrated measurement of the impact on the various sectors of national life -- economic, political, social, and developmental. What is possible here is to record those responses given by the voters on the attitudinal questions which deal with some aspects of performance and the attitude voters have about the government in general. Broadly, the perception of the electorate is analyzed here by asking the following questions which deal with voters' attitudes toward the government officials, Panchayat government, and interim government: Whether government officials at the lower level were doing well in the respondents' villages and towns (Question 31)? Whether higher government officials were doing their job well (Question 32)? Whether the government was better now than in the past during Panchayat period (Question 33)? Whether the respondents' families were better off or worse now than in the past (Question 34)? To study the effects of government on the respondents a few questions were asked to study whether there was any effect of national government on respondents' daily lives and whether the respondents felt better "without government" (Questions 35-36).

Comparison Between Panchayat Government and Interim Government

On the positive side, the voters clearly support the political change -- the transformation of Panchayat system to a multi-party system. The approval rating is seventy percent. Closely linked to the success of the multi-party system is the overwhelming conviction of voters (76-85%) that parties and elections are "necessary". Given this positive attitude, how do the voters compare the performance of the interim government and the Panchayat government under two types of political system? The responses given by the voters are not encouraging. Two questions were asked: "Do you think the government we have during the past year is better or worse than the Panchayat government we had before then? Are you and your family better off or worse off now than last year when there was a Panchayat Government?" Around one-third of the respondents in the first question consider the interim government better. In the second question, a negligible percentage of respondents (6%) think that their family conditions have improved (Table 1).

To almost 3 out of 4 respondents the family conditions of the general public seem to remain the same without any improvement. The comparison between the two sets of attitude show some degree of dissatisfaction. It can be fairly assumed that the dissatisfaction is characterized more by expectancy than negativism. Given the short time frame of the interim government, it would be premature to make

Table 1. Evaluation of Interim Government and of Family Conditions Compared with Panchayat Government

	Better	Worse	Same	Don't Know	Total
Interim Government better or worse than Panchayat Government	34	12	45	9	100
Present Family Conditions better or worse than during Panchayat government	6	13	72	9	100

an objective assessment of government performance on the basis of these data alone. For instance, there is a large percentage of respondents who consider their family conditions to be the same as during the Panchayat government. This type of response may be treated in either positive or negative way. Positively, it may be claimed that the situation has not deteriorated further in view of the larger challenges the interim government faced, namely to bring political stability by formulating a new constitution and holding an early election. Negatively, if related to the working character of the interim government, it may be interpreted such that the interim government did not show the kind of image the public expected, especially after what was achieved through a long struggle of the people. The rating of the interim government to be the same as the previous Panchayat government suggests a low rating of government efficiency.

When we further probe into the types of respondents who evaluate the interim government relative to the Panchayat government, and classify them according to their family conditions, it is clear that the respondents are found to be dissatisfied (Table 2).

Table 2. Attitude Towards Performance of Interim Government by Attitude Towards Economic Conditions of Respondents' Families

Economy Compared to Ten Years Ago	Performance of Interim Government			
	Better	Same	Worse	Total
Better	17	70	14	100
Same	1	91	8	100
Worse	1	57	42	100

According to Table 2, those who state that their family conditions have become worse believe that the interim government is similar to the Panchayat government or worse than it. Those whose family conditions have remained the same have an overwhelming opinion that the interim government is not much different from the previous government. Lastly, those whose family conditions have improved are the only ones who rate the interim government to be better.

Interrelation of National and Local Performance

The low performance of the government can be further testified by the relation between two questions: [A] "What do you think of the government officials in this village or town - are they doing their job well, or not? [B] And, what about government officials at higher levels - are they doing their job well, or not?" The association between the two responses in these questions is quite significant: The Kendall Tau-b is 0.56 (Table 3).

Table 3.   Attitude Towards Performance of Government Officials in the Villages and Towns and Attitude Towards Performance of Higher Government Officials

| | Performance of Higher Government Officials | | |
	Doing Well	Not Doing Well	Total
Performance of Local Gov. Officials:			
Doing well	51	49	100
Not doing well	3	97	100

By cross tabulating the two sets of attitude we gain a more precise information which further proves that the interim government did not perform well. Thus two proposition may be stated. First, in the judgement of the voters, the table shows there are three categories (1) those thinking the government is doing well at both levels, (2) those thinking it is doing well only at the low level, and (3) those thinking it is not doing well at any level. Secondly, the performance of both the interim government and the Panchayat government was considered fairly poor.

Economic Factors in Dissatisfaction

An important index of government performance is provided by respondents' economic conditions. Such an index is tangible and visible. In the voters' survey more than fifty percent of the respondents originating from the lowest income bracket or the richest income bracket consider the political transformation to be "better" for the country. Those with small houses do not see much difference between the partyless Panchayat system and multi-party system (Table 4). Regarding the impact of government policies on R's economic conditions, there is no significant change recorded on the living conditions of three-quarters of the population, an average for the whole population. Strangely, only those without a house have noted an improvement in their living conditions (Tables 4 & 5).

Table 4. *Attitude Towards Interim Government in Comparison to Panchayat Government by Respondents' Estimated Value of the House (Q. 33)*

	The Government is Better or Worse Than the Past Panchayat Government				
	Better	Worse	About Same	Don't Know	Total
Estimated Value of House					
No House	52	11	28	9	100
Less Than Rs 25,00	24	15	55	6	100
Rs 25,000- 49,000	29	10	51	10	100
Rs 50,000-149,000	35	9	47	9	100
Rs 150,000-349,000	45	15	18	22	100
Rs 350,000 or more	56	10	25	9	100

Table 5. *Evaluation of R's Economic Conditions by R's Estimated Value of the House (Q.34)*

	R's Economic Conditions				
	Better	Worse	About Same	Don't Know	Total
Estimated Value of House					
No House	15	9	64	12	100
Less Than Rs 25,000	1	17	76	6	100
Rs 25,000- 49,000	5	12	65	18	100
Rs 50,000-149,000	10	10	75	5	100
Rs 150,000- 349,000	3	7	87	3	100
Rs 350,000 or more	8	20	66	6	100

For the successful functioning of democracy, the middle class plays an important role of balancer between the rich and the poor income groups. The voter's study reveals a critical situation in which the transition to a stable democratic society can be quite difficult as the lower middle class have not experienced any direct economic benefit from the political transformation. Also, the middle class elite who hold important positions in governmental bureaucracy cannot remain committed to democracy nor can they be responsive to the electorate if public expectations are found soaring and the government performance is low.

Social Position and Satisfaction of National Government

Looking into a few variables which describe the social position of the respondents and their attitude towards the performance of government, we notice important variations. By place of origin, the respondents from rural areas show a slightly less dissatisfaction with the government than those from urban areas by saying either the interim government is better than the Panchayat government or "same" as the Panchayat government. About the actual performance of government, a low percentage of both the urban and rural respondents (1 out of 7) equally think that the higher government officials are doing well or the government is worse than the Panchayat system. However, when place of origin is dichotomized into mountain and Terai, it is clear that a higher percentage of mountain respondents (7 out of 10) state that the higher government officials are not doing well than the Terai respondents. Also, when urban-rural variable is controlled by place of origin (mountain and Terai), it is clear that the urban respondents are much more dissatisfied, especially the respondents from the urban Terai (Table 6).

Table 6. Attitude Towards Performance of Higher Government Officials by Urban or Rural Residence by Mountain and Terai Districts

	Mountain		Terai	
	Urban	Rural	Urban	Rural
Higher Government Officials Are:				
Doing Well	11	11	9	14
Not Well	73	70	78	53
Don't Know	16	19	13	33
Total	100	100	100	100

By age, the younger people; i.e., those below the middle age group, are slightly more euphoric than the older people regarding the recent political transformation. They rate the interim government to be better than the Panchayat government though they are convinced that the government has not done well when it comes to performance. Comparatively, it is in the middle aged bracket we find the lowest percentage of voters who give poor rating of the government. Also, there are more number of people in this age group who consider the new government to be worse than the Panchayat government. They are the most negative age group. It may be mentioned here that age as an explanatory variable is not significant.

By schooling too, there is very little that can be said. Comparatively, those without schooling are more negative about the government when it comes to performance than those who have some kind of schooling. Also, those who are more educated tend to support the political transformation slightly more by confirming that the new government is better than the Panchayat government. A proposition may be mentioned here that the higher the educational level of voters the greater is the support for the transformation.

140

By sex, the female population give a slightly higher degree of support to the government than the male population (Table 7).

Table 7. *Performance of Government and Comparison Between Panchayat Government and Interim Government, by Sex of Respondent*

	Doing Well	Better than Panchayat	Same as Panchayat	Worse than Panchayt	Total
Male	10	29	47	13	100
Female	18	32	41	9	100

In Table 7 and 8 we have combined the responses to two questions so as to form four groups of respondents. It can be seen that the women are more numerous compared with the men in the two relatively positive groups holding that at least the Interim government was better than the Panchayat government.

Satisfaction and Party Choice

In cross tabulating these attitudes by party choice of voters, there are expected differences in opinion (Table 8).

Table 8. *Attitude Toward Performance of Government, by Choice of Party*

	Govt Doing Well	Better than Panchayat	Same as Panchayat	Worse than Panchayat	Total
United People's F	8	49	23	20	100
CPN-UML	10	25	55	10	100
Congress	17	37	35	11	100
National Dem.	24	4	61	11	100
Sadvabana	11	22	42	25	100
Other	2	19	70	9	100

In Table 8 the National Democratic parties have the largest percentage of voters who believe that the performance of the interim government was the same as that of the Panchayat government (61%), and also the lowest percentage of voters who believe that the new government is better than the Panchayat government (4%). On the other hand, a high number of NDP voters (24%) thought the government was doing well conforming that the Interim government was doing well. A small percentage of the leftwing voters, trailing behind Nepali Congress voters, believe that the government was doing well and it was better than the Panchayat government. However, over half of the voters supporting CPN-UML believe that the interim government was the same as the Panchayat government. This figure is fairly high compared to United People's Front voters among whom almost half (49%) believe that the Interim government was better than the Panchayat government. In general the supporters of the Nepali Congress party are evenly divided between those who believe that the Interim government was better than the Panchayat government and that it was the same as the Panchayat government. Among Sadvabana voters, every 1 out of 4 voters believe that the interim government was worse than the Panchayat government.

Role of Mass Media in Public Evaluation of Government

In advanced industrial democracies the role of mass media during the time of election is crucial in determining which party is likely to influence the voters. In the less developed societies of the Third World, such may not be the case as there is a large number of illiterate people who cannot read or write, or the newspapers, radios and televisions are inaccessible to many. The question of spreading public dissatisfaction over government policies by the instruments of mass media do not arise as radio and television stations are generally controlled by the ruling government. In Nepal, the mass media is influenced by the public agencies which are regulated by government rules, funds and personnel.

In our interviews with the Nepalese voters we asked two questions whether they followed newspapers and listened to radios. These questions after cross tabulating with attitude towards government performance suggest the extent of influence mass media has over the attitude of voters towards the interim government. (Table 9).

Table 9. Frequency of Radio Listening and Newspaper Reading of Respondents by Attitude towards the Interim Government

	Follow Radio				Read Newspaper			
	Many	Few	None	Total	Many	Few	None	Total
Better	15	56	29	100	7	35	58	100
Worse	11	43	46	100	2	20	78	100
Same As Before	9	54	37	100	3	24	73	100
Don't Know	1	39	60	100	--	34	66	100

Table 9 clearly reveals that radios are more influential than newspapers in influencing the attitude of voters. Also, respondents who are radio listeners and newspaper readers are less critical of the interim government. Those who say that the interim government is "worse" than the Panchayat government or that the interim government is the "same as before" tend not to be listeners of radios or readers of newspapers.

142

Next, when we probe further on how the radio listeners and newspaper readers evaluate the performance of government officials at the higher and local level, we notice that, on the whole, a very critical evaluation is done regarding how well the government officials performed at higher level or in towns and villages. Among those saying local officials were doing well, only 8% had followed many radio broadcasts; among those saying local officials were doing badly, the corresponding figure was 12%. The difference is even more striking when it comes to evaluation of higher officials. Those saying higher officials were doing well had listened very little to radio broadcasts. But when it comes to newspapers, reading "a few times" seemed to favour a positive evaluation of higher officials (Table 10).

Table 10. Frequency of Radio Listening and newspaper reading of Respondents by Attitudes Toward Performance of Government Officials in Towns and Villages and Performance of Government Officials at Higher Level

	Follow Radio				Read Newspaper			
	Many	Few	None	Total	Many	Few	None	Total
[A] Performance of Government Officials at Local Level								
Doing Well	8	61	31	100	4	20	76	100
Not Well	12	54	34	100	5	31	64	100
Don't Know	7	33	60	100	1	21	78	100
[B] Performance of Government Officials at Higher Levels								
Doing Well	1	30	69	100	1	61	38	100
Not Well	14	55	31	100	6	31	63	100
Don't Know	8	39	52	100	2	19	79	100

Also, there is a contrasting impression of those who do not listen to radios and those who do not read newspapers. A low percentage of the former group and high percentage of the latter group is recorded, stating that the government officials are doing well in towns and villages. But, this is not true of the same group. A higher percentage of those who never listen to radio state that the government officials at higher level are doing well. Those registering a favourable attitude towards higher government officials of doing well is a small percentage.

Effect of Performance on Support for Democracy

Despite the low performance of the interim government and the minimal impact it had on the livelihood of the general voters, there is a strong public faith in democracy. The general voters believe that the political parties are necessary and the adoption of the multi-party system was good for the country (Table 11 & 12).

Table 11. Attitude Towards the Performance of Interim Government by Attitude Towards Multi-Party System

| | Type of Party System Desired | | | | |
	Only One Party	More Than One Party	Don't Know	Total	N
Interim Government Better or Worse Than Panchayat					
Better	26	69	5	100	309
Worse	15	80	5	100	94
Same	14	74	12	100	388
Don't Know	20	50	30	100	73

Table 12. Attitude Towards R's Economic Conditions by Attitude Towards Multi-Party System

| | Type of Party System Desired | | | | |
	Only One Party	More Than One Party	Don't Know	Total	N
R's Economic Conditions					
Better	25	70	5	100	55
Worse	15	78	7	100	114
Same As Before	19	72	9	100	614
Don't Know	23	50	27	100	79

In comparing the interim government with that of the Panchayat in Table 11, three out of four respondents clearly believe in the multi-party system even when the performance of the former is "worse" or the "same" as the Panchayat. The support for the multi-party system does not decrease despite the fact that the respondents' economic conditions has deteriorated. In Table 12 we can clearly observe that a large majority (3 out of 4 respondents) do not see any improvement in their economic conditions yet they support a multi-party system.

Conclusions

The interim government was not an elected government although it represented movements pledged to democracy. Its performance, therefore, cannot be judged as one judges democratic governments, as responsible to the voters. In the judgement of the Nepalese voters the interim government was on balance a step forward, but from the very poor performance of the Panchayat government; but it must not be overlooked that around half the Nepalese voters saw no difference (Table 1).

The evaluation of local government officials is less negative than the evaluation of higher officials; and a positive evaluation of local officials seems to be a precondition for giving positive evaluations of higher officials (Table 3).

Those who follow radio broadcasts and read newspapers are more satisfied with the interim government than those not following these media (Table 9). But they are also more critical of officials as a general rule (Table 10), and it is unfortunately the adherents of a one-party state who regard the interim government as a step forward (Table 12); the explanation may be that the interim government gave the communists a chance of influence which they feared to lose once more after the parliamentary election. Hence it seems important that the new government does not bereave the leftwing opposition of all influence.

CHAPTER 9

NEPALESE POLITICAL CULTURE

The term political culture refers to the typical beliefs held by people in a society about their basic political institutions. These institutions comprise, for example, the government, parliament, elections, parties, courts of justice, and citizens' rights and duties in regard to political participation. In order to explain the political behaviour that characterizes a society and sets it apart from other societies - including the outcome of that behaviour such as power distributions and political stability - researchers often look for some key political values and skills that are assumed to be installed in people from their childhood or youth as part of a more general process of socialisation. The political culture of a society thereby changes only slowly, and democratic norms tends to develop in the course of several generations. Thus Almond and Verba (1963), who coined the term political culture, found that Germans, Italians, and Mexicans were each in their own way marked by the experiences of an authoritarian regime whereas Englishmen and Americans, having grown up in old democracies, had adopted a more participatory and confident approach to politics.

In the case of Nepal we may expect to find a rather confused and deficient political culture in regard to democratic participation, since the Nepalese voters were denied the opportunity to appreciate how a democracy will function. The experience with democracy in 1959-60 was brief and on the whole negative; the ensuing Panchayat system was given legitimate shape by a majority of the voters in the referendum of 1958; and according to tradition Nepal is a Hindu Kingdom with the King as a reincarnation of the god Vishnu. Our study includes several questions about the old and new political institutions. It should therefore provide a good occasion for testing the assumptions of political-culture theory. In this chapter we analyze the following survey questions:

*   Preference for monarchy or republic (Q.28-29 in the voter survey)
*   Religious legitimation of the monarchy (Q.30)
*   Support for Elections and Parties (Q.23-26)
*   Perceptions of the effect of government on society (Q.35-36)
*   Trust in politicians (Q.37)
*   Feelings of citizen competence (Q.38)
*   Tolerance of unconventional political behaviour (Q.39)

All of these questions, in one way or the other, may be employed to construct "indicators" of the extent of democratic thinking and feeling in the Nepalese public, and in subgroups thereof. We need to study not one but several such indicators

146

because democracy is much too complex to be measured by using a single question as a yardstick; and our indicators need to be studied not only one by one but also in their interrelation as a coherent set in order to pay full attention to that complexity. But even this will not be sufficient for an assessment of Nepalese democracy. In addition to studying the indicators and their internal relationship for the Nepalese public as an aggregated whole, we need to study them for critical subgroups such as age, sex, caste, and educational groups on one hand, and partisan groups on the other hand. This is necessary because democratic thinking and feeling may differ very much from one group to the next, and this difference can be presumed to be consequential for the future working of Nepalese democracy. If, for example, major parts of the population should turn out to be quite alienated from the new democratic institutions - or, even worse, if there should be a compact resistance against the forces of democracy in some quarters - this would be a sign of danger. If, on the other hand, our study will show a scattered allegiance to democracy in all major subgroups, we should be more confident that given some time for the new system to demonstrate its virtues, Nepalese democracy will survive in the long run.

The Constitutional Issue

As our first indicator of democratic attitudes we shall study to what extent allegiance to the monarchy may raise obstacles to the acceptance of the new political system by the Nepalese public. The April 1990 revolution was an uprising against the absolute monarchy, and during the entire period of the interim government the position of the King stood in the centre. On a number of constitutional issues, such as the King's emergency powers, his authority over the army, or his veto power in the legislative process, the parties had the opportunity of making their positions known. They aligned themselves with the communist parties on one side as adherents of a republic, the Nepali Congress party in the middle as adherents of a symbolic or constitutional position, and the National Democrats as reluctant to rob the monarchy of its power.

Table 1 demonstrates that the constitutional issue was not lost on the voters. It may be noted from the outset that the three first of these positions can be reconciled with democracy. Certainly it cannot be assumed that a republic is more democratic than a constitutional monarchy; indeed, most of the old European democracies are constitutional monarchies. Only the fourth position, which is to give (back) more power to the King, represents a step away from the democratic development.

Of the percentage figures, the first column indicates the proportion in different parties wanting Nepal to become a republic. Among the Communists there is a

Table 1.   Position on the Constitutional Issue, by Party Vote (Percentages)

	Republic	King Symbol	Same as Now	King More Power	Total
United Peoples F	47	9	44	0	100
Communist UML+U	52	6	36	6	100
Congress	10	6	53	31	100
National Dem.	15	10	31	44	100
Sadvabana	21	9	40	30	100
All	27	7	43	23	100

slight majority for this position, but in the other parties and especially in the Nepali Congress party there is only a small minority for a Nepalese republic.

In the other three columns the respondents are arranged in positions of increasing royal power. Only between 6 and 10 percent want to keep the king as merely a figurehead with symbolic functions. The status quo, represented in the third column, attracts a majority of the Nepali Congress voters, but it is interesting that it is a very popular solution also among many of the Communist voters. The issue is therefore hardly one that might release intense conflict in the course of the next years.

Finally, the fourth position of strengthening the royal power is chosen by almost one third of the Nepali Congress voters and close to one half of the National Democratic voters. This is natural in light of the traditional norms. However, the fact that almost none in the Communist parties prefer this position indicates that it might indeed create a conflict if the Nepali Congress government attempts to strengthen the monarchy.

One can interpret this relationship in different ways. To claim that the constitutional issue had a pretty strong effect on the vote would be one interpretation, but it overlooks two possibilities. The first is that the issue does not stand isolated but is part of the value dimension to which we referred in Chapter 2, namely the dimension of modernism/traditionalism; consequently we should control for this dimension before we judge the more direct effect of the constitutional issue. The second possibility is that the causal chain may well go in the reverse direction: from partisanship to stand on the constitutional issue. In favour of this interpretation is that it seems highly unlikely that so many Nepalese would be republicans if the Communist parties had not been in the forefront in the opposition against the monarchy and systematically advocated the abolition of it.

Our data permit only an analysis of the first possibility, and that analysis suggests that the constitutional issue has a slightly stronger correlation than the modernism/traditionalism dimension with the three-way vote (Communist-Congress-National Democratic). Therefore it certainly exerts an independent effect on the vote. And when the respondent's stand on the constitutional issue and his stand on the modernism/traditionalism dimension are combined into an additive index, the tau b correlation between this index and the vote rises to 0.50. It is especially telling that among those respondents, numbering one quarter of the sample, who identify with new ideas and at the same time are republicans, the communist parties obtain 87 percent of the vote. Were we to predict whether a respondent would vote communist or not solely by having information on his position on these two variables, we would predict 77 percent of the respondents correctly.

Religious Legitimation of the King

The constitutional issue touches on two critical and related questions. First, are the republicans on the left and the royalists on the right just as good democratic citizens as the constitutionalists in the two middle categories? Before we discuss this question, however, we will deal with another which has to do with the role of religion, especially Hindu religion, in Nepalese politics. To what extent is the constitutional issue associated with religious feelings about the legitimate role of the king? Indeed, to what extent are the left wing parties, and the values and "new ideas" with which the left wing is associated, related with secularization? This question will be taken up at this place.

We shall study whether the respondent's position on the constitutional issue, and through that his partisan choice and allegiance to "new ideas" is associated with religious beliefs about the divinity of the King. According to tradition, the Nepalese king is a descendant of the god Vishnu. The liberal atmosphere of the election permitted us to ask a question whether the respondent believed this to be true (Question 30), a question which would almost surely have caused severe trouble for the investigation a year earlier. Table 2 breaks down the responses according to respondent's vote.

Table 2. Belief in Divine Descendance of the King, by Party Vote (Percentages)

| | King Reincarnation of Vishnu? | | | |
	True	False	Don't Know	Total
United People's Front	20	71	9	100
Communist UML+U	33	61	6	100
Nepali Congress	45	49	6	100
National Democratic	68	24	8	100
Sadvabana	48	45	6	100
All	43	50	7	100

149

reincarnation of Vishnu, as shown in the bottom row. The belief in the King's divine descendance rises steadily from left to right, from 20 percent among the United People's Front to 68 percent among the National Democratic voters. Within the Nepali Congress party the division is almost like the national average, and in the Sadvabana party the attitude is slightly more secular than the grand average.

Understandably, the Nepali Congress leaders have not spoken up on this matter, as they would offend a great deal of their followers whichever position they took. But the other parties will probably also play the subject of the King's religious legitimacy softly, the National Democrats because they have the distinct minority position, and the Communists because after all almost one quarter of the religious legitimists vote for them.

There is a fair association between the positions taken by respondents in Table 1 and Table 2. The belief in the King's reincarnation certainly implies a stand on the constitutional issue by which the King has more power than at present. Reversely, those not believing in the King's reincarnated origin find it easier to support a transition to a republican state. Furthermore, the religious issues are associated with the contrast between the modern urban culture and the traditional rural culture. For example, in the towns (with more than 10,000 inhabitants) only 10 percent want the King to have more power, whereas in the rural areas it is 24 percent; and in the towns only 27 percent believe in the divine origin of the King, as against 44 percent in the rural areas.

Thus indirectly religious or secular beliefs come to have an effect on party politics although the leaders attempt to keep them apart from practical politics. But it would be going much too far to contend that traditional religion has been the main barrier in preventing an earlier democratic development, or that it will be a major obstacle in the future. We are inclined toward the perhaps unorthodox view that religious feelings in the majority group (the Hindus) are not among the most important factors in the basic political development of Nepalese society.

Support for Elections and Parties as Institutions

For our next indicator, four questions in our survey tapped the support for elections and parties, "Do you think elections are necessary here in Nepal, or not necessary?" (Q.23), "Do you think elections make the government pay attention to the people, or don't you think so?" (Q.24), "How about political parties - do you think they are necessary in Nepal, or not necessary?" (Q.25), and "...Which do you think is necessary - only one party or more than one party?" (O.26).

The responses to these four questions turned out to be closely interrelated, and for that reason they were added up to an index varying from 0 to 4. Respondents who thought that elections were necessary, that they made the government pay attention, that parties were necessary, and that it was necessary to have more than one party, were scored the maximum value of 4. Each of these responses were in huge majority, which is why the score of four was by far the most common, attained by 57 percent of the respondents.

Table 3 displays the percentage scoring 0-2, 3, and 4 in various subgroups of the sample.

Table 3. *Support for Elections and the Multiparty System as Measured by Four Questions (Percentages)*

| | No. of Positive Responses | | | |
	0-2	3	4	Total
School Education				
No schooling	38	38	31	100
Primary or low secondary school	23	24	53	100
High secondary or more	10	20	70	100
Age Group				
18-29 years	25	26	49	100
30-44 years	32	31	37	100
45 years or more	36	30	34	100
Vote at Election				
United Peoples F	63	26	11	100
Communist UML+U	26	36	38	100
Nepali Congress	26	23	51	100
National Democratic	36	34	30	100
Sadvabana	22	14	64	100
All	33	29	38	100

From the upper set of percentages one gathers that the democratic support varies strongly with level of education. Among those without schooling only 31 percent give democratic responses to all four questions, whereas among those with high secondary schooling 70 percent do so.

The next set of figures show that the young are more inclined to give democratic responses than are the older generations. This of course has to be seen in connection with the higher educational level among the young.

In the lower set of figures one sees that the Sadvabana voters and the Nepali Congress voters gave the most democratic responses, while voters of the left wing (United People's Front) gave the least democratic support.

Cognition of the Effect of Government

In a democracy the citizens control the policy of the government both directly by indicating their policy preferences and indirectly by supporting those parties whose policy stands coincide with their own. This presupposes that the citizens are sensitive to government policy, that is, that they feel that the policies have an effect upon themselves. Following Almond and Verba (1963) we have attempted to measure this sensitivity to politics by asking, "Thinking about the national government in Kathmandu, about how much effect do you think its activities, the laws passed and so on, have on your daily life - do they have a great effect, some effect, or none?" (Question 35). For those indicating that the government activities had at least some effect, the questionnaire went on, "On the whole, do the activities of the national government tend to improve conditions in this country, or would we be better off without them?" (Question 36). On the basis of the responses to the first of these two questions we may classify the respondents in the way indicated by Table 4:

Table 4. Perceived Effect of Government on Respondent's Daily Life (Percentages)

	Great Effect	Some Effect	No Effect	Don't Know	Total
School Education:					
No schooling	4	6	43	47	100
Primary or low secondary	7	13	50	30	100
High secondary or higher	9	30	40	21	100
Residence:					
Urban	7	15	48	30	100
Rural	4	8	44	44	100
Gender:					
Male	6	10	48	36	100
Female	4	8	40	48	100
All	5	9	44	42	100

According to the bottom line, a tiny minority of 5 percent think that the government has a great effect on their daily lives. Almost twice as many think it has some effect, almost half think it has no effect, and a considerable portion, 42 percent, are unable to judge about the effect of government.

These figures from the weighted sample can be compared with the five nations covered by the Almond-Verba survey mentioned earlier. This comparison shows Nepal to be far behind these societies except possibly Mexico. Combining the first two columns, 85 percent in the U.S.A. perceive at least some effect of government,

73 percent in the U.K., 70 percent in Germany, 54 percent in Italy, and 30 percent in Mexico. In Nepal the corresponding figure is 14 percent. However, the Mexican figure is probably too high since it includes almost no "don't know" responses, whereas the Nepalese figure includes almost half.

Still, the average Nepalese voter certainly perceives only a faint echo of the political initiatives taken by the national government in Kathmandu. In part this is because of the low level of literacy and education characterizing most voters, but in part it is also because actually very little has been done to penetrate the local communities with national institutions. In other words the figures are affected both by subjective and by objective factors. If we look at the figures as describing the result of a communication process in which the state communicates to the citizens, the result will depend on both sender and receiver. Therefore we may expect the perception of government effects to be stronger in advanced societies, where national institutions and government programmes play a large role, and we must expect them to be stronger among those voters having the best receptive equipment, that is, the best educated and most politically involved.

The upper set of figures show that this is the case with regard to the level of education. Among those without schooling only 10 percent perceived any effect of government, among those with primary or low secondary school it was 20 percent, and among those with high secondary schooling it was 39. Clearly this huge difference is not caused by the objective impact of government being so much higher on the well-educated than on the uneducated. In all likelihood the difference is one of greater sensitivity to politics among the well-educated.

Compared with educational differences, the differences between urban and rural respondents, and between men and women, are minor, as shown in the other two sets of figures. Also, the differences between age groups (not shown) are small.

General Political Support or Alienation

Political alienation is the feeling of being outside of politics. Political leaders are regarded as playing a complicated game far above the heads of ordinary citizens. Often, the leaders are regarded with a mixture of fear and distrust: they have lost touch with the people, they work only in their own interest, they do not keep their promises, they are corrupt, etc. These ideas are coupled with a feeling of powerlessness and meaningless concerning the participation of ordinary voters in politics.

Political alienation is, of course, an attitude which is dangerous for democracy if it is widespread and lasting. The alienated voter is not motivated to fight for democracy, and he or she tends to see a transition from authoritarian rule to democracy or the reverse as being of no real consequences.

153

Our measure of voters' perception of the effect of government, discussed in the previous section, can be regarded a measure of alienation. However, we have sought to measure alienation more systematically by means of four attitudinal items in the Nepalese survey (Question 37):

a. In general the politicians care too little about what the voters think.
b. One can generally trust the politicians to make the right decisions for the country.
c. By voting in an election people like me can really take part in deciding how the country is run.
d. Politics is so complicated that people like me don't understand what goes on.

On all four items the respondents were asked to say whether they agreed, disagreed, or were undecided. In addition, allowance was made for Don't Know responses.

It should be noted that the two first statements deal with politicians, while the last two deal with ordinary voters, or "people like me". Thus they measure the attitude toward two different objects. In the literature on political alienation these two attitudes are sometimes called external and internal political efficacy, respectively, or the former is called political distrust or political cynicism, to distinguish from the latter, which is then called political powerlessness or (in its reverse form) political efficacy or political competence. These two attitudes are ordinarily related with one another, but that need not always be the case. For example, a feeling of distrust toward political leaders coupled with a feeling of political efficacy is sometimes found among activists of protest movements.

It should also be noted that statements (a) and (d) are phrased negatively, so that agreement with these statements indicated a negative attitude, whereas statements (b) and (c) are phrased positively, indicating a positive attitude. Hence it follows that in order to show extreme political alienation the respondent has to respond Yes, No, No, and Yes to the four statements in that precise order, an exercise which insures that he or she really has been attentive to the content of the statements.

Such an exercise may have been a little to demanding of most of our respondents, most of whom had of course never been exposed to people who were interested in hearing their opinions on political matters. Whatever the reason, we find almost no correlation between the responses to item (a) and item (b). Respondents who agreed with item (a) were just as likely to agree with item (b) as were respondents who disagreed with item (a). The same was true of responses to items (c) and (d), the response to one of these two items being of no use in predicting the response to the other. Thus we cannot say that there was even the beginning of a scale in people's attitudes of political trust or political efficacy. There was, however, a positive relationship between the responses to items (a) and (d), and between the responses to items (b) and (c). That is, people who agreed with one positive statement tended to agree with the other positive statement, and people who agreed with one negative statement tended to agree also with the other negative statement. By scoring the responses to each item either 1 (the alienated response), 2 (undecided), or 3 (the unalienated response), and summing up the scores for all four items, we therefore arrived at a tolerably good measure of what we shall term general political support, the reverse of political alienation. This measure has a range from 4 to 12 for the individual respondent.

Before using this index of general political support we shall, however, present the crude level of agreement with each of the four items. In Table 5 we indicate the percent of respondents in various categories who agree, disregarding the rest who responded either disagree, undecided, or don't know.

Table 5. Agreement with Positive and Negative Statements on Political Alienation, by Respondents' Level of Education and Party Choice (Percentages)

| | Percent Agreeing That: | | | |
	Politicians Care Too Little	One can Trust Trust Pol's	By Voting I Can Decide	Politics Is So Complicated
Level of Schooling:				
None	80	65	70	68
Primary or low secondary	67	70	78	61
High secondary or higher	63	73	86	41
Party Choice:				
Leftwing	79	67	75	68
Congress	70	64	75	55
National Dem.	78	66	58	76
Sadvabana	88	70	69	68
Nonvoters	80	82	79	73
All	76	67	73	64

A comparison between respondents with different levels of schooling (upper section of table) shows that in regard to all four items the well-educated are not nearly as alienated as the uneducated. This is especially the case with item (d) in which 68 percent of the uneducated but only 41 percent of the well-educated agree that politics is too complicated for "people like me". The difference between the educational groups is smallest in the case of item (b) in which 67 percent of the uneducated and 73 percent of the well-educated agree that one can generally trust the politicians to make the right decisions. The entire pattern of relationship between these responses and the level of education conforms to what might be expected,

155

and what is found in other societies: the educated strata are in general less alienated from politics than the uneducated strata, and in particular when it comes to feelings of competence or personal efficacy.

The lower section of the table suggests that political alienation also has some overtones of partisan politics - in other words, that these statements have the character of being political issues. The criticism of politicians voiced in item (a) is at a minimum among Nepali Congress voters, and it attains maximum among voters of the Sadvabana party. The confidence in the representative system implied by item (c) is much lower among National Democratic voters and voters of the Sadvabana party than among voters of the Nepali Congress party and the leftwing parties. This presumably reflects the feeling that the two large parties are more sure of being represented in the Nepalese election system than are voters of the minority parties. The feeling that politics is too complicated, item (d), is widespread especially among nonvoters and among National Democratic voters, and least pronounced among Nepali Congress voters, all of which is quite in line with our preconceived notions. Only with regard to item (b) the differences between partisan groups are vague and insignificant.

In general, however, our four items on political support or alienation seem to work in a meaningful way and to measure roughly the same attitude even though the responses to them are only weakly related. If these responses are combined into our index of general political support, the measurement becomes more exact and reliable. Table 6 presents some results of using this index. The figures shown in the table are percent of the respondents scoring 9-12 on the index, the total range of which as previously stated is from 4 to 12.

When the respondents are classified by their level of education (top section of table) one finds a marked tendency for the well-educated to give general support to politics compared with the uneducated, just as we saw in the previous table with regard to the individual items composing the index. With regard to age, one might have expected this factor to operate in the direction of a higher general support among the young than among the old, since the young tend to be the well-educated. But the difference between the age groups is not large, and in statistical terms it is not significant. With regard to partisan differences, we might again point toward the low political support given by the Sadvabana voters (18 percent supportive) compared with for example voters of the Nepali Congress or voters of the United People's Front (both 38 percent).

In the lower sections of the table we have classified the respondents according to their responses on questions which are logically related with general political support. Question 31 of the survey questionnaire read, "What do you think of the government officials in this village or town - are they doing their job well, or not?"

Table 6. General Political Support in Various Groups (Percentages)

Level of education:	
No schooling	27
Primary or low secondary	39
High secondary or more	53
Age group:	
18-29 years	36
30-44 years	29
45 years or more	31
Party Choice	
United People's Front	38
Communist UML or U	25
Nepali Congress	38
National Democratic	28
Sadvabana	18
Nonvoters	25
Evaluation of government performance	
Doing well here	46
Not doing well here	29
Don't know	21
Doing well at higher levels	41
Not well	31
Don't know	28
Support for elections and multiparty system	
0-3 positive responses	23
4 positive responses	44

This was followed by a similar question about government officials at higher levels. Consequently we have two measures of the respondent's evaluation of the perform-ance of the government. It would be natural if a negative evaluation should colour the respondent's general political support, even though the object of the attitude has been shifted from "government officials" to politicians and ordinary voters at a more general level. The table shows that indeed such a colouring takes place: especially those who think that the government officials are doing a good job in their own village or town tend to show general political support (46 percent sup-portive), as against those thinking that the officials are not doing well (29 percent supportive) and those who answered don't know (21 percent supportive).

Finally, the last figures in the table provide the link with the preceding analysis. General political support tends to go hand in hand with support for elections and the multiparty system. Of those giving positive answers on all four points in the previous section, 44 percent give general political support as we have defined it here; of those giving less than four positive answers, only 23 percent give general political support.

Tolerance of Unconventional Behaviour

The Nepalese multiparty democracy was won through unconventional behaviours like protest meetings and marches, strikes, and underground press issues which culminated in the Spring of 1990. Consequently these activities were popular in large sectors of the public. But where do people draw the line between acceptable and unacceptable means of expressing their opinions - and who are the most tolerant sectors of the Nepalese population?

A series of questions in the Nepalese survey attempt to measure the acceptance of different kinds of unconventional behaviour. The answers show that the public readily differentiates between nonviolent and peaceful means on one hand, and violent or obstructive political steps on the other hand. Table 7 indicates the percent in the weighted sample who would allow eight different types of behaviour.

Table 7. Acceptance of Different Types of Unconventional Political Behaviour (Percentages)

	Should Be Allowed	Should Not Be Allowed	Don't Know	Total
Organise public meetings to protest against the government	80	9	11	100
Publish pamphlets to protest against the government	70	14	16	100
Organise protest marches and demonstrations	66	18	16	100
Organise a nationwide strike of all workers against the government	56	25	19	100
Write slogans on walls defaming the government	19	66	15	100
Occupy a government office and stop work there for several days	16	67	17	100
Take up arms against the government	6	81	13	100
Seriously damage government buildings	3	81	16	100

The first four are accepted by more than half the population and should properly be regarded as lying within the civil rights supplied with a democratic constitution. The next two, illegal but nonviolent measures, are accepted by one out of five or six voters, and the last two, which are in the violent end of the unconventional repertoire, are accepted by only a tiny minority.

These rates of acceptance can be compared with data from Western countries, since our questions have been quoted from the International Social Survey Programme (ISSP) 1985, a series of surveys which were conducted in a number of countries. In the first row showing that 80 percent accepted protest meetings and 9 percent rejected, that is, an acceptance ratio of 9:1, is practically the same as in West Germany and Great Britain, whereas in the USA and Italy the acceptance ratio is lower, 4:1 or 3:1. In the second line dealing with pamphlets, the Nepalese acceptance ratio is 5:1, which is similar to Britain and Italy and actually higher than in West Germany or the USA, where it is around 3:1. The third row, dealing with marches and demonstrations, has an acceptance ratio in Nepal of almost 4:1 as against approximately 2:1 in Britain, USA or Italy (in Germany more than half wanted to outlaw marches and demonstrations!) Finally, the acceptance ratio of more than 2:1 for nationwide strikes is higher than in all the four Western countries mentioned above - only Italy approaches the same ratio.

We may conclude that taken together, these legal and democratic forms of popular protest met with a higher degree of acceptance in the Nepalese public than in any of these Western countries. The same, however, seems to be true of

Table 8. No. of Voters Accepting from 0 to 4 Legal Types of Unconventional Political Behaviour (Percentages)

	No. of Activities Accepted					
	0	1	2	3	4	Total
Sex:						
Male	16	10	10	12	52	100
Female	14	9	15	19	43	100
Age Group:						
18-29 years	8	6	9	22	55	100
30-44 years	16	11	10	16	47	100
45 years or more	17	10	15	13	45	100
School Education						
No School	17	10	13	14	46	100
Primary or low secondary	9	9	12	20	49	100
High secondary or higher	6	3	7	16	68	100
Party Choice:						
United People's F	10	15	18	11	46	100
Communist UML or U	7	6	4	17	66	100
Nepali Congress	19	9	15	15	42	100
National Dem.	24	6	14	19	37	100
Sadvabana	18	10	4	13	55	100
All	15	9	12	16	48	100

the other protest forms listed in the table. The Nepalese acceptance rate of about 1:4 for occupying government offices, for example, should be compared with ratios around 1:10 for Western countries. In short, across the board Nepalese voters are more ready to allow unconventional behaviour.

In order to study the general acceptance in various subgroups of those activities lying within the scope of civil rights, we have constructed an index simply by counting how many of these activities are accepted by a given respondent. The breakdown of this index is presented in Table 8.

The gender difference is quite interesting, the women tending to accept two or three activities in comparison with the men, who tend to accept either none or all four activities.

The age pattern shows that the young generation is distinguished by its acceptance of three or four activities, compared with the middle-aged and older voters.

The educational pattern is equally clear, those without schooling tending to accept none of the four activities (17 percent) compared with the two other groups. Of these, the group with low education disproportionably accept 3 activities (20 percent) whereas the well-educated tends to accept all four activities (68 percent). Thus the acceptance rises markedly with rising education.

Finally, when the respondents are grouped by their party preference, quite substantial differences turn up. Voters of the leftwing United People's Front disproportionably accept one or two activities out of the four. Voters of the Communist UML or U parties are the most tolerant of all, almost two-thirds accepting all four activities. The Nepali Congress voters are much more cautious with only 42 percent accepting all four activities and as many as 19 percent accepting none of them. The National Democratic voters on the right wing are by far the least tolerant, almost one quarter accepting none of the four activities. And of the Sadvabana voters somewhat over the average accept all four activities.

We can easily see from these figures that acceptance of these unconventional means is influenced by both education and by party, the latter especially such that the Communist parties allow for a wider repertoire of political means.

The Readiness to Act

The fact that one tolerates a certain type of unconventional behaviour does not mean that one is also ready to engage in that behaviour oneself, although presumably it will facilitate such behaviour. We will end our review of Nepalese political culture by studying the respondent's readiness to act, using a question which was used in the Almond-Verba study almost forty years ago, and which has been used in many later studies. The question reads, "Suppose a law was being considered by the parliament which you considered to be very unjust or harmful. What do you think you could do?" (Question 38 in the Nepalese questionnaire). Those who indicated something they could do were asked, "Anything else you could do?" (Question 38A).

In view of the theory of "civic culture" put forth by Almond and Verba, our results are truly surprising. According to that theory Nepalese society, being 80-90 percent agrarian and having only rudimentary prior experience with public political participation, should be dominated by a mixture of the parochial and the subject political culture but with only a dash of the participant culture in the case of the well-educated strata and the party activists. This expectation was fortified by our previous finding that few Nepalese voters perceived any effect of government on their daily lives. However, when investigating the readiness to engage in political action among the Nepalese voters we are almost inclined to turn the theory of the civil culture upside down by claiming that in a society undergoing rapid democratization a surge of political involvement requires neither any previous socialisation nor any cognition of an impact of government. The message of the mobilising campaign seems to be that a maximal utilisation of the suffrage and the new civil rights to participate is a precondition for changing the society to the better.

Table 9 reports what the Nepalese respondents thought they could do to stop an "unjust or harmful" law from being passed by the parliament.

Table 9. Suggested Action against an Unjust or Harmful Law (Percentages)

	Action 1	Action 2
Go to a party leader or official	40	24
Go to a government official	6	8
Go to a locally influential person	9	13
Write a letter to a newspaper	3	3
Talk with friends and neighbours	18	11
Protest (in some way)	6	12
Other suggestions	1	1
I could do nothing	7	13
Don't know	10	15
Total	100	100

The large majority of voters were able to suggest not only one but two types of action, and the parties were seen as the most important vehicle for carrying grievances upward in the system - or, in the language of political science, as the most important input medium. Other rather common suggestions were the "clientelist" procedure of talking to some local influential, and the "parochial" procedure of talking with friends and neighbours. Less frequent were the suggestion of talking to a government official, and even less frequent the suggestion of writing to newspapers. In view of the low level of literacy one should not be surprised at the low reliance on mass media for taking grievances upward toward the decision-making layers.

Totalling these suggestions and the unspecified one of "protesting", we find that 83 percent mentioned at least one type of action, and 72 percent mentioned two types. This astoundingly high readiness to act is not generally found in older democracies, and it contrasts with the idea that participatory ideas evolve only slowly in the population during the process of democratization.

Since the readiness to act comprised the large majority, there are no dramatic differences between social or political groups. Still, differences there are, and Table 10 summarizes them by indicating how many in a given group offered one and two suggested actions.

Table 10. Number of Suggested Actions in Various Groups (Percentages)

	None	One	Two	Total
Sex:				
Male	12	23	65	100
Female	12	21	67	100
Age group:				
18-29 years	8	22	70	100
30-44 years	12	23	65	100
45 years or more	13	22	65	100
Educational level:				
No schooling	14	25	61	100
Primary/low sec.	6	20	74	100
High secondary	3	8	89	100
Party choice:				
United People's F	14	29	57	100
Communist UML or U	8	22	70	100
Nepali Congress	9	21	70	100
National Dem.	13	28	59	100
Sadvabana	7	20	73	100
Residence:				
Urban	13	18	69	100
Rural	12	23	65	100
All	12	22	66	100

The readiness to act is slightly higher among the female respondents than among the male ones, although the difference is not statistically significant. It is definitely higher among the young than among the middle-aged and older respondents, and as one might expect it is much higher among the well-educated than among those having no schooling. Looking at the different partisan groups we find a pattern whereby the Sadvabana voters and the voters of the two large parties are more ready to act than are voters on the right and left. From one perspective this is surprising: voters of the extremist parties are ordinarily more inclined than voters of moderate parties toward protest behaviour. But from another perspective it makes sense: the two large parties have penetrated almost all communities with their organisation, and consequently their voters have some party leader in a nearby village or town quarter.

The readiness to act, as we have measured it here, is associated with our previously discussed indicators of political culture. Those who suggest one or two ways of acting tend to be the same who give democratic responses to the four questions about elections and parties. They also tend to be the ones who give general political support on the questions about politicians and voters. Third, they tend more than other voters to perceive an impact of government. And fourth, they tend to accept more types of unconventional behaviour. Thus there is an over-arching dimension reaching from those who have an active and participatory orientation to politics and those with a more passive mind. In the concluding section we shall take a more general look at these orientations and their social and political determinants.

Conclusion

Nepalese political culture as indexed by these cognitive and affective measures does not conform to the picture painted by previous political culture studies, from Almond and Verba's 1963 study onward. But since none of these studies have been conducted in the circumstances of rapid democratization of an agricultural society, we may here be facing a case unforeseen and unimaginable for the conventional study of political culture. The chief finding setting out study apart may be summarized as follows:

In the first place, very few perceive any effect of government on their daily lives. This extremely low 'output cognition', to apply Almond and Verba's language, is one of the hallmarks of a parochial political culture. When almost ninety percent of the population are agrarian, scattered in small communities separated by mountain ranges, so that the capital comprises only around 2 percent of the population, this weakness in the penetration of government or "the state" might perhaps be expected.

In the second place, however, this fits badly with the strong support for "democracy" and the confidence that a citizen can and should act when the government or parliament passes laws against their interest. And the majority of the Nepalese public look to the parties as the chief intervening link between the citizen and the decision-makers, which seems to imply that they want first of all to see what can be done through the means of parliamentary representation before turning to extra-parliamentary methods.

It may be that what we are here witnessing is a transitory political culture, affected by the party propaganda of the first election campaign. It seems fair, however, to question the conventional picture of democracy as evolving slowly out of autocracy. The young Nepalese generation does not bear the stamp of generations of obedience to the royal authority. Unlike the Italian and German voters found in the interviews of the late 1950s, the Nepalese voters of the 1990s are in no way handicapped by an authoritarian past in utilising every available means of democratic political expression. This "explosion" of civil politics may naturally lead to a later disappointment and a backlash in the form of sympathies with a strong man. The main burden seems to lie with the parties. At the moment, they are clearly looked at as the critical forces of democracy. Sound government and sound opposition may over the years lead to a stable democracy even in the face of that economic hardship which is unavoidable for the Nepalese society.

CHAPTER 10

ABOUT THE SURVEY

The election survey on which this study is based was planned in July 1990. It was one out of a number of projects sponsored by the Danish Foreign Aid Service (Danida) on occasion of the political system change taking place in Nepal in April 1990 and the anticipated democratization of Nepalese politics. The survey was carried out under the auspices of the Political Science Association of Nepal (Polsan). The director of the project was Chitra K. Tiwari, with Sushil R. Panday as project co-ordinator and Ole Borre as Danish consultant.

Time Schedule and Administration of the Survey

The project began officially on March 1, 1991. Prior to that date, however, the project headquarters in Kathmandu had been leased and computer equipment in the form of two PC's ordered. Also, some initial drafting of the questionnaire had taken place. The month of March was spent mainly in finishing the questionnaire in its English form and in hiring field surveyors, each of whom would be responsible for one of the ten sampling districts. Most of the field surveyors were recruited from the university staffs not only of Tribhuvan University in Kathmandu but also from several provincial universities.

April was occupied by instructing the field surveyors and making them familiar with the computers, which was a new experience to them. The questionnaire was translated into Nepali, and then back-translated into English to make sure that the two versions were so far as possible identical in their meaning. Pilot interviews were conducted with outside voters, and the field surveyors interviewed one another with the double purpose of becoming familiar with the interviewing technique and spotting errors and dubious questions or code categories in the questionnaire. Finally, the Nepali version of the questionnaire was printed in sufficient quantity for the survey of 1,000 respondents.

May 12 had been fixed as Election Day, and about one week in advance the field surveyors began to depart for their districts, where they were to set up a local headquarters and hire assistants. Due to the mountainous country and the generally poor transport facilities of Nepal, most field surveyors took two or three days in getting to their districts. The interviewing began immediately following the election, and the intensity of the interviewing culminated four days after the election (see the Appendix, Question 72). About one week later the surveyors began to return to the project headquarters in Kathmandu, carrying their filled-in questionnaires.

Preparation and coding of the questionnaires took place in the project headquarters, the field surveyors generally preparing and coding the questionnaires of their own district. A coding scheme was constructed for coding the responses to the open-ended questions about important political problems (Questions 1 and 2). The codes were added on the margins of the questionnaire rather than being transferred to another form. The codes were then entered into a database program on the two computers simultaneously and checked for illegal codes. Such codes were then corrected by the field surveyors themselves by going back to the original questionnaire. As it turned out that the illegal codes were disproportionably frequent on two districts, all questionnaires from these districts were recoded.

By June 10 the database was ready for analysis. It was then translated into an SPSS systems file, which would be used for printing the report with marginal distributions. At the same time, some initial analytic tables were prepared for the field surveyors to comment on at a public seminar. By June 25, printing of the report began. The project came to an end by June 30 when the report and database were finished.

How the Questions Were Selected

Researchers who are familiar with mass surveys of political behaviour will recognize many of the questions we have included in the questionnaire. From the very beginning it was stated as an important objective that the Nepalese election survey should be comparable with other surveys and especially with the great comparative surveys (Borre, 1990). Notwithstanding the fact that the survey would be the first of its kind to take places in Nepal, and that it would take place under unusual political circumstances, it was judged that as far as possible, the questionnaire should include items that had worked well in other and more normal settings. The argument was that if both the items and the setting were new, it would not be possible to ascertain whether the findings should be ascribed to one or the other.

Yet there are theoretical concepts and corresponding operational measures that were judged from the outset as having little relevance in the Nepalese context. For example, measuring party identification by an item such as "Do you usually consider yourself an adherent of any particular party?" seems to have little meaning when parties stand for election for the first time. Similarly, asking respondents to place themselves on a left-right scale from 1 to 10 was judged to presuppose a Western-type political culture that would be alien to all but a few Nepalese voters.

Referring to the Appendix, in which the questions are listed, Questions 1 and 2 are the standard means for obtaining respondents' views of which problems are the most relevant political problems on the national and local level. These questions are open-ended and are asked as a beginning in order not to influence the responses by mentioning issues preselected by the researcher.

Questions 3-8 deal with respondent's exposure to political communication during the election campaign. With the exception of Question 4B, "Did anyone read from the newspapers to you?", which is motivated by the low level of literacy in especially the older Nepalese population, these questions are very similar to those appearing in Western surveys. On Question 6, asking whether the respondent were visited by campaign workers, we did not anticipate the intensity of the campaign; had we done so, we would have differentiated the response categories better.

Question 9 is the standard question dealing with political interest, whereas Question 10 is the only knowledge question in the survey, dealing with respondent's knowledge of the Nepalese party symbols figuring on the ballot. After Questions 11-13, which deal with past political behaviour, comes the central Question 14 on the voting choice at the 1991 election. This is followed by other questions on the voter's decision process.

Issues and policy positions are the topic of Questions 19-22. Regarding respondent's own position we have chosen to present them as "proposals that have come from the parties", inviting respondent to say whether they are good and important, good but unimportant, or bad. This is the method used in election surveys from a number of countries.

Questions 23-40 seek to measure respondent's attitude toward some central political institutions: parties, elections, the monarchy, politicians and the government, and various forms of political protest. They are part of the political culture in the widest sense of the concept. Several of these questions correspond with the International Social Science Programme 1985 or 1990 (for example, the eight forms of unconventional behaviour mentioned in Question 39), whereas others appear in most election surveys, and Questions 35, 36, 38, and 38A are taken from the five-nation study by Almond and Verba (1963).

Question 41-50 deal with the voters' perceptions of election fraud of various types. Some of them correspond with questions in the Eldersveld and Ahmed study of Indian elections (1978), whereas others are novel and take up topics discussed during the Nepalese election campaign.

The questions from Question 52 onward unravel background information about respondent's family and social position.

Sampling and Representativity

To provide a fairly representative sample of Nepalese voters, ten administrative districts were selected of the 75 into which Nepal is divided. As can be seen from

Question 70 in the interview questionnaire the districts were Doti, Banke, Rukum, Rupandehi, Tanahun, Chitwan, Rasuwa, Sindhupalchok, Saptari, and Ilam. These districts, shown in Diagram 2, represented 29 out of the total of 205 constituencies. The sampling districts were selected with a view to obtaining a balance with regard to religious and ethnic composition, literacy rate, geographical or regional distribution, and urban versus rural population. Thus the selected districts were scattered from the extreme western to the extreme eastern Nepal, and from the low-lying Terai plain bordering on India to the high Himalayas. The sample of districts, however, did not include any from the Kathmandu valley. This decision can be defended on the ground that this valley, the traditional centre of Nepal, only holds five percent of the population. Yet in retrospect it would have been preferable to include a Kathmandu district, since the voting behaviour in the capital may be different from the rest of the country.

Within each district it was decided to interview 100 voters by means of quota sampling. Quota sampling is naturally inferior to random sampling, in which respondents are picked at random from a list of electors. It was judged, however, that there would be serious disadvantages associated with relying on election lists. In the first place, obtaining such lists would require the cooperation of elections officials and create political attention to the survey. Second, the lists would be subject to

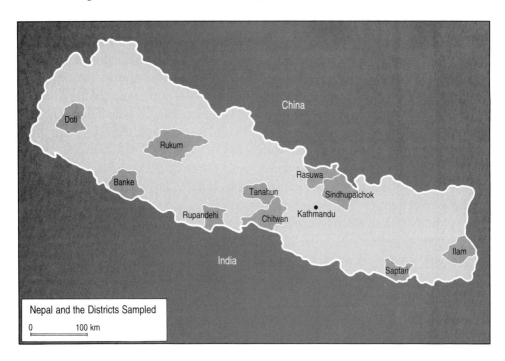

Nepal and the Districts Sampled
0   100 km

many errors; for example, in Kathmandu alone, 50,000 voters had complained that they were not included on the election list, and very likely a similar proportion were listed twice or even more times. In our study, 94 respondents were aware that they were listed in another constituency, and 30 said they had not voted because they were not listed. Thirdly, the lists did not contain the addresses of the electors, and therefore would be useless when the interviewer attempted to locate the electors.

The interviewers were to complete 100 interviews in their district. They were instructed to seek out young and old electors, rich and poor, men and women in rough proportion to their actual number in the district. However, there was no up-to-date statistics available by which these target proportions could be fixed. Thus the interviewers were conceded some leeway in determining who to interview. The result was a sample with a marked bias toward men and educated persons, and for that reason any estimate of the Nepalese electorate made on the basis of the survey should be weighted (see the below section on weighting). In other respects the sample is not seriously biased. For example, 26 percent of the sample comes from towns above 10,000 inhabitants and 74 percent from villages below this size. The religious distribution is 80 percent Hindi, 14 percent Buddhist, and 4 percent Moslem. In ethnic composition, 25 percent are Brahmin, 21 percent Chhetri, and 12 percent Newar. All of these proportions are fairly close to the official statistical figures for the whole country.

Most importantly, the sampling distribution by partisan choice is not seriously off the official election result, as the following table indicates:

Party	Official	Sample
Nepali Congress	39.5%	43.5%
Communist UML	29.3	26.7
NDP (Thapa)	5.6	1.8
NDP (Chand)	6.9	7.9
Sadvabana	4.3	4.2
Communist Dem.	2.5	4.5
United People's Front	5.0	8.9
Other parties	2.5	0.9
Indep. candidates	4.4	1.6
Total	100.0%	100.0%

The unweighed sample contains an over-representation of voters of the Nepali Congress party, the Communist Democratic party, and the United People's Front, and an under-representation of voters of the Communist UML party, "other parties" and independent candidates. But the distortion is not serious.

169

Conditions for Interviewing

Interviewing mostly took place in the respondent's home. A problem that was antici-pated was that in some cases the interviewer spoke a dialect or language which the interviewer needed an interpreter to translate. Mostly, indigenous persons with some education such as teachers were used as interpreters or as assistant interviewers.

Another problem was that the interview situation often attracted friends and neighbours who might intervene or merely, by their presence, cause the respondent to respond different from what he or she would do if no one was listening. This was anticipated, and the last item in the questionnaire records whether anyone was present during the interview. From the marginal distribution it appears that in almost half the interviews, there were others present (apart from small children), but that they generally did not interfere.

It took an average of 1 hour and 15 minutes to complete a questionnaire.

Coding Problems

The Nepali questionnaire which was used during the interviewing was pre-coded with regard to the large majority of questions and response categories. As mentioned above, the coder (identical with the field surveyor in charge of the particular district) wrote the Arabic numbers corresponding to the responses in the margin of the original questionnaire, page by page. Thus no special coding form was used, a procedure which made the checking of the codes easier.

As a first step the questionnaires for each district were identified by district no. and a serial no. for administrative reasons. This of course does not inflict upon the anonymity of the respondents since the names of the respondents were neither asked nor recorded. The identification appears as Field 1 in the database and Variable 1 in the SPSS file.

In the case of a few questions the response categories of the Nepali questionnaire deviate from those of the English questionnaire, especially so that the former contains 3 or 4 where the latter contains 9 for a Don't Know response. These errors were not discovered before the Nepali questionnaire went to the printer. The database in these cases conform with the Nepali questionnaire whereas the SPSS file conforms with the English questionnaire recorded in the Appendix.

A few questions were open-ended and their response categories thus not pre-coded. This is the case with National Problem 1-3 and Local Problem 1-3 (Questions 1-1B and 2-2B, respectively), and Issues Mentioned by the Nepali Congress, the Communist UML, the NDP (Thapa), and the NDP (Chand) candidate standing in the particular district (Questions 20A-20D). For these ten variables the same coding scheme was employed. This coding scheme originated from lists provided by the coders on which he listed all the responses that occurred in the questionnaires from his district. The lists were combined into a coding scheme which was then circulated to the coders. A similar procedure was employed with regard to Question 64, respondent's ethnic group. Since the respondents mentioned castes or groups not anticipated at the time when the questionnaire was printed, the pre-coded list of numbers was extended with some extra groups.

A number of questions have pre-coded categories termed "Other" on which the interviewer has supplied information on the response. This information has not been entered in the database, and to study that information one must go back to the original questionnaires.

Missing information has been coded 0 in the SPSS file, and there are no remaining illegal codes. However, where the interviewer has made a mistake in the branches existing in the questionnaire (such as asking an adherent of a republic how he wants the monarchy to function in Questions 28-29), we have not tried to make the coding consistent because it is not possible to tell which of the responses is bad.

Weighting the Data

The survey is heavily biased toward male and educated voters. This bias was not intended but to some extent anticipated. Although the interviewers were instructed to seek out the richer and poorer quarters of their districts in rough proportion to their size, and to attempt to interview as many women as men, they ended up with a clear over-representation of males at medium and higher levels of schooling. This means that all estimates of the aggregate or marginal distributions have to be weighted. On the other hand it should be appreciated that estimates for people with secondary schooling and higher education have a lower sampling variance than what an unbiased sample would produce.

The weighting is done according to the following schemes:

Table 1. Educational Distribution

Educational Category	Official No.	Per cent
Illiterate	9,346	76.7
No Schooling	670	5.5
Total		82.2
Primary, 1-5 years	1,380	11.3
Low secondary, 6-7	261	2.1
Secondary, 8-10	324	2.7
Higher	199	1.6
Total	12,180	100.0

The first column of figures shows the no. of people over six years in the various categories according to official statistics (Statistical Yearbook of Nepal 1991, p. 118, in thousands), whereas the second column is a breakdown of these figures in percentages.

However, the latest statistics at the time of writing was from 1981, and since then the Nepalese school system has expanded greatly. We decided therefore to increase the proportions in the last four categories, those having at least primary schooling, by 50% for our weights.

With regard to the sex distribution, our sample contains 63.7 percent male and 36.3 percent female respondents. Since the correct figure seems to be 53 percent male and 47 percent female, we assigned such weights to the sexes as to arrive at this distribution.

The weighting scheme combining sex and educational level is presented in Table 2.

Within each category there are three figures. The first shows the actual number of respondents, the second (in parentheses) the computed no. which should be used in the subsequent analysis. The third figure shows accordingly the weight by which the first figure has to be multiplied in order to arrive at the second figure.

Table 2. Weights Applied to the Analysis

	Men	Women	Total
No schooling	130	135	265
	(388)	(345)	(733)
	2.98	2.55	
Primary school	103	41	144
	(90)	(80)	(170)
	0.87	1.95	
Low secondary	77	25	102
	(17)	(15)	(32)
	0.22	0.60	
Secondary	167	69	236
	(22)	(19)	(41)
	0.13	0.28	
Higher education	163	93	256
	(13)	(11)	(24)
	0.08	0.12	

It will be seen from the weights that the persons of both sexes having no schooling are under-represented by a factor of almost three for males and about two and a half for females. The next set of figures shows that there were also too few females with primary education, only about half the estimated figure, so that these should be weighted upward too. Those with more than secondary education are all over-represented and should be weighted downward. In particular there seems to have been approximately ten times as many persons with higher education than there should be.

Although of course a heavily biased sample always gives some problems, we want to point out that it also has certain advantages. If the educated were represented in their true proportion, we would not be able to say very much about them. As it is, 256 respondents with higher education provides a good base for studying the most opinionated and significant portions of Nepalese society. In the other end, had we ended up with over 700 respondents without schooling, we would have an enormous frequency of Don't Know responses to deal with in every table.

Relation to Other Nepalese Surveys

As it emerges from tables in several of the foregoing chapters, many questions from the voter survey have found their way into other Nepalese surveys. In particular three such surveys should be mentioned:

1. Simultaneously with the voting survey, ten elite persons were interviewed in each of the ten sampling districts, thus providing a sample of 100 persons. A mixture of local notabilities entered into this sample, which should be regarded only as a tentative control group for the voter sample.

2. About 800 party members of different parties were interviewed in March 1992.

3. Finally, Nepalese parliamentarians were interviewed, also in the beginning of 1992.

The two latter surveys belong to another project, which might be regarded as a sort of successor to the present one.

APPENDIX

English Questionnaire with Marginal Distribution of Responses

This appendix indicates the question no., the (English translation of) the wording of the questions and responses, the variable name (v) in the SPSS system file, and for each response, the absolute frequency or no. of respondents, the unweighted percentage, and the weighted percentage. Concerning the weights applied, see Chapter 12. These percentages have been rounded so as to add up to 100 wherever possible. Missing data indicate that the question was not asked, either by mistake or because some respondents were filtered out by previous questions. Missing data are generally coded as 0 and not included in the percentage breakdown.

Introduction: Hello, I'm from the National Election Survey Office of the Nepal Political Science Association. We are conducting research on the elction. The study is related to the election and we want to find out what the people of this country think of the government and politics. We seek your help to make this research successful. We request you to help us by answering our questions. All your answers will be kept confidential and used only for statistics.

		Frequency	%	Weighted
1.	In your opinion, what is the most important problem facing Nepal today? (If vague answer:) Could you say it a little more specifically? (v2)			
1	Violence	22	2	1
2	Official graft	93	9	6
3	Lack of fertilizers	56	6	9
4	Unemployment	275	27	27
5	Afforestation	13	1	1
6	Drinking water	85	9	13
7	Irrigation	47	5	7
8	Health, sanitation	24	2	3
9	Education	136	13	13
10	Ethnic problems	22	2	2
11	National sovereignty	52	5	4
12	Peace and security	39	4	3
13	Relations with India	12	1	1
16	Roads and transport	15	2	1
19	Poverty	26	3	1
	Other responses*	60	6	2
99	Don't know	27	3	6
	Total	1004	100	100

*These responses were coded: 14-Relations with China, 15-Electricity, 17-Price rise, 18-Communication, 20-Industrialisation, 21-Exploitation, 22-Food shortage, 23-Food and shelter, 24-Problems of the landless, 25-Agriculture, 26-Fuel shortage, 27-Black market, 28-Alcohol, drunkenness, 29-Dowry, 30-River diversion, 31-Political stability, 32-Political consciousness, 39-Other problems.

1.A   (If problem mentioned in Q. 1:) Can you mention a second important problem facing Nepal? (v3)

		Frequency	%	Weighted
1	Violence	14	1	1
2	Official graft	48	5	4
3	Lack of fertilizers	43	4	4
4	Unemployment	166	17	13
5	Afforestation	34	3	4
6	Drinking water	96	10	15
7	Irrigation	91	9	9
8	Health, sanitation	71	7	8
9	Education	173	17	18
10	Ethnic problems	43	4	4
11	National sovereignty	28	3	1
12	Peace and security	59	6	5
13	Relations with India	13	1	1
16	Roads and transport	25	3	3
19	Poverty	7	1	0
	Other responses (see v2)	63	6	2
99	Don't know	30	3	6
	Total	1004	100	100

1.B   (If two problems mentioned:) And a third? (v4)

		Frequency	%	Weighted
1	Violence	9	1	1
2	Official graft	43	4	3
3	Lack of fertilizers	38	4	5
4	Unemployment	123	12	13
5	Afforestation	38	4	4
6	Drinking water	69	7	7
7	Irrigation	73	7	11
8	Health, sanitation	87	9	11
9	Education	141	14	15
10	Ethnic problems	38	4	3
11	National sovereignty	47	5	3
12	Peace and security	102	10	6
13	Relations with India	33	3	3
16	Roads and transport	32	3	3
19	Poverty	10	1	1
	Other responses (see v2)	88	9	5
99	Don't know	42	4	7
	Total	1004	100	100

2.   Thinking now of your village or town, which is the most important problem facing you here? (If vague answer:) Can you say it a little more specifically? (v5)

		Frequency	%	Weighted
1	Official graft	68	7	6
3	Lack of fertilizers	103	10	11
4	Unemployment	159	16	15
5	Afforestation	19	2	2
6	Drinking water	207	21	24
7	Irrigation	108	11	13
8	Health, sanitation	65	7	6
9	Education	73	6	7

		Frequency	%	Weighted
10	Ethnic problems	22	2	1
12	Peace and security	32	3	2
15	Electricity	27	3	3
16	Roads and transport	37	4	2
Other responses (see v2)		81	8	8
99	Don't know	3	0	0
Total		1004	100	100

2.A   (If problem mentioned in Q. 2:) Can you mention a second important problem facing you in this village or town? (v6)

		Frequency	%	Weighted
2	Official graft	26	3	1
3	Lack of fertilizers	46	5	4
4	Unemployment	157	16	14
5	Afforestation	39	4	4
6	Drinking water	180	18	20
7	Irrigation	113	11	10
8	Health, sanitation	150	15	19
9	Education	134	13	14
10	Ethnic problems	24	2	2
12	Peace and security	23	2	1
15	Electricity	32	3	3
16	Roads and transport	28	3	3
Other responses (see v2)		47	5	3
99	Don't know	5	0	1
Total		1004	100	100

2.B   (If two problems mentioned:) And a third? (v7)

		Frequency	%	Weighted
2	Official graft	24	2	2
3	Lack of fertilizers	52	5	6
4	Unemployment	113	11	10
5	Afforestation	41	4	4
6	Drinking water	89	9	10
7	Irrigation	96	10	9
8	Health, sanitation	143	14	15
9	Education	174	17	19
10	Ethnic problems	42	4	3
12	Peace and security	70	7	6
15	Electricity	29	3	3
16	Roads and transport	42	4	5
Other responses (see v2)		73	8	6
99	Don't know	16	2	2
Total		1004	100	100

3.   Before the election there were broadcasts on radio and television in which the parties were talking. Did you follow many of these broadcasts, only a few, or none at all? (v8)

		Frequency	%	Weighted
1	Many	181	18	10
2	Only a few	584	58	47
3	None at all	194	19	33
9	Don't know	44	5	10
0	Missing data	1	-	-
Total		1004	100	100

		Frequency	%	Weighted
4.A.	Did you read in the newspapers about the parties many tims, a few times, or never? (v9)			
1	Many times	142	14	4
2	A few times	471	47	23
3	Never	303	30	56
9	Don't know	87	9	17
0	Missing data	1	-	-
	Total	1004	100	100

4.B	Did anybody read from the newspapers to you? (v10)			
1	Yes, many times	30	3	2
2	Yes, a few times	353	35	27
3	Never	476	48	51
9	Don't know	140	14	20
0	Missing data	5	-	-
	Total	1004	100	100

5.	Did you go to meetings where the candidates or the party spokesmen made speeches? (v11)			
1	Yes, many times	243	24	11
2	Once or a few times	502	50	45
3	No	243	24	40
9	Don't know	15	2	4
0	Missing data	1	-	-
	Total	1004	100	100

6.	Did any candidate or party worker come to your house and talk to you? (If Yes:) From which party? (v12) [circle one only]			
0	No	213	21	26
1	Yes, from Congress party	184	18	19
2	Yes, from United Marxist-Leninists	89	9	7
3	Yes, from National Democrats (Thapa)	0	0	0
4	Yes, from National Democrats (Chand)	22	2	4
5	Yes, from Goodwill Party	13	1	1
6	Yes, from another Party: Which?	42	4	5
7	Yes from two or more parties	426	43	36
9	Don't know	15	2	2
	Total	1004	100	100

7.	Before the election, did you talk about parties and politics with your family, friends, neighbours, colleagues, or other persons? (If yes:) With whom? [Circle two or more if needed]			
1	Family (v13)	734	73	71
2	Friends (v14)	673	67	47
3	Neighbours (v15)	652	65	57
4	Colleagues at work (v16)	158	16	8
5	Housewives (v17)	143	14	15
6	Students (v18)	82	8	3
7	Social workers or volunteers (v19)	132	13	6
8	School teachers (v20)	104	10	5
9	Religious leaders (v21)	22	2	1
10	Local notables (v22)	145	14	9
11	Others (v23)	41	4	5

(v13-v23 are coded 1=yes, 0=no; frequencies of yes are indicated)

8.A Did you work in the campaign in any of the following ways? (v24)
[Circle one in each column)

		Frequency	%	Weighted
1	House to house canvassing	190	19	14
2	Help voters get to polling station	43	4	4
3	Raise money for a party	14	1	1
4	Help organize an election meeting	18	2	2
5	Join a procession or demonstration	85	8	6
6	Distribute polling cards or literature	6	1	0
7	Other ways	14	1	1
8	More than one way	166	17	8
0	No, none of these ways, or don't know	468	47	64
	Total	1004	100	100

8.B Did anyone in your household work in the campaign in any of these ways? (v25)
[Circle one in each column)

		Frequency	%	Weighted
1	House to house canvassing	148	15	14
2	Help voters get to polling station	42	4	4
3	Raise money for a party	24	2	2
4	Help organize an election meeting	33	3	3
5	Join a procession or demonstration	79	8	4
6	Distribute polling cards or literature	7	1	1
7	Other ways	12	1	0
8	More than one way	129	13	10
0	No, none of these ways, or don't know	530	53	62
	Total	1004	100	100

9. How interested are you in politics? (v26)

		Frequency	%	Weighted
1	Very interested	263	26	15
2	Somewhat interested	344	34	25
3	Only a little interested	198	20	23
4	Not at all interested	163	16	28
9	Don't know	34	4	9
0	Missing data	2	-	-
	Total	1004	100	100

10. Can you remember the symbols of different parties and tell me some of them? (Probe:) Any more?
[Do not mention specific symbols of parties; circle each correctly identified symbol]

		Frequency	%	Weighted
1	Tree=Congress (v27)	979	98	95
2	Sun=United ML (v28)	858	86	75
3	Cow=NDP Thapa (v29)	690	69	59
4	Plough=NDP Chand (v30)	712	71	62
5	Hand=Goodwill Party (v31)	297	30	15
6	Drum=Labour Peasant party (v32)	235	23	12
6	Other symbol= _____ (v33)	413	41	35
7	Other symbol= _____ (v34)	204	20	18

(v27-v34 are coded 1=yes, 0=no; frequencies of yes are indicated)

11. During panchayat rule, were you then affiliated with banned political parties?

178

		Frequency	%	Weighted
(If yes:) Which party? (v35)				
1	No	802	80	93
2	Yes, Party: _____	188	19	6
9	Don't know	11	1	1
0	Missing data	3	-	-
Total		1004	100	100

12. During last year's people movement, led by Nepali Congress and United Left Front, did any protest meeting or demonstration take place in this village/town? (v36)

1	Yes	390	39	23
2	No (go to Q.13)	516	51	60
9	Don't know (go to Q.13)	96	10	17
0	Missing data	2	-	-
Total		1004	100	100

[Note: In the Nepali questionnaire, Don't know is coded 3]

12.A (If Yes in Q.12:) Did you participate? (v37)

1	Yes: In what capacity? _____	180	45	28
2	No: Why not? _____	201	50	66
9	Don't know	18	5	6
0	Missing data	605	-	-
Total		1004	100	100

13. Did you vote in the 1980 referendum? (If yes:) For which side? (If no:) Why not? (v38)

1	Too young to vote	283	29	15
2	Did not vote because lacking political interest	23	2	5
3	Did not vote for other reasons	68	7	7
4	Voted for panchayat rule	209	21	34
5	Voted for multi-party rule	320	32	23
9	Don't know or remember	92	9	17
0	Missing data	9	-	-
Total		1004	100	101

14. Now we are coming to the recent election of 12 May. Many people voted in that election, but there were also many who did not vote. How about you - did you vote? (If Yes:) For which party or candidate? (v39)

00	Did not vote (go to Q. 17)	43	4	5
01	Congress Party [Tree]	402	40	35
02	Communist UML [Sun]	248	25	23
03	National Democratic (Thapa) [Cow]	17	2	3
04	National Democratic (Chand) [Plough]	73	7	13
05	Goodwill (Sadbhawana) [Hand]	39	4	3
06	Labour Peasant (Majdoor Kisan) [Drum]	1	0	0
07	Communist Democratic [Sickle]	42	4	4
08	United People's Front (Samyukta Janamorcha) [Sickle and hammer]	82	8	10
09	National People's Liberation Front (Rastria Janamukti Morcha) [Man]	0	0	0
10	Communist (Verma) [two knives crossed]	3	0	0
11	National People's Party (Rastria Janata) [Fish]	1	0	0
12	Communist (Amatya) [Sickle and corncobs]	0	0	0

179

13	People's Front (Janabadi Morcha) [Oil Lamp]	1	0	0
14	Independent candidates	15	2	2
98	Refuses	34	4	2
99	Don't know (Go to Q.17)	3	0	0
Total		1004	100	100

15. (If voted:) When did you decide to vote for that party? Was it ... (v40)

1	Before the campaign started	562	59	44
2	During the campaign, or	211	22	27
3	In the last days before the election	164	17	26
9	Don't know	20	2	3
0	Missing data	47	-	-
Total		1004	100	100

16.* (If yes:) Which other party did you think of voting for? (v42)

16A* (If No in question 16:) If somehow you could not vote for your party or candidate, which is the second best party to you? (v42)

[Circle one only]

00	No alternative or second best party	249	25	22
01	Congress Party [Tree]	111	11	11
02	Communist UML [Sun]	176	18	13
03	National Democratic (Thapa) [Cow]	39	4	5
04	National Democratic (Chand) [Plough]	50	5	7
05	Goodwill (Sadbhawana) [Hand]	24	2	2
06	Labour Peasant (Majdoor Kisan) [Drum]	16	2	1
07	Communist Democratic [Sickle]	20	2	1
08	United People's Front (Samyukta Janamorcha) [Sickle and hammer]	56	6	4
09	National People's Liberation Front (Rastria Janamukti Morcha) [Man]	7	1	0
10	Communist (Verma) [Two knives crossed]	5	1	0
11	National People's Party (Rastria Janata) [Fish]	0	0	0
12	Communist (Amatya) [Sickle and corncobs]	1	0	0
13	People's Front (Janabadi Morcha) [Oil Lamp]	1	0	0
14	Independent candidates	41	4	3
98	Refuses	68	7	6
99	Don't know (Go to Q.17)	140	14	25
Total		1004	102	100

16C* (If R voted:) Is there a party which you would never vote for? (If yes:) Which party is that? (v43)

[Circle one only. If R mentions several parties, circle the largest i.e. the lowest no]

00	No	310	31	37
01	Congress Party [Tree]	99	10	8
02	Communist UML [Sun]	64	6	4
03	National Democratic (Thapa) [Cow]	92	9	6
04	National Democratic (Chand) [Plough]	74	7	5
05	Goodwill (Sadbhawana) [Hand]	95	9	6
06	Labour Peasant (Majdoor Kisan) [Drum]	0	0	0
07	Communist Democratic [Sickle]	3	0	0
08	United People's Front (Samyukta Janamorcha)			

		Frequency	%	Weighted
	[Sickle and hammer]	29	3	2
09	National People's Liberation Front (Rastria Janamukti Morcha) [Man]	0	0	0
10	Communist (Verma) [Two knives crossed]	8	1	0
11	National People's Party (Rastria Janata) [Fish]	1	0	0
12	Communist (Amatya) [Sickle and corncobs]	1	0	0
13	People's Front (Janabadi Morcha) [Oil Lamp]	3	0	0
14	Independent candidates	6	1	1
98	Refuses	75	7	7
99	Don't know	144	14	23
	Total	1004	98	99

[Now go to Q. 18)

17. (If R did not vote:) Did you not vote because of one of the following reasons (v43a)

1	The leaders of the parties requested you not to vote	1	2	2
2	You did not have the time to go to the polling station	7	16	22
3	You are not interested in politics	0	0	0
4	There was no suitable party or candidate	2	5	1
5	You feared being intimidated	2	5	5
6	Possibility of violence on election day	1	2	2
7	The government is inefficient	0	0	0
8	Your name was not listed	30	68	63
9	None of these reasons, or don't know	1	2	5
0	Missing data	960	-	-
	Total	1004	100	100

18. (Ask all:) Which party did the leaders of your caste, ethnic or occupational group support in this election? (v44)

00	No party in particular	242	24	23
01	Congress Party [Tree]	315	31	26
02	Communist UML [Sun]	165	16	13
03	National Democratic (Thapa) [Cow]	6	1	1
04	National Democratic (Chand) [Plough]	51	5	8
05	Goodwill (Sadbhawana) [Hand]	37	4	2
06	Labour Peasant (Majdoor Kisan) [Drum]	1	0	0
07	Communist Democratic [Sickle]	29	3	3
08	United People's Front (Samyukta Janamorcha) [Sickle and hammer]	57	6	8
09	National People's Liberation Front (Rastria Janamukti Morcha) [Man]	2	0	0
10	Communist (Verma) [Two knives crossed]	0	0	0
11	National People's Party (Rastria Janata) [Fish]	1	0	0
12	Communist (Amatya) [Sickle and corncobs]	0	0	0
13	People's Front (Janabadi Morcha) [Oil Lamp]	0	0	0
14	Independent candidates	11	1	1
98	Refuses	0	0	0
99	Don't know	87	9	15
	Total	1004	100	100

19. Do you think there are important differences in the politics and programs of different parties? (v45)

		Frequency	%	Weighted
1	Yes	645	65	42
2	No	126	13	15
9	Don't know	222	22	43
0	Missing data	11	-	-
Total		1004	100	100

20.A* What issues did the parties and candidates talk about in this district? First, the Congress party candidate - what did he or she talk about? (v46)
[Circle only one in each column. If R mentions more than one, probe for the most important]

1	Violence	21	2	2
2	Official graft	53	5	4
3	Lack of fertilizers	32	3	4
4	Unemployment	167	17	11
5	Afforestation	21	2	3
6	Drinking water	97	10	13
7	Irrigation	32	3	3
8	Education	74	7	6
9	Ethnic problems	19	2	1
10	National sovereignty	62	6	4
11	Peace and security	38	4	1
12	Relations with India	82	8	4
Other responses (see v2)		58	6	4
99	Don't know	247	25	40
0	Missing data	1	-	-
Total		1004	100	100

20B* Next, the United M-L candidate? (v47)

2	Official graft	59	6	3
3	Lack of fertilizers	19	2	2
4	Unemployment	278	28	20
6	Drinking water	21	2	3
7	Irrigation	17	2	2
9	Education	67	7	8
10	Ethnic problems	42	4	3
11	National sovereignty	52	5	2
13	Relations with India	46	5	2
14	Relations with China	15	1	1
23	Food and shelter	15	1	0
Other responses (see v2)		60	6	5
99	Don't know	311	31	49
0	Missing data	2	-	-
Total		1004	100	100

20C* Next, the NDP (Thapa) candidate? (v48)

6	Drinking water	24	2	3
10	Ethnic problems	19	2	1
11	National sovereignty	29	3	1
12	Peace and security	54	5	3
13	Relations with India	23	2	1
16	Relations with China	16	2	1
Other responses (see v1)		86	9	8

		Frequency	%	Weighted
99	Don't know	750	75	82
0	Missing data	3	-	-
Total		1004	100	100

20D* And finally, the NDP (Chand) candidate? (v49)

		Frequency	%	Weighted
6	Drinking water	32	3	4
7	Irrigation	29	3	3
9	Education	23	2	2
10	Ethnic problems	23	3	1
11	National sovereignty	76	7	7
12	Peace and security	60	6	5
13	Relations with India	28	3	2
Other responses (see v1)		59	6	4
99	Don't know	672	67	72
0	Missing data	2	-	-
Total		1004	100	100

21.* Some parties want to preserve old tradition, while others stand for new ideas, and still others are in-between. Where would you put:

A. The Congress party? (v50)

	Frequency	%	Weighted
Tradition	352	35	30
New ideas	181	18	19
In-between	326	33	23
Don't know	145	14	28
Total	1004	100	100

B. United M-L? (v51)

	Frequency	%	Weighted
Tradition	67	7	6
New ideas	648	64	55
In-between	99	10	5
Don't know	190	19	34
Total	1004	100	100

C. The NDP (Thapa)? (v52)

	Frequency	%	Weighted
Tradition	550	55	47
New ideas	19	2	2
In-between	85	8	5
Don't know	350	35	46
Total	1004	100	100

D. The NDP (Chand)? (v53)

	Frequency	%	Weighted
Tradition	578	58	52
New ideas	29	3	3
In-between	113	11	8
Don't know	284	28	37
Total	1004	100	100

E. And where would you put yourself? (v54)

	Frequency	%	Weighted
Tradition	152	15	22
New ideas	503	50	42
In-between	296	30	25
Don't know	52	5	11
Missing data	1	-	-

183

		Frequency	%	Weighted
	Total	1004	100	100
	Missing data			

22.* I will now read you some proposals that have come from the parties. Please tell whether you think it is
[Circle one in each item]

A.	To improve our relationship with India (v55)			
1	A good proposal, important that it be done	759	79	75
2	A good proposal, but not so important	119	12	11
3	Or a bad proposal that should not be done	24	3	2
9	Don't know	60	6	13
0	Missing data	42	-	-
Total		1004	100	101

B.	To improve our relationship with China (v56)			
1	A good proposal, important that it be done	525	54	46
2	A good proposal, but not so important	298	31	30
3	Or a bad proposal that should not be done	40	4	3
9	Don't know	104	11	21
0	Missing data	37	-	-
Total		1004	100	100

C.	To use more money for afforestation programs (v57)			
1	A good proposal, important that it be done	857	87	84
2	A good proposal, but not so important	107	11	13
3	Or a bad proposal that should not be done	2	0	0
9	Don't know	16	2	3
0	Missing data	22	-	-
Total		1004	100	100

D.	To improve the quality of the drinking water (v58)			
1	A good proposal, important that it be done	941	94	92
2	A good proposal, but not so important	48	5	5
3	Or a bad proposal that should not be done	1	0	0
9	Don't know	11	1	3
0	Missing data	3	-	-
Total		1004	100	100

E.	To have a better health service (v59)			
1	A good proposal, important that it be done	957	96	93
2	A good proposal, but not so important	29	3	4
9	Don't know	12	1	3
0	Missing data	6	-	-
Total		1004	100	100

F.	To create more jobs for young people (v60)			
1	A good proposal, important that it be done	776	81	70
2	A good proposal, but not so important	129	14	21
9	Don't know	51	5	9
0	Missing data	48	-	-
Total		1004	100	100

G.	To maintain Nepal as a Hindu kingdom (v61)			
1	A good proposal, important that it be done	601	62	63

		Frequency	%	Weighted
2	A good proposal, but not so important	149	15	13
3	Or a bad proposal that should not be done	189	20	18
9	Don't know	28	3	6
0	Missing data	37	-	-
Total		1004	100	100
H.	To have proper utilization of our resources (v62)			
1	A good proposal, important that it be done	815	85	75
2	A good proposal, but not so important	77	8	9
3	Or a bad proposal that should not be done	5	0	0
9	Don't know	65	7	16
0	Missing data	42	-	-
Total		1004	100	100
I.	To develop roads and transportation (v63)			
1	A good proposal, important that it be done	939	94	92
2	A good proposal, but not so important	46	5	6
3	Or a bad proposal that should not be done	2	0	0
9	Don't know	8	1	2
0	Missing data	9	-	-
Total		1004	100	100
J.	To give the same wage to women and men for the same job (v64)			
1	A good proposal, important that it be done	760	78	74
2	A good proposal, but not so important	171	18	18
3	Or a bad proposal that should not be done	24	2	3
9	Don't know	19	2	5
0	Missing data	30	-	-
Total		1004	100	100
K.	To give women same right to inherit as men have (v65)			
1	A good proposal, important that it be done	644	67	62
2	A good proposal, but not so important	204	21	20
3	Or a bad proposal that should not be done	87	9	10
9	Don't know	33	3	8
0	Missing data	36	-	-
Total		1004	100	100
L.	To keep the Indo-Nepalese frontier open (v66)			
1	A good proposal, important that it be done	487	51	54
2	A good proposal, but not so important	194	20	17
3	Or a bad proposal that should not be done	213	23	16
9	Don't know	52	6	13
0	Missing data	58	-	-
Total		1004	100	100
M.	To improve creative work for rural and community development (v67)			
1	A good proposal, important that it be done	752	79	71
2	A good proposal, but not so important	112	12	10
3	Or a bad proposal that should not be done	14	1	2
9	Don't know	78	8	17

			Frequency	%	Weighted
0	Missing data		48	-	-
Total			1004	100	100

N. To maintain Gorkha recruitment (v68)

			Frequency	%	Weighted
1	A good proposal, important that it be done		227	24	25
2	A good proposal, but not so important		229	24	26
3	Or a bad proposal that should not be done		403	43	31
9	Don't know		89	9	18
0	Missing data		56	-	-
Total			1004	100	100

O. To demand work permits for Non-Nepalese (foreigners) (v69)

			Frequency	%	Weighted
1	A good proposal, important that it be done		661	69	61
2	A good proposal, but not so important		149	16	15
3	Or a bad proposal that should not be done		89	9	9
9	Don't know		62	6	15
0	Missing data		43	-	-
Total			1004	100	100

23. Do you think elections are necessary here in Nepal, or not necessary? (v70)

		Frequency	%	Weighted
1	Necessary	918	92	85
2	Not necessary	52	5	7
9	Don't know	32	3	7
0	Missing data	2	-	-
Total		1004	100	99

24. Do you think elections make the government pay attention to the people, or don't you think so? (v71)

		Frequency	%	Weighted
1	Yes	700	70	57
2	No	154	15	16
9	Don't know	150	15	27
Total		1004	100	100

25. How about political parties - do you think they are necessary in Nepal, or not necessary? (v72)

		Frequency	%	Weighted
1	Necessary	869	87	76
2	Not necessary	81	8	13
9	Don't know	49	5	11
0	Missing data	5	-	-
Total		1004	100	100

26. Some people think it is necessary to have only one party to determine what all the people want. Others think it is necessary to have more than one party to find out what the people want. Which do you think is necessary - only one party or more than one party? (v73)

		Frequency	%	Weighted
1	Only one party	125	14	19
2	More than one party	756	82	71
9	Don't know	38	4	10
0	Missing data	85	-	-
Total		1004	100	100

27. Are you a member of any party? (If yes:) Which party? (v74)

		Frequency	%	Weighted
00	No	684	68	83

186

		Frequency	%	Weighted
01	Congress Party [Tree]	144	14	6
02	Communist UML [Sun]	97	10	5
03	National Democratic (Thapa) [Cow]	5	1	1
04	National Democratic (Chand) [Plough]	12	1	1
05	Goodwill (Sadbhawana) [Hand]	9	1	0
06	Labour Peasant (Majdoor Kisan) [Drum]	1	0	0
07	Communist Democratic [Sickle]	8	1	0
08	United People's Front (Samyukta Janamorcha) [Sickle and hammer]	23	2	2
09	National People's Liberation Front (Rastria Janamukti Morcha) [Man]	4	0	0
10	Communist (Verma) [Two knives crossed]	1	0	0
11	National People's Party (Rastria Janata) [Fish]	0	0	0
12	Communist (Amatya) [Sickle and corncobs]	0	0	0
13	People's Front (Janabadi Morcha) [Oil Lamp]	0	0	0
14	Independent	4	0	0
98	Refuses	2	0	0
99	Don't know	10	1	1
	Total	1004	99	99

28.* There are opinions in this country which call for radical change toward a republican state. What is your opinion in this regard - are you in favour of or against Nepal becoming a republic? (v75)

1	In favour (Go to Q.30)	315	31	23
2	Against	561	56	54
9	Don't know	126	13	23
0	Missing data	2	-	-
	Total	1004	100	100

29.* (If against) If you are against Nepal being a republic, how do you want the monarchy to function in Nepal? (v76) Do you prefer:

1	The king to be symbolic head of state only	117	17	7
2	His power to be limited by the constitution, as it is now, or	380	56	48
3	Should the king be more powerful in politics than he is now?	115	17	25
9	Don't know	70	10	20
0	Missing data	322	-	-
	Total	1004	100	100

30. Some people in this country believe that the king is the reincarnation of Lord Vishnu. Do you think this is true or false? (v77)

1	True	263	26	42
2	False	686	68	51
9	Don't know	54	6	7
0	Missing data	1	-	-
	Total	1004	100	100

31. What do you think of the government officials in this village or town? Are they doing their job well or not? (v78)

1	Doing well	177	18	19
2	Not doing well	727	72	65

187

		Frequency	%	Weighted
9	Don't know	98	10	16
0	Missing data	2	-	-
Total		1004	100	100

32. And what about government officials at higher levels - are they doing their job well or not? (v79)

1	Doing well	108	11	10
2	Not doing well	716	71	64
9	Don't know	199	18	26
0	Missing data	3	-	-
Total		1004	100	100

33. Do you think the government we have had during the past year is better or worse than the panchayat government we had before then? (v80)

1	Better	490	49	34
2	Worse	96	10	12
3	About the same (volunteered by R)	363	36	45
9	Don't know	54	5	9
0	Missing data	1	-	-
Total		1004	100	100

34. Are you and your family better off ow worse off now than last year when there was a panchayat government? (v81)

1	Better off now: Why? _____	85	8	6
2	Worse off now: Why? _____	146	15	13
3	About the same (volunteered by R)	723	72	72
9	Don't know	49	5	9
0	Missing data	1	-	-
Total		1004	100	100

35. Thinking about the national government in Kathmandu, about how much effect do you think its activities, the laws passed and so on, have on your daily life - do they have: (v82)

1	A great effect	84	9	5
2	Some effect, or	203	20	9
3	None? (Go to Q.37)	424	42	44
9	Don't know (Go to Q.37)	290	29	42
0	Missing data	3	-	-
Total		1004	100	100

36. (If a great or some effect:) On the whole, do the activities of the national government tend to improve conditions in this country, or would we be better off without them? (v83)

1	Improves conditions	206	55	34
2	Better off without them	77	21	20
9	Don't know	90	24	46
0	Missing data	631	-	-
Total		1004	100	100

37. Please tell me whether you agree or disagree with the following statements:
A. In general the politicians care too little about what the voters think (v84)

1	Agree	617	61	58
2	Disagree	207	21	15
3	Undecided	66	7	3

188

		Frequency	%	Weighted
9	Don't know	114	11	24
Total		1004	100	100

B. One can generally trust the politicians to make the right decisions for the country (v85)

1	Agree	619	62	48
2	Disagree	183	18	17
3	Undecided	69	7	6
9	Don't know	133	13	29
Total		1004	100	100

C. By voting in an election, people like me can really take part in deciding how the country is run (v86)

1	Agree	737	73	57
2	Disagree	85	9	13
3	Undecided	77	8	8
9	Don't know	105	10	22
Total		1004	100	100

D. Politics is so complicated that people like me don't understand what goes on (v87)

1	Agree	467	47	53
2	Disagree	346	34	22
3	Undecided	105	10	7
9	Don't know	86	9	18
Total		1004	100	100

38. Suppose a law was being considered by the parliament which you considered to be very unjust or harmful. What do you think you could do? (v88)
[Circle only one in each column. Do not read the list to R]

1	Could go to a party leader or official	468	47	40
2	Go to a government official	34	3	6
3	Go to locally influential person	75	7	9
4	Write a letter to a newspaper	57	6	4
5	Talk with friends and neighbours	130	13	18
6	Protest (in some way)	121	12	6
7	Other suggestions	20	2	1
8	I could do nothing	40	4	7
9	Don't know	56	6	10
0	Missing data	3	-	-
Total		1004	100	101

38.A (If something mentioned by R:) Anything else you could do? (v89)

1	Could go to a party leader or official	232	23	24
2	Go to a government official	58	6	8
3	Go to locally influential person	110	11	13
4	Write a letter to a newspaper	106	11	3
5	Talk with friends and neighbours	114	11	11
6	Protest (in some way)	184	18	12
7	Other suggestions	28	3	1
8	I could do nothing	81	8	13
9	Don't know	89	9	15
0	Missing data	2	-	-
Total		1004	100	100

39. There are many ways people or organizations can protest against a government action they strongly
     oppose. Now I shall read some of these methods. For each, please tell me whether it should be
     allowed or not. Here comes the first:
     [Circle one for each item]

A.   Organize public meetings to protest against the government (v90)

		Frequency	%	Weighted
1	Allowed	878	88	80
2	Not allowed	78	8	9
9	Don't know	45	4	11
0	Missing data	3	-	-
Total		1004	100	100

B.   Publish pamphlets to protest against the government (v91)

1	Allowed	813	81	71
2	Not allowed	115	12	13
9	Don't know	73	7	16
0	Missing data	3	-	-
Total		1004	100	100

C.   Organize protest marches (v92)

1	Allowed	786	78	66
2	Not allowed	140	14	17
9	Don't know	76	8	16
0	Missing data	2	-	-
Total		1004	100	99

D.   Organize a nationwide strike of all workers against the government (v93)

1	Allowed	664	66	56
2	Not allowed	238	24	25
9	Don't know	101	10	19
0	Missing data	1	-	-
Total		1004	100	100

E.   Occupy a government office and stop work there for several days (v94)

1	Allowed	162	16	16
2	Not allowed	746	75	67
9	Don't know	93	9	17
0	Missing data	3	-	-
Total		1004	100	100

F.   Seriously damage government buildings (v95)

1	Allowed	27	3	3
2	Not allowed	890	89	81
9	Don't know	86	8	16
0	Missing data	1	-	-
Total		1004	100	100

G.   Write slogans on walls defaming the government (v96)

1	Allowed	195	19	19
2	Not allowed	720	72	66
9	Don't know	88	9	15
0	Missing data	1	-	-
Total		1004	100	100

H.   Take up arms against the government (v97)

190

			Frequency	%	Weighted
1	Allowed		88	9	6
2	Not allowed		837	83	81
9	Don't know		77	8	13
0	Missing data		2	-	-
Total			1004	100	100

40. All systems of justice make mistakes, but which do you think is worse: (v98)

		Frequency	%	Weighted
1	To convict an innocent person, or	337	34	30
2	To let a guilty person go free	92	9	10
3	Equally bad [volunteered by R]	535	54	53
9	Don't know	32	3	7
0	Missing data	8	-	-
Total		1004	100	100

41. Have you any knowledge that any of the following forms was used to nuy votes during the election: [Circle more than one if needed. Do not circle if R says Don't know]

		Frequency	%	Weighted
1	Feast with liquor? (v99)	269	27	22
2	Money payment? (v100)	367	37	32
3	Promise of employment? (v101)	221	22	18
4	Other forms? Which? _____ (v102)	58	6	4

(v99-v102 will be coded 1=yes, 0=no)

42. Did any party or candidate offer you cash? (v103)

		Frequency	%	Weighted
1	Yes: Which party? _____	55	6	7
	How much? _____			
2	No	873	89	83
9	Refuses, or Don't know	50	5	10
0	Missing data	26	-	-
Total		1004	100	100

43. Do you think the government machinery was used to influence voters in favour of certain candidates? (v104)

		Frequency	%	Weighted
1	Yes	85	9	6
2	No (go to Q.45)	634	65	58
9	Don't know (go to Q.45)	250	26	36
0	Missing data	35	-	-
Total		1004	100	100

[Note: In the Nepali questionnaire, Don't know is coded 3]

44. (If yes:) How was it done? (v105)
[Circle one only]

		Frequency	%	Weighted
1	Police were seen to harass certain candidates	7	8	9
2	Polling officers directed voters to vote for a particular candidate	19	21	24
3	Government employees canvassed in favour of the parties	5	5	1
4	Government officials engaged in disinformation campaigns against certain candidates or parties	5	5	1
5	Government vehicles were used to transport voters of a certain party	11	12	6
6	Other: _____	28	30	49

191

		Frequency	%	Weighted
7	More than one way mentioned	10	11	2
9	Don't know how it was done	7	8	9
0	Missing data	912	-	-
Total		1004	100	101

45. Are you listed in a constituency other than this one? (v106)

		Frequency	%	Weighted
1	Yes	94	9	5
2	No, or don't know	909	91	95
0	Missing data	1	-	-
Total		1004	100	100

46. Do you think there were malpractices at the polling stations?(v107)

		Frequency	%	Weighted
1	Yes	174	17	11
2	No (go to Q.48)	649	66	66
9	Don't know (go to Q.48)	165	17	23
0	Missing data	16	-	-
Total		1004	100	100

47. (If yes:) What method was used? (v108)
[Circle one only]

		Frequency	%	Weighted
1	False polling	65	36	32
2	Capture of booths	25	14	9
3	Restricting voters from reaching the polling station	6	3	0
4	Making false rumours about the victory of a candidate	27	15	21
5	Other: _____	24	14	20
6	More than one way mentioned	26	15	8
9	Don't know	6	3	10
0	Missing data	825	-	-
Total		1004	100	100

48. Have you heard of rigging of votes in your constituency? (v109)

		Frequency	%	Weighted
1	Yes	240	24	17
2	No (go to Q.51)	576	58	57
9	Don't know (go to Q.51)	178	18	26
0	Missing data	10	-	-
Total		1004	100	100

49. (If yes:) What method was used? (v110)
[Circle one only]

		Frequency	%	Weighted
1	Boxes were changed	4	2	3
2	Valid votes were counted	4	2	2
3	Invalid votes were counted	3	1	2
4	Someone was seen or heard to vote in someone else's name	120	51	44
5	Votes were cast in the name of absentees (deceased, living abroad, or persons not present on election day)	41	17	18
6	Other: _____	14	6	9
7	More than one way mentioned	47	20	20
9	Don't know	4	2	2

		Frequency	%	Weighted
0	Missing data	767	-	-
	Total	1004	101	100

50. Is there any particular party you believe to have rigged the election (v111)

		Frequency	%	Weighted
1	Yes: Which party? _____	196	74	69
2	No	8	3	6
9	Don't know	61	23	25
0	Missing data	739	-	-
	Total	1004	100	100

51. (Ask all:) Do you think the new government to be formed after the election will last for the whole election period of five years? (v112)

		Frequency	%	Weighted
1	Yes	323	32	21
2	No	287	29	20
9	Don't know	387	39	59
0	Missing data	7	-	-
	Total	1004	100	100

52. Now I want a little information about yourself and your family. First, how old are you? (v113)
____ Years
00   Refuses [or question not asked]

53. Are you married? (v114)

		Frequency	%	Weighted
1	Yes	822	82	94
2	No	177	18	6
9	Refuses	2	0	0
0	Missing data	3	-	-
	Total	1004	100	100

54. How many children do you have? (v115)

	Frequency	%	Weighted
0	244	24	12
1	101	10	8
2	164	16	15
3	176	18	19
4	143	14	19
5	85	9	12
6	39	4	6
7	33	3	6
8	10	1	2
9	6	1	1
10	2	0	0
12	1	0	0
Total	1004	100	100

55. Are you living in a joint family or a separate family, or do you live single? (v116)

		Frequency	%	Weighted
1	Joint family	577	58	50
2	Separate family	382	38	45
3	Single	42	4	5
9	Refuses	1	0	0
0	Missing data	2	-	-
	Total	1004	100	100

193

56. How long have you been living in this town/village? (v117)

		Frequency	%	Weighted
1	Have always lived here (go to Q.59)	686	69	74
2	Ten years or more, but not all my life	161	16	15
3	Five years, but not ten years	60	6	5
4	Less than five years	58	6	3
9	Refuses	32	3	3
0	Missing data	7	-	-
	Total	1004	100	100

57. (If not born here:) Where did your family come from? (v118)

1	Terai	35	11	9
2	Hills	212	67	67
3	Himalaya	3	1	2
4	India	18	6	5
6	Other places	15	5	5
9	Refuses	32	10	12
0	Missing data	689	-	-
	Total	1004	100	100

58. (If not born here:) Was it an urban or a rural area? (v119)

1	Urban (more than 10,000 inh.)	48	15	13
2	Rural	239	75	76
9	Refuses	30	10	11
0	Missing data	687	-	-
	Total	1004	100	100

59. (Ask all:) What is your family's main occupation? (v120)

1	Agriculture (go to Q.61)	741	75	78
2	Manufacturing, factory work	14	1	2
3	Commerce, trading	81	8	7
4	Hotels, banks, other services	34	3	3
5	Teaching, social work, nursing	39	4	1
6	Government administration	27	3	2
7	Other: _____	56	6	8
9	Refuses	2	0	0
0	Missing data	10	-	-
	Total	1004	100	101

60. Is your family in private or in public employment or is it self-employed? (v121)

1	Private employment	99	20	19
2	Public employment	108	21	9
3	Self-employed	291	58	69
9	Don't know	5	1	3
0	Missing data	501	-	-
	Total	1004	100	100

61. (If agriculture:) Are you a landlord, a tenant farmer, an owner-tiller, or a mixture of these? [Circle two or three if needed]

1	Landlord (v122)	103	10	9
2	Tenant(v123)	61	6	10

		Frequency	%	Weighted
3	Owner-tiller (v124)	695	69	69

(v122-v124 are coded 1=yes, 0=no)

62. (If family owns land:) How large is your family's landholding, and which region is it in?
    Terai: _____ bighas (v125)
    Hills: _____ ropanees, murees (v126)
    Himalaya: _____ ropanees (v127)
    (v125-v127 will be coded with three digits each)

63. How do you estimate the cost or value of your house, including the ground where it stands, at current prices? (v128)
    [If R does not know, Interviewer should estimate value]

		Frequency	%	Weighted
0	Does not have a house	62	6	10
1	Less than 25,000 Rupees	190	19	28
2	25,000-49,000 R	213	21	25
3	50,000-149,000 R	264	27	24
4	150,000-349,000 R	142	14	6
5	350,000 R or more	133	13	7
	Total	1004	100	100

64. Which ethnic group do you belong to? (v129)

		Frequency	%	Weighted
01	Brahmin	252	25	16
02	Chhetri	208	21	20
03	Kiratis	16	2	2
04	Newar	122	12	8
05	Gurung	39	4	4
06	Thakali	8	1	1
07	Sherpa	16	2	1
08	Magar	49	5	6
09	Yadav	33	3	2
10	Vaishya	24	2	1
11	Muslim	41	4	5
12	Tharu, Mandal,Chaudari, Rai	19	2	3
13	Artisan: Kami, Damai, Sarki, Kasai, Mushuhar, Biswarkarma, Sujikar, Kumalai, Theli	63	6	13
19	Others: Bengali, Marwari, Shikh, Baniya, Barai, Khatawai, Giri, Puri, Bharati, Garai	112	11	19
0	Missing data	2	-	-
	Total	1004	100	100

65. Do you or does your family have the following items:
    [Mention each item separately, and circle if yes]

		Frequency	%	Weighted
1	Radio (v130)	757	75	55
2	Television (v131)	178	18	7
3	Small press (v132)	7	0	0
4	Telephone (v133)	100	10	2
5	Car (v134)	6	1	1
6	Motorcycle (v135)	58	6	2
7	Refrigerator (v136)	46	5	2
8	Stereo recorder (v137)	103	10	5

195

		Frequency	%	Weighted
9	Washing machine (v138)	7	1	0
10	Power tiller or tractor (v139)	7	1	1
11	Bicycle (v140)	341	34	19
12	Water pump (v141)	47	5	2
13	Bus, lorry or truck (v141a)	15	2	0

(v130-v141a are coded 1=yes, 0=no)

66.* As for yourself, did you go to school? (If yes:) What education did you get? (v142)

1	No schooling	265	26	73
2	Primary school only	144	14	17
3	Lower secondary school	102	10	3
4	Secondary school	236	24	4
5	Higher education	256	26	2
0	Missing data	1	-	-
Total		1004	100	99

67.* Are you employed? (If yes:) What is your occupation?
(If unemployed or retired:) What was your former occupation? (v143)

01	Farmer	318		46
02	Farm worker	43		9
03	Servant, waiter	63		4
04	Worker	37		8
05	Clerk, shop assistant	10		1
06	Teacher, social worker, nurse	116		2
07	Craftsman	13		3
08	Shopkeeper	82		10
09	Non-academic professional, middle level civil servant	29		1
10	Academic profession	13		1
11	Businessman, salesman	37		3
12	Housewife	62		10
13	Student	101		2
14	Unemployed	36		2
99	Refuses	1		0
0	Missing data	43	-	-
Total		1004	100	100

68.* What is your religion? (v144)

1	Buddhism	142	14	24
2	Hinduism	803	80	70
3	Islam	43	4	5
4	Christianity	1	0	0
5	Nature worship	1	0	0
6	Not religious	9	1	0
7	Other	5	1	1
Total		1004	100	100

Thank you very much. Now I just have to make a few notes.
[Interviewer notes:]

69.* Sex of respondent (v145)

1	Male	640	64	53

196

		Frequency	%	Weighted
2	Female	364	36	47
Total		1004	100	100

70. District no. (v146)

		Frequency	%	Weighted
01	Doti	103	10	13
02	Banke	101	10	7
03	Rukum	100	10	16
04	Rpuandehi	100	10	4
05	Tanahun	100	10	7
06	Chitwan	100	10	9
07	Rasuwa	99	10	19
08	Sindhupalchok	101	10	13
09	Saptari	100	10	7
10	Ilam	100	10	5
Total		1004	100	100

70.A Constituency no. within district (v146a)

	Frequency	%	Weighted
1	416	41	49
2	418	42	42
3	169	17	9
4	1	0	0
Total	1004	100	100

71. Town or village? (v147)

		Frequency	%	Weighted
1	Town (above 10,000 inh.)	258	26	12
2	Village	746	74	88
Total		1004	100	100

72. Date of interview: (v148)
29   Election day
30-31, 01-14 Subsequent dates

73. Was anybody present during the interview? (v149)

		Frequency	%	Weighted
1	No one except respondent (plus small children)	489	49	40
2	Family/neighbours present bud did not interfere	485	48	57
3	Family/neighbours present and interfered	25	3	3
4	Other comments about interview situation	2	0	0
0	Missing data	3	-	-
Total		1004	100	100

197

LITERATURE

Almond, Gabriel, and Sidney Verba. *The Civic Culture: Political Attitudes and Democracy in Five Nations*. Princeton, N.J.: Princeton University Press, 1963.

Borre, Ole. "Election Surveys and Voter Types". *Essays on Constitutional Law*, vol. 3. Kathmandu: Nepal Law Society, 1990.

Borre, Ole, Sushil R. Panday and Chitra K. Tiwari. "The Nepalese Election of 1991." *Electoral Studies*, vol. 10 no. 4 (December 1991).

Eldersveld, Samuel J., and Bashiruddin Ahmed. *Citizens and Politics: Mass Political Behavior in India*. Chicago: University of Chicago Press, 1978.

Joshi, Bhuwan Lal, and Leo E. Rose. *Democratic Innovations in Nepal. A Case Study of Political Acculturation*. Berkeley, Cal.: University of California, 1966.

Lipset, Seymour Martin. *Political Man*. London: Heinemann, 1960.

Nepalese Voters. A Survey Report. Kathmandu: Nepal National Election Survey, 1991.

Shaha, Rishikesh. *Politics in Nepal 1980-1990*. Kathmandu: Ratna Pustak Bhandar, Bhotahity, 1990.

INDEX

Political culture 1-2, 4-5, 99-100, 109, 112, 146-164, 166-167
Political Science Association of Nepal 165
Poverty problem 100-105, 108, 112
PPEC Committee 18, 21, 34
Pradhan, Sahana 33
Pratinidhi Sabha (Lower House) 36, 41
Price rise 98-105, 107-108, 112
Prithvi Narayan Shah 6, 72
Protest marches 44, 158-159
Protest meetings 158-159
Proximity voting 56-57

Queen Aishworya 22, 23
Quezon, Manuel L. 11

Radio 17, 70, 80-84, 91, 95, 142-143, 145
Radio Nepal 17, 81
Rallies, political 79-80, 82-86, 91, 95
Rana, Bir Shamsher 127
Rana, Jung Bahadur 6
Rana, Mohan Shamsher 7, 116
Rana, Subarna Shamsher 13
Rastriya Sabha (Upper House) 36, 41
Rasuwa district 69-70, 91, 119, 168
Referendum 1958 146
Referendum 1980 17-19
Regional differences in issue positions 124, 126-127, 130
    -- -- in political support 140
    -- -- in result of election 40
    -- -- in voting 64-65
Reincarnation 1, 146, 149-150
Religion 3, 69, 110, 120, 122, 149-150
Religious differences in party choice 69
Residential community 3
Rigging of elections 44
Rising Nepal, The, newspaper 17
Roads and transportation issue 99, 101, 103-107, 111-112
'Rohit', Narayan Man Bijukchhe 23
Royal Nepal Academy 32, 34